At My Mother's Knee . . .

and other low joints

www.**rbooks**.co.uk

At My Mother's Knee . . .
and other low joints

Paul O'Grady

BANTAM PRESS

LONDON · TORONTO · SYDNEY · AUCKLAND · JOHANNESBURG

TRANSWORLD PUBLISHERS
61–63 Uxbridge Road, London W5 5SA
A Random House Group Company
www.rbooks.co.uk

First published in Great Britain
in 2008 by Bantam Press
an imprint of Transworld Publishers

This book is a work of non-fiction based on the life, experiences and recollections of
Paul O'Grady. In some limited cases names of people, places, dates, sequences or the
detail of events have been changed solely to protect the privacy of others. The author
has stated to the publishers that, except in such minor respects not affecting the
substantial accuracy of the work, the contents of this book are true.

A CIP catalogue record for this book
is available from the British Library.

ISBN 9780593059258 (cased)
ISBN 9780593059883 (tpb)

All the photographs were kindly supplied by the author, except for the three views of
Birkenhead which are reproduced by kind permission of Birkenhead
Reference Library.

Addresses for Random House Group Ltd companies outside the UK
can be found at: www.randomhouse.co.uk
The Random House Group Ltd Reg. No. 954009

The Random House Group Limited supports The Forest Stewardship
Council (FSC), the leading international forest-certification organization. All our
titles that are printed on Greenpeace-approved FSC-certified paper carry the FSC logo.
Our paper procurement policy can be found at www.rbooks.co.uk/environment

Typeset in 11.5/15pt Sabon by
Falcon Oast Graphic Art Ltd.

Printed and bound in Great Britain by
CPI Mackays, Chatham, ME5 8TD

4 6 8 10 9 7 5

In memory of the Savage Sisters – Mary, Anne and Christine – without whom my world would've been a much duller place to grow up in.

ACKNOWLEDGEMENTS

I'd like to thank Doug Young at Transworld for his patience, my sister Sheila for coping with the endless questions and phone calls at all hours of the day and night when I needed information about the clan, and everybody who put up with my moaning as I sat writing this bloody thing when all I really wanted to do was to go out and play.

CHAPTER ONE

A T HOME I'VE GOT A BOX CONTAINING WHAT I SUPPOSE YOU might call the Family Archives. Family Archives sounds very grand but it's actually just an ordinary cardboard box containing an assortment of birth certificates, letters, old diaries and sepia photographs – the flotsam and jetsam of lives past. There's even a pair of yellowing false teeth wrapped up in a handkerchief. God knows who they belonged to. It could have been any one of my long-dead forebears.

When I was growing up in Birkenhead, nearly every adult I knew had false teeth or at least had a couple of fake choppers on a dental plate – either that or no teeth at all. My mother, christened Mary but known to everyone as Molly, had every tooth in her head extracted when false teeth became available on the National Health. She came from a generation where a poor diet and only the most primitive dental hygiene had taken its toll on working-class teeth, therefore a set of gleaming white gnashers courtesy of the NHS was a highly desirable acquisition.

In the early sixties, when she was only forty-four, she under-went this extreme dentistry. I remember her then as being quite slim and pretty, though I can't recall what condition her teeth were in. She used to say that the reason she'd had them all taken out was because she had a mouthful of teeth 'like a row of

1

bombed houses', which was a slight exaggeration. Like everyone else, she had all her teeth out because it was fashionable.

The sight of her lying in bed, moaning softly, a tea towel pressed to her swollen mouth and a bucket for blood on the floor beside her, horrified me. That nightmare scene put me off going to the dentist for life. Nothing and nobody could persuade me to go, and I'm still the same today. OK, I might not develop rigor mortis, throw myself on the front-room floor and hold my breath until my face turns a vivid scarlet at the mere suggestion of a check-up any more, but if a tooth is playing up I'll stupidly ignore it until the final hour. When I'm defeated by the pain and my cheek is as swollen as Popeye's I'll give in and go for treatment.

My patient dad would try and gently coax me into taking the trip to see Mr Aboud, our dentist, inevitably with no luck. Eventually my mother, exasperated by my carry-on, would get me there by means of devious trickery. On the pretext of visiting a clothes shop called Carson's that just happened to be close to Aboud's House of Torture, she'd whip me into his surgery with the speed and efficiency of the Childcatcher before I realized what was happening.

Mr Aboud, a dapper little man who wore neroli oil in his hair and spoke with an exotic accent – if he had chosen acting instead of dentistry he would have made the perfect Hercule Poirot – would place me firmly in his chair and press the foul-smelling rubber mask over my nose and mouth, telling me to 'Close your eyes, child, and breathe deeeeply, deeply . . .' To my ears he sounded just like Bela Lugosi in the Dracula films I'd seen on the telly. The gas would take effect and, slipping into a coma for what felt like hours but was actually only seconds, I would have wild, technicolour dreams and come to with a start on the leather bench in the waiting room, retching from the after-effects of the gas into a bloodied bowl held by my mother.

Dentistry has a come a long way since the sixties. I've been through more dentists than I have socks over the years, but now I've finally found a sympathetic marvel I'm a lot better. I still won't have an anaesthetic though; I don't like the after-effects. The dentist's creed back then was 'rip them out'. My aunty Chris, who kept all her extracted teeth wrapped in tissue in a jewellery box in her bedroom and was always threatening to have the poisonous-looking fangs made into a necklace, could never understand 'why anyone would want to spend their lives rootin' around people's gobs' and dismissed all dentists as butchers.

After she'd had weeks of soup and soggy toast, the long-awaited day came when Mr Aboud proudly presented my mother with her brand new set of dentures. She went straight from the dentist's to her sisters, Annie and Chrissie, and the new teeth were premiered in their back kitchen.

'Come on then, Moll, give us a gander at the new choppers,' said Annie, rubbing her hands together like a bookie with a hot tip. My mum, lips pursed tightly, removed her headscarf and arranged herself by the kitchen sink so that the light from the window would catch the full effect of the revelation. She ran her tongue back and forth across the teeth, cleared her throat and then slowly curled back her top and bottom lips, rather like a camel, to expose a set of startling white tombstones. For a moment, nobody spoke. You could have heard a pin drop.

'Jesus tonight,' said Aunty Chris, 'it's Mr Ed.'

My mum hated those teeth. They joined the ranks of her bêtes noires. The reasons she loathed the teeth were many. They were agony. They crucified her, it was like having a mouthful of barbed wire wrapped around your gums. She couldn't eat with them, they fell out when she talked and she wasn't bloody wearing them for no amount of sodding money so you can shove that in your pipe, sunbeam, and smoke it.

She was forever taking them out when she was around the

3

house and then forgetting where she'd put them. 'Where's me teeth?' was a familiar cry around the halls of Holly Grove. These peripatetic choppers would turn up in the most unlikely places, sometimes with embarrassing consequences.

In my teens, I'd go for a night on the razz, clubbing it over in Liverpool. If I'd managed to pull a bloke with a car, I'd try to convince him that giving me a lift home through the Mersey Tunnel would be well worth his time. Inevitably, such was my gratitude at being spared the hell of the tunnel bus, I would ask him in for a 'cup of tea' – a familiar euphemism for a grapple on the front-room couch, but a quiet one because my mum was upstairs in bed. During the preliminary necking session I would open one eye and to my utter mortification spy the Teeth, wedged down next to a cushion or grinning up at me obscenely from the pages of an upturned library book. As I tried to hide them by dropping them on the floor and pushing them under the sofa with my foot I'd be completely thrown off my stride.

Once I even found them biting into a toilet roll on top of the cistern and another time Jacko, a neighbour's Labrador, a lovely, friendly old hound who had a habit of coming into the house and helping himself to anything he fancied, found her teeth on the side of the bath. 'Where's me bloody teeth?' came the gummy enquiry just before she glanced at Jacko and had hysterics. Jacko was sat in the back yard gurning at her, his tail wagging, proudly showing off a muzzle full of false teeth.

Sometimes, as she sat on the sofa chatting and shaving an apple into wafer-thin membranes so that she could eat it with some semblance of dignity, the top set would unexpectedly slip their moorings and fall out into her lap, causing me, callous little swine, to fall about laughing. Sighing Garboesquely, she'd pick them up and, tossing them across the front-room floor, she'd moan, 'These bloody teeth, why did I ever get them?'

In retrospect, I realize that she sometimes did the teeth act purely to entertain me.

I was born in the Tranmere Workhouse during a violent thunderstorm on 14 June 1955. That's only partly true, I just fancied a bit of melodrama. I was actually born in St Catherine's Hospital, which in its day had been a workhouse. The weather had been stormy but by the time I arrived at 7.30 a.m., a disgusting hour to make one's debut, the storm had subsided and the sun was cracking the flags. According to my mother, the midwife who delivered me interpreted the storm clearing and the sun coming out as a promising omen. My mother, possessing an inherent pessimism, hoped that she was right.

St Cath's was to feature heavily in the lives of our family. Operations for ulcers and varicose veins were performed there. My father died in St Cath's after a heart attack. My sister nursed in maternity. My mother did a spell in the laundry and later she was an auxiliary nurse on the children's ward – at least until the day the hated deputy matron, a vicious little gnome of a woman loathed by staff and patients alike, hit a child across its bare legs. Mum lost her temper and after she walloped Miss Brindle on the head with a bedpan she lost her job too.

I sold newspapers and cigarettes around the wards for Prescott's, the newsagents across the road from the hospital. I wasn't allowed to go into maternity so instead I would position myself at the end of the ward and roar '*ECHO!!*' at the top of my lungs. I was accused of bringing on many an overdue labour. Now I come to think about it, I did them a favour.

I nearly had my first sexual experience on one of the psychiatric wards. An unwelcome one, with an extremely tall male nurse who was married to a Thumbelina of a woman. We frequently saw this incongruous couple shopping in our local Co-op, when my mother would remark, 'Every pan has a lid.' The male nurse made a lunge at me in the sluice, offering me sixpence if I'd 'just slip my hand' into his open trousers. Even at the tender age of eleven I realized that the going rate for a quick ham shank was a lot more than a tanner so I declined. What would Emma Peel do? Or Napoleon Solo? A rampant fan of secret agent programmes, I knew exactly how to react – I gave him a swift kick in the goolies that would've done any Avenger proud and said no more about it. I doubt if anyone would've believed me if I had run home screaming child abuse and besides, strange as it seems, I didn't want to get him into trouble. I saw him not as a dangerous paedophile but more as someone to be pitied. He certainly kept his distance from me after that.

The better part of St Cath's has long been demolished. Only the old annexe, treating long-term psychiatric patients, remains. The once-smart little porters' lodge is now a needle exchange centre for addicts. Poor old St Cath's.

A week after I was born I was allowed home to 23 Holly Grove, Higher Tranmere, Birkenhead. I grew up in this little house with my sister Sheila and brother Brendan, the youngest child of Molly and Paddy O'Grady. I was the Last Kick of a Dying Horse, an unexpected bonus, or a curse, depending on how well disposed towards me my ma was feeling that day. There's an eleven-year gap between me and my sister. My mother had no idea she was pregnant until she went to the doctor complaining of indigestion. Once she got over the shock, she quite warmed to the notion of becoming a mother again at thirty-nine. (It was in later years that I disappointed her when I failed to match up to her lofty and sometimes unreasonable expectations.) My parents couldn't decide on a name. My dad wanted to call me James, after his uncle; my mother aspired to Damien. Thank God my dad put his foot down on that one! With the advent of the film *The Omen* I can't imagine the stick I'd have got with a moniker like that. In the end they settled on Paul James, boring but adequate, and I was duly christened at St Joseph's Church.

Holly Grove was, and still is, at the top of Sydney Road, a steep hill that my mother once pushed a pram up, loaded with coal gathered from the railway sidings by Cammell Laird's after a direct hit in the Second World War. When she got to the top of the hill she stopped for a moment, exhausted by the long haul from the dock road and irritated by the inconvenience of the perpetual air raids. She stuck two fingers up to the night skies.

'Take this back to Hitler,' she shouted at the planes above her, 'you miserable shower of bastards, bombing women and babies!'

An ARP warden came running up the hill, wondering what this mad woman with a pram was doing, shouting abuse to the skies in the middle of a raid. Shining his torch on the contents of the pram, he realized. 'Gerrin, you daft cow, before you get nicked for looting,' he said, obligingly pushing the pram up the Grove for her.

Number 23 was the third house from the end of a winding row of houses cut into the side of the hill. They were built in the early 1930s on the site of an old quarry and there were signs of subsidence everywhere. Ominous cracks would appear in the walls and ceilings overnight and my mum was convinced that one day she'd come home from work to a pile of rubble. In front of the house was a grass bank leading down to the road. From this I would watch the great Cunard liners sailing up the Mersey and look across to Liverpool, another world when I was little. I used to stand there and listen for the one o'clock gun, a cannon in the Morpeth Dock that was fired electronically from the Bidston Observatory every day promptly on the hour.

Number 23 was like a doll's house inside. Two rooms, a bathroom and a kitchen extension that my dad built after the war downstairs, and three bedrooms and a toilet upstairs, with a postage-stamp garden in the front and a small yard at the back. There were only two power points in the entire house, one in the front room and a deadly old round-pinned Bakelite antique in the kitchen that sometimes gave off electric shocks.

All the electrical appliances in the house were fed from these two sockets. Fuses blew regularly. My mother had a fear of electricity; it was something else on her long list of what was 'not to be trusted'. Everything had to be unplugged before we went to bed. It was a waste of time her ever turning in for an early night as she couldn't relax until the rest of the family had gone up. She'd ask repeatedly if we'd 'turned all the lights out and pulled all the plugs out'.

'Yes, Mam,' I'd assure her, night after night.

'Are you sure?'

'Yes, I'm sure,' I'd reply absently.

'Are you sure you're sure?' she'd ask again. 'Go downstairs and check, just in case.'

For my eighteenth birthday a power point was installed upstairs on the landing wall so that I could play records in my bedroom and my mother could have an electric blanket. She was paranoid about that blanket. Even though it provided her with the luxury of a warm bed she viewed it as a death trap. At around 8.30 p.m. the Ceremony of the Electric Blanket would begin. First she'd ask you to pop upstairs and turn her blanket on. Ten minutes later she'd ask if you'd done it and make you go back upstairs to check. This went on all night. I was up and down like a whore's drawers. Sometimes she'd fall asleep on the sofa or become so engrossed in her latest Jean Plaidy that she'd forget the blanket was still on and when she did suddenly remember, usually halfway through *News at Ten*, she would react as if a time bomb was about to go off.

'Jesus Christ!' she'd scream, hurling herself off the couch and rattling the dinner service in the china cabinet, a present brought back from Hong Kong by my cousin Mickey. 'Me blanket! Gerrup them stairs and turn it off! Quick! Before the bloody bed catches fire.'

One night she fell asleep and forgot to turn it off. She awoke hours later 'gasping for air' and 'sweating cobs', with the bed 'burning the back off her'. After that incident she banished the electric blanket to the top of the wardrobe and took to using a hot-water bottle instead. Like its predecessor the blanket, it was not to be trusted. The bottle had to be bent nearly double in case air got in as she held it by the neck with a tea towel and filled it from a kettle of scalding water over the draining board. She had a theory that if air got inside the bottle it would explode later on in the bed. After she'd filled it to her exact safety standards and screwed the top back on tightly, she would shake it vigorously, upside down, to check that there weren't any leaks. She would then wrap it in an old hand towel and I would be dispatched to put it in the bottom of her bed. The bottle didn't last long. It failed to provide sufficient warmth for that iceberg of a bed. The blanket was soon reinstalled and we reverted to the old routine.

It was always cold, that house. No, not cold – freezing. You could've hung meat in the bedrooms during the winter months. On a bitterly cold morning the frost created strange patterns on the inside of the window pane. I'd lie in bed, the blankets pulled tightly around me for warmth, desperate for an early morning pee but holding out for as long as possible before daring to make the dash to the arctic conditions of the lav. It was a damp house as well, very damp. When the windows weren't frozen up they were running with condensation. Tea towels lined the window sills to soak up the lakes of water that formed. I'm surprised we didn't have a family of otters move into the back bedroom – the conditions were perfect.

The house had no central heating – that was unheard of. The only form of heating was a coal fire in the front-room grate, which also heated the water. If you wanted a bath you first used the poker to pull the damper down at the back of the grate, then, after a wait of two or three hours, you could take your bath. A bath, Holly Grove style, usually meant sitting in two inches of lukewarm water, flinching each time an ice-cold drip fell from the wet washing hanging out to dry on the pulley above you and hit you on the bare back.

On mornings when the temperature had dropped to Siberian levels, my mother would give in and get the electric fire out from the cupboard under the stairs. She didn't like using the electric fire as she claimed that it 'ate electricity'. She would panic if it was on for what she considered an unnecessary length of time. If you really wanted to send her into orbit you switched on both bars of the fire. She'd immediately go into her act.

'Jesus tonight, the heat in here,' she'd complain, coming in from the kitchen, fanning her face with the *Daily Mirror* and opening her cardigan. Two minutes earlier she'd been shivering like Pearl White on an ice floe. 'There's no need for an extra bar, turn it off before I suffocate. If that meter goes we're buggered because I haven't got a shilling, so get it off.'

She never had a shilling for the meter. I was always being sent round the neighbours' houses with a fistful of pennies to see if any of them had 'a single shilling for me mam, please'.

In extreme weather, when the water in the toilet bowl froze over, a paraffin heater that belched out stinking fumes sat on the upstairs landing. My mother instantly declared this a death trap. Just like the blanket, the heater needed watching, only more so, and it became another perfectly valid reason to tear me away from the telly and send me running up and down stairs to 'have a little look to see if it's OK'.

As the house was at the top of a hill and close to the River Mersey, we took the brunt of the worst weather. A mist from the river would creep up the hill and mingle with the smoke pouring out of every chimney pot in Birkenhead, mutating into a freezing, acrid fog that burned the back of your throat. This was before the Clean Air Act put a stop to coal fires, which in turn meant the loss of a familiar sight around the back alleys: the coalman.

The weekly delivery of coal was a ritual that all the women

in the area looked forward to. They would fluff up their hair and apply a little face powder and lipstick in readiness. The lid of the coal bunker would be flung back in preparation, the back-yard door would be opened wide and the women, purses in hand, would stand on the step and peer down the alley waiting for Alf, the Chippendale of coalmen. Good-natured and with a cheeky line in patter, Alf had the ladies of Holly Grove eating out of the palm of his hand. He was tall and handsome, with a set of magnificent white teeth (his own) and startling blue eyes enhanced by the thick layer of coal dust that covered his face. He wore a leather jerkin open to the waist, revealing a well-defined hairy chest, and a leather cap perched at a jaunty angle covered his greasy black curls. He had two side-kicks, 'the miserable one' with a lugubrious expression and 'the bit of a lad' who was very young and blushed under the coal dust whenever a woman spoke to him. I thought that Alf and his cronies were part of *The Black and White Minstrel Show* on the TV, a suspicion that was confirmed by Alf's repertoire of popular tunes. He fancied himself as something of an opera singer and his powerful rendition of 'The Toreador Song' echoed around the yards and alleys, transforming them for a moment into the back streets of Seville and my mother and the other women into Carmens.

'What do I owe you, Alf?' my mother would coyly ask as he tipped the sack of coal that he had draped nonchalantly over his shoulder into the bunker with a sly smile.

'Run away with me to New Brighton for a night of passion and a fish supper and we'll call it quits,' he'd reply with a dirty wink, making her blush and sending her into a fit of girlish convulsions. He said the same line to all the housewives, making them feel like desirable women again even if only for a moment.

During the winter, regardless of how well prepared my dad had been with his primitive loft insulation of newspapers and old coats, the pipes always froze and burst, inevitably during the night. Water cascaded through my parents' bedroom ceiling. The neighbours, awoken by the commotion, would arrive, their clothes hastily pulled over their nightwear, armed with buckets and mops to help clean up the mess. My dad vanished into the loft to assess the damage and my mother, soaked to the skin and looking slightly demented, pushed the wet hair from her face with the back of her hand and began mopping up the flood. I'd be evacuated to Mary and Frank's, our next-door neighbours'. Mary worked in the brewery and got on my mother's nerves because she used to 'pop in', unannounced and uninvited, while we were eating our tea and hang over the back of a chair, fag in hand and reeking of Guinness, expounding some crying shame. Mary was an ardent movie fan and loved a good 'fillum'.

'There's a marvellous Bette Davis fillum on the telly this afternoon, Molly,' she'd say to my mum over the back-yard fence as she ran some washing through a mangle so big that she had to jump as she turned the handle. '*Now, Voyager*, with Paul Henreid.' She'd pause from her leaping for a moment to remove the Capstan Full Strength from her lower lip, taking an enormous pull on it first. 'It was Bette Davis that got me smoking, you know,' she'd reflect proudly, exhaling a cloud of smoke in a manner emulating her heroine. '"Oh, Jerry, why ask for the moon when we have the stars . . ." *Now, Voyager* . . . they don't make fillums like that any more.'

As a testimony to her love of the silver screen, Mary had developed a corned beef leg. The skin on the side of her left leg had turned shiny and tight, red and mottled like corned beef from a lifetime of sitting too close to the fire with her stockings rolled down to watch fillums on the telly. According to my mother, corned beef leg was the mark of a slut. So was going about with your stockings rolled down to your ankles, a fag dangling out of the corner of your mouth and more than a hint of Guinness and whisky on your breath. To be seen running to the shop for the *Echo* in your slippers and a pair of men's socks was inexcusable. Mary, staggering home from work slightly the worse for wear one night, fell over the bin in the back yard and revealed that her choice of lingerie was an old pair of her husband's underpants, grey with age and secured at the waist with a large nappy pin. This damning evidence was enough to condemn Mary as a slut of the Highest Order of Sluttery for life. Out taking his daily wander, Jacko the Labrador strolled into Mary's kitchen one afternoon and helped himself to Frank's tea, a nice piece of yellow fish. He was halfway down the back alley, fish in mouth, before Mary caught up with him and retrieved it. She rinsed it under the tap, said nothing and served it up later that night with mashed potatoes. Frank was none the wiser.

I liked Mary and her good-natured husband. They never had children of their own, which was a shame as they were great around children. Mary was a child's delight, always up for a bit of fun. She'd make ice-cream floats with lemonade and vanilla ice and we'd sit on the back-yard step drinking them. She taught me how to play cards and knew the filthy version of 'Maggie May'. Frank, a diabetic, let me watch him inject himself with his daily insulin and, as he shaved in a mirror over the kitchen sink with a cut-throat razor, told me stories of his miserable childhood and how he survived the cruel regime in the orphanage where he grew up. Frank's orphanage tales worried me. My mother was always threatening to put me in a home if I didn't behave. I didn't want to eat bread and dripping and be beaten with a belt by nuns so I'd be on my best behaviour for a while, making my mother instantly suspicious. 'What have you broke?' she'd ask.

My mother didn't share Mary's enthusiasm for fillums and wasn't very keen on going to the cinema. She'd been 'touched up' (her words) during a showing of *The Blue Angel* and it had put her off. The film had been on at 'the Colly', the Coliseum Cinema on Old Chester Road, known locally for obvious reasons as 'the Bug House', and during the show a man had put his hand on her leg. She had not screamed out but had sat in the dark, terrified, unable to move from fear. After that her visits to the cinema were rare. It was my dad who sat through all the Disney cartoons with me, not that he had to endure the likes of *Sleeping Beauty* for very long. We'd be back on the street within ten minutes, for as soon as the villainess appeared on screen I'd shoot up the aisle like a bullet to get away from her and back to the safety of Number 23.

Whenever I dream of that damp little house, and I occasionally still do, I recall it in vivid and minute detail. I visualize it as I saw it when I was a child. Like an old movie shot in monochrome, I can see a small boy sat on top of his sister's Dansette record player watching the condensation running down the front-room window, protected from the heat of the coal fire by a fire guard hung with damp washing. I loved that little house. It was the backdrop for my formative years. It's in my blood still.

CHAPTER TWO

SIFTING THROUGH THE JUNK THAT IS OVER A CENTURY OF family memorabilia, I came across relics from my own distant past that acted like jump leads on the rusty engine of my memory. They brought an instant recall of incidents from my childhood, not vague, dim recollections but crystal clear images of times that I thought I'd long forgotten. I found an old school report of mine from the sixties. Reading it, I was transported back down the years, to Corpus Christi High School during an Eng lit lesson. My teacher, Dora Doughty, a well-corseted and glamorous siren with big hair who looked as if she was formed from the same mould as Elsie Tanner, sat cross-legged on her desk wafting powerful fumes of scent as she expounded the wisdom of Proust to an uninterested Class 5S. Pearls before swine, I'm afraid. We were far more taken with Miss D's magnificent bosom than anything Marcel had to say for himself. But now, years later, sitting in the loft, absorbed by the account of a fourteen-year-old schoolboy who was once 'bright and chatty but needed to try harder at maths' and whom I can't imagine ever being, I can hear and see it all.

A girl at the front of the class, egged on by her mates, has got her hand up in the air. 'Miss, what's that perfume you've got on called?'

'Do you like it?' replies Miss Doughty, sniffing her wrist. 'It's called Ambush,' and producing a bottle from her handbag she proceeds to spray it liberally into the air. 'Now tell me, class, what does that smell bring to mind?'

After a long pause and a lot of theatrical sniffing, the pupils slowly give their opinions.

'Perfume, miss.'

'Toilet cleaner.'

'Me nan.'

'It reminds me of a particular Bonfire Night.' This comes from Dougal, the class creep.

'And why is that, Dougal?' enquires Miss Doughty, silencing our groans with a wave of her hand.

'Because it smells of burnt toffee, and we had toffee apples at our last bonfire party,' Dougal answers, surveying the class smugly.

More groans and catcalls.

'Dougal is right,' Miss Doughty triumphantly announces. 'Smell is the key that unlocks the secrets of the mind. Indeed, as Proust himself believed, the most profound memory is triggered off by smell.'

Funny the crap you remember. I can't remember my mobile phone number but I can rattle off my mother's Co-op dividend number: 28171 in case you are interested.

Proust was right, for inside an old red leather purse that once belonged to my mother, nestling among the bus tickets and holy medals, I came across a tiny bottle that had once contained perfume. It was Honeysuckle, and after Tweed by Lentheric it was her favourite smell.

I removed the minuscule rubber stopper and took a sniff. Even after all these years, there was still a faint trace of Honeysuckle. I closed my eyes, inhaled deeply and instantly called to mind one of my earliest memories. I was staring up at a ceiling, lying on my mother's knee in my dad's armchair, listening to the radio.

'This is the BBC Home Service for mothers and children at home . . . *Dong de dong, dong de dong, dong, dong* . . . Are you sitting comfortably? Then we'll begin.'

I imagine *Listen with Mother* is a familiar memory to those of a certain age. I never missed it. Every weekday afternoon at 1.45, I'd haul myself up on to my mum's knee for a quarter of an hour's ecstasy with George Dixon and Daphne Oxenford.

My mum would sing along with them, 'This is the way the old men ride, Hobble-dee, hobble-dee, hobble-dee and down into a ditch.'

Because George and Daphne were very posh my mum would adopt a highly refined tone for these elegant nursery rhymes. It was the voice that she used when she was feeling flush and shopped at Stubb's, a smart confectioner's and baker's at the top of Grange Road West. It was her society voice.

'Tu skanes end a farncie pliss,' she would ask politely, pointing towards the scones and sticky pink and blue fancies that sat tastefully displayed on paper doilies in the shop window. The crumbling assistant in her little white pinny and faded black dress, with a white lace cap pinned to what was left of her hair in testimony to her years of servitude rather than for reasons of hygiene, would flutter behind the counter like a moth under glass. She would incline her head graciously as an acknowledgement of my mother's order and then, with the speed and dexterity of a close-up magician, would make up a little box out of a flat piece of card. I always wanted to reward this outstanding display of origami with a round of applause but Stubb's was not the place for such spontaneous outbursts of enthusiasm.

The assistant would then lean effortlessly into the window and, using a cake slice, scoop the skanes and farncies delicately into the box. The climax of this enviable performance came

17

when she took a roll of red and gold ribbon that hung by the side of the ornate till and deftly wrapped a length around the box, tying it in a bow.

As far as I was concerned, this woman was wasted behind the counter of Stubb's. She should've been on *Opportunity Knocks*. My mum would only enter the hallowed portals of Stubb's if she was dressed appropriately in her smart woollen coat with the shawl collar and big buttons. She'd rather be strapped naked to the altar of St Werburgh's than cross the threshold of Stubb's dressed in her 'scruff'.

Not that she ever really was. She was always smart when she went into town. After she died and I went through her wardrobe I was amazed at how many beautiful clothes she had, most of them hardly worn.

She could be pretty scary if caught en déshabillé first thing in the morning though. I remember one morning when I was about thirteen. I was awoken from my slumbers at the crack of dawn by the sound of frantic banging on the front-room window, accompanied by shrieks of 'Shoo!' and 'Gerrof me bloody plants!' I ran downstairs to find my mum bent over the gas fire like a malevolent crone, sucking on a piece of dry toast, deep in thought. She wasn't looking her best in her flannelette nightgown and derelict bedjacket, her teeth safe for once in the pocket, and a solitary roller, around which she'd absently rolled a couple of strands of hair as she'd said her prayers the night before, swinging drunkenly in the middle of her forehead. This perfunctory attempt at beauty maintenance was meant to ensure that, when she awoke the next morning, the fine hair she'd been cursed with from birth would be transformed into a mass of fascinating curls. A mug of tea perched precariously on the end of the mantelpiece and a slice of burnt toast smeared with a scraping of marmalade sat on a saucer in the hearth as she turned slowly towards me.

'That damn cat's been at me plants again' was all she said, staring forebodingly out of the window.

My mum's pride and joy was her little front garden. She had a way with plants that unfortunately, try as I may, I haven't inherited. She knew instinctively what to do with the delicate cuttings that she nicked on her many excursions to the stately homes of England, accompanied by her partner in crime, my aunty Anne.

'Keep your eyes peeled, Annie, while I get a couple of cuttings off this beautiful little astilbe,' she'd hiss to her nervous sister as she surreptitiously stashed the contraband inside her furled umbrella.

Aunty Anne would react as if they were smuggling heroin out of Istanbul, her eyes wide with panic, her mouth set in a maniacal grin as they walked out past the security guard on the gate.

'Goodbye, thank you.' My mum would wave cheerily to the guard as she elbowed my aunty Anne hard in the ribs and on to the coach for home.

She could identify most plants by their Latin name and had a knowledge of the medicinal properties of herbs that would have impressed Culpeper. A visit to the doctor would be a last resort. She was distrustful of doctors and hospitals and preferred to self-medicate from the dispensary of pills and potions that she'd accumulated over the years and kept hidden under the bathroom sink. If she didn't have a suitable pill for what ailed you, she had a neat sideline in home remedies that would either kill or cure you.

Bread poultices and hot cabbage leaves would bring a boil to a head and draw out the infection, and tea made from raspberry leaves would help induce a pregnancy that had gone beyond full term. She used lavender for burns, oranges for constipation, and the water from a boiled onion mixed with a little ginger and cayenne pepper for the treatment of catarrh.

Two hundred years earlier and she most likely would've been burned as a witch. As it was, she went about the garden treating me to an impromptu botany lesson.

'How did the dandelion get its name?' she'd ask, as she tore the unfortunate weed out of the flower bed and dropped it on to a sheet of newspaper. 'It's from the French. *Dent-de-lion*, meaning lion's tooth. You can eat the leaves, you know, but if you eat too many your wee turns blue.' I don't know where she'd acquired all this unusual information but I found it fascinating, particularly when it came to the deadlier residents of her patch.

'This is a bugger, this stuff,' she'd say, waving a large bunch of small pinky-white flowers with long stems that she'd hacked at with the carving knife. Thinning, she called it. 'It's a herb really.' She was warming to her theme. '*Valeriana officinalis*, otherwise known as valerian. The root is good for the guts but it can also be a lethal sedative, a killer. It grows like wild mint, you have to keep an eye on it otherwise it's inclined to take over. Bit like her,' she said, nodding in the general direction of Rose Long's house. Rose Long lived next door but one and was not my ma's favourite person. 'If anyone needed sedating it's her . . . permanently.'

'You see this plant?' She'd point to a large pink foxglove. '*Digitalis purpurea*, used in the treatment of heart disease, also known as dead man's bells, and do you know why?' she'd ask dramatically. 'Because it can kill you, that's why. It's deadly poisonous, and at its most toxic just before it flowers. Pretty-looking thing, isn't it?' She'd stand back and gaze lovingly at the plant with more than a hint of admiration in her voice. Thanks to my mum, I was an expert toxicologist by the time I was ten and could've poisoned half of Birkenhead if I'd felt like it.

'D'ya fancy a trip to Bidston Hill?' meant get your coat, we're going to steal leaf mould for the roses. In the early sixties, Bidston was still untouched by the spreading urban desecration of council estates and bypasses. It was a film location manager's dream; you stepped back in time as you entered this ancient village with its cobbled courtyards, farmhouses and thatched cottages. The village shop had a huge, heavily studded wooden door that wouldn't have looked out of place in a Harry Potter saga. Inside the shop, all was order and calm. My mother would put on her society voice and ask the old lady behind the counter for 'Two Pendleton's ice creams, pliss, one cornet, one wafer, think yew.' We'd eat these as we strolled at a snail's pace up towards Bidston Hill, stopping as always to stare at the carving of a horse hewn into a rock at the side of the path just as you turned into the woodland.

'That was carved in one hundred AD,' she'd say through a mouthful of Pendleton's, 'and some swine has gone and defaced it,' gesturing disgustedly to the words 'Thomo is a wanker' scrawled across it in black marker pen. 'They want horsewhipping in the street – no, hanging, horsewhipping's too good for them.' Had she been a magistrate God knows what sentence she would have passed on a serious offender, say a murderer. Probably he'd be hung, drawn and quartered very slowly after a period of prolonged torture.

There was another carving on a flat rock, further up towards the observatory. This was of a sun goddess, older than time and nearly five foot in length. I didn't like to hang around the sun goddess for very long; she always left me feeling unsettled. I had an eerie sensation that someone or something was observing me. I felt that this ancient deity should be shown more respect, that it wasn't quite right to be standing on a rock casually looking at her.

I always enjoyed a day out to Bidston Hill, even if it did mean a return trip carrying my own body weight in leaf mould. Bidston Hill was a glorious adventure playground and it catered to my overactive imagination. Tales of Robin Hood and William Tell were played out as I ran through the woods, accompanied by appropriate sound effects as I dodged the imaginary arrows of the sheriff's men. The windmill that sat on top of a rock was transformed in my mind's eye into the lair of the Evil Queen, so I'd re-enact the death of Snow White, playing the parts of the huntsman and Miss White respectively. My mother was busy shovelling trowels of leaf mould into a laundry bag and muttering to herself as she went about her work.

'Look at this,' she'd coo fondly at a shovelful of earth, waving it towards me. 'Isn't that the most beautiful leaf mould you've ever seen? Marvellous for the roses! Come and have a sniff.'

Holding a handle apiece we'd drag this bag of earth home with us, hauling it off the bus and up Sydney Road. 'If your dad asks,' she'd say conspiratorially, pausing to get her breath as we hiked up the hill, leaning against the wall and grabbing her chest for effect, 'tell him it's a bag of washing.' And in case he happened to look into the bag, not that he would, she would wrap her cardigan over the top of the earth to make it look more 'convincing'.

She spent hours in that garden tending to her flowers. Roses were her speciality; she grew almost every variety from the delicate tea roses to the big blowzy blooms that truly intoxicated you with their heady perfume. Refusing to wear gardening gloves, she preferred to feel the soil with her bare hands. After an afternoon spent pruning her roses, she would emerge from the garden weary but content and, standing in the front room, would hold out her cut and bloodied arms and hands wearing the martyred expression of a nun with stigmata.

'Do you think I should go for a tetanus?' she'd ask, the blood running down her arms from various thorn wounds, 'or should I chance it with a bit of Dettol?'

She always chanced it.

No sensible cat within a five-mile radius of our house would chance it near Molly O.'s garden though. No cat in its right mind would put a paw inside the garden gate for fear of bitter and sometimes deadly reprisals. The neighbourhood moggies had obviously passed a message around the feline grapevine telling all members to keep away from the madwoman at Number 23's garden regardless of how inviting the beds of flowers and tasty blackbirds looked.

She loved to listen to the birds. There was a robin that she was particularly soft on, and she would lovingly buy him mealworms from the fishing tackle shop in town.

'Do you know why the robin's breast is red?' Without bothering to wait for an answer, she would go on to relate the tale of the robin's breast as she had done countless times before.

'When Jesus was on the cross,' she would say, adopting her pious voice, 'the brave little robin, who was brown all over in them days, tried to ease poor Jesus's suffering by pulling out the nails in his poor bloodied hands. As he tugged at those hard iron nails, red with Jesus's blood, he stained his breast and that's why it's red today, as a testament to that little bird's undying bravery and loyalty. So think on, my lad, and don't start screaming like a bloody big ciss when that plaster on your knee has to come off tonight, think of poor Jesus.'

Mum enjoyed telling this fable of the robin. I'm still reminded of it whenever I see a robin in the garden and they are my favourite birds, just as they were hers. I also think of Jesus when I'm pulling a plaster off my leg, a lot more painful since I hit puberty. As the plaster is ripping chunks of hair out of my leg, I even shout his name, the full title: 'JESUS CHRIST!'

All was harmonious in the garden of Number 23 until the arrival of a strange black and white tomcat, an enormous beast that was oblivious to all of my mother's frantic protestations from the front-room window. The monster would pause momentarily as it strolled across the postage-stamp lawn and, with a yawn, would glance up contemptuously in her direction before it moved on at a leisurely pace to have a nice lie-down on a bed of pansies. Completely ignoring her, it would stretch out its paws luxuriantly and roll around, flattening the flowers with its massive girth.

'Me pansies!' My mother would be driven insane by this effrontery and the air would turn every shade of blue as she charged out of the house, hurling a lump of coal at the creature with the speed of a fast bowler at Lord's. She would invariably miss. My dad said there was more coal in the garden than there was in the coal bunker in the back yard. It was beginning to look like a slag heap. The battle raged, and as the weeks progressed the garden began to show the wear and tear of an urban war zone.

The cat would lie in wait for the birds, hidden in a bed of lavender and poised to pounce. It would pee scornfully against the front door and on the coal in the bunker, which made the entire house stink of cats. Cocking its insolent arse in the air it would crouch behind the roses and defecate, digging up delicate plants as it buried the evidence.

My mother was wild with fury. She set up defence headquarters in her bedroom and maintained a permanent vigil. Standing close to the open window, her face half hidden by the net curtains, she waited patiently, surveying the garden with gimlet eyes for any sign of the Hun, armed with an artillery of rocks and coal.

Each morning daily bulletins of how the war was progressing were shouted up the stairs to me.

'That bloody cat's had all me sweet peas down and it's done its business right behind the gate again, the filthy swine. I'll have to throw this slipper out now.'

Blithely the seemingly unassailable cat carried on using her garden as if it were its own personal property, acknowledging her presence only by spitting viciously when a lump of coal, fired with great force from the bedroom window, miraculously scored a bullseye.

The final straw came on that dreadful day when, looking out of the window, she saw the behemoth sprawled out on the grass before her, its tail lashing back and forth, proudly taunting her with its recent kill. Hanging limply from its mouth by the tip of its wing was the lifeless body of Her Robin. She let out a strangled scream and was out of the house and into the garden like a woman possessed. By the time she got there the enemy had fled, leaving behind the sad little casualty of war.

She was genuinely distressed by what she considered an unprovoked act of cruelty on the part of the cat and was unable to stem the tears of frustration that flowed as she buried the broken corpse of her old friend, lovingly wrapped in a sheet of blue toilet paper.

'I know it's a natural instinct for a cat to kill a bird,' she moaned, 'but why didn't its owners put a bell on the cat's collar? Robbie would've heard it coming then and flown off.'

As she mourned the loss of the bird, she blamed herself for encouraging it to come into the garden. My poor mother had tried every repellent known to man to keep the cat out; the place was a minefield. If you bent to sniff a rose you collapsed in a violent sneezing fit thanks to the amount of pepper that she'd sprinkled about the flower beds to deter it from 'doing its business'. All to no avail: the moggy was impervious to her attempts. Defeated by this last sickening blow, she took to her bed.

She lay under the counterpane for a few hours, her mind seized by dark thoughts. A solution slowly dawned on her and she began, I believe, to hatch an evil plan that would rid her of her adversary once and for all. Over the next few days she observed the hated creature from the front-room window as it stalked the occupied territory of the garden, destroying what was left of her beautiful flowers and plants.

I would catch snatches of the curses she was muttering to herself as she watched it prowl among her flowers. 'That's right, me lad, you help yourself,' she'd say grimly, tapping her foot. 'Just you wait.'

One morning I returned home from my paper round earlier than usual. As I turned the corner to go up the path my mother suddenly appeared from behind the garden hedge, dressed in her nightie, holding a dead cat by the tail.

'Ooh! You nearly gave me a bloody heart attack,' she complained, clutching her chest. 'What d'ya think you're doin', creeping around at this hour of the bloody morning?'

'I've been doing me paper round,' I answered, 'and what are you doing creeping around the garden in your nightie swinging a dead cat in your hand?'

'What cat?' she asked innocently, playing for time. 'Oh, this . . .' her voice trailing off as she surveyed her nemesis with more than a glint of satisfaction in her eyes. 'I've just found it . . . dead, poor thing. I was opening the bedroom window and I saw it lying there motionless, in a funny position like . . . so I came down to investigate, and that's why I'm in my nightie. Now, if you don't mind, keep your bloody voice down and your big trap shut in case they hear you,' she hissed, glancing nervously up to Dot next door's bedroom window, 'and help me get rid of the bloody thing.'

Indicating for me to hold open a bin liner that she just happened to have with her, she dropped the dead cat into it, instructing me to dispose of the corpse in the bin chambers of the block of flats on Sydney Road.

'Serves it bloody right,' she sniffed, as she hurried back indoors before the neighbours saw her. 'It must have eaten something.'

It wasn't until a few weeks later, when I was searching in the scary recesses of the cupboard under the kitchen sink for a tin of shoe polish, that I came across the evidence that let the cat out of the bag, so to speak. Hidden behind the assorted bottles and tins that gather under kitchen sinks I found a tin of Kitekat and a half-empty medicine bottle containing an extremely suspect concoction.

I confronted her with the evidence.

'Give me that bottle,' she said, snatching it out of my hand. 'You haven't got any on your skin or drunk any, have you?' she added, starting to panic.

'Did you poison that cat?' I asked, looking her straight in the eye.

'Don't be so stupid,' she retorted, feigning outrage, and claimed that the cat food was for 'that poor undernourished creature that sometimes comes in the back yard' and that the dubious contents of the bottle were for 'the drains'. Who did I think I was?

Did this Birkenhead Borgia poison that unfortunate cat? She always hotly denied it but I still have my doubts. I wouldn't put it past her. She hated that cat with a passion and couldn't have, wouldn't have, stood by and let it destroy her beautiful garden and all the hard work she'd put into it without a fight. Then there was the killing of 'her robin', an act that I think finally tipped her over the edge and sounded the death knell for the poor moggy. As she herself was wont to say, 'Desperate times call for desperate measures.'

An Alsatian dog was kept permanently chained up in the back yard of a house to the rear of ours and it barked incessantly, twenty-four hours a day. All the neighbours complained, the couple who owned the hound were reported to the RSPCA, the police were called out when it escaped one day from its back-yard prison and supposedly attacked George Long, but still nothing was done about this poor dog who barked all day and all through the night. After we'd endured two years of sleepless nights, the wretched hound was found dead one morning in strange and inexplicable circumstances.

At the time I was temporarily delivering papers for Henshaw's, our local newsagent-cum-grocer's. Eileen Henshaw liked to adopt a superior attitude, the sort she imagined befitted a grocer's wife. My mother said she was common and that she gave herself airs above her station. She was forever bragging about her son's scholastic achievements and the fact that he went to a grammar school. 'The teachers reckon the way he's going on it'll be head boy for him in a few years,' she'd say to my mother as she sliced into a lump of Cheshire cheese with a length of wire. 'He's a child prodigal,' she'd add, picking crumbs of cheese off the board and chewing on them, smiling pityingly all the while over the counter at me.

'Common cow,' my mother would say on her way home, 'you'd think she ran Harrods instead of a shitty backstreet midden.' My mother hated going into Henshaw's but it was the only shop locally that sold newspapers. She didn't go in there often, she usually sent me instead. She much preferred to shop at Mrs Profitt's, but that good lady had sold up and gone to live with her daughter, selling the house-cum-shop to the couple who owned the dog.

Every Wednesday Mrs Profitt made her own meat and potato pies in her little kitchen behind the shop. Her pies had the distinction of being the 'talk of Tranmere' and deservedly so, for I've yet to taste a better one. Her other claim to fame was finding a tropical spider in a box of Fyffes bananas. As she took the lid off the box and pulled aside the straw, a hairy-legged monster hopped out and crawled across the shop floor, causing more than a little fuss among the women waiting to be served. Mrs Profitt, however, was as cool as ice and calmly covered the spider with an upturned washing-up bowl and called the police. The spider was later identified by Chester Zoo as relatively harmless but it rocketed Mrs Profitt to fame. She ended up in the *Birkenhead News*, photographed outside her shop holding a big bunch of Fyffes bananas in one hand and a meat and potato pie in the other, under the headline SHOPKEEPER CATCHES DEADLY TARANTULA.

Mrs Profitt was a real lady, not some jumped-up trollop who didn't have an arse in her trousers, a pot to piss in or a window to chuck it out of until she married that old nit, George Henshaw . . . My ma had a pretty low opinion of Eileen Henshaw.

Eileen had a nasty habit of 'shouting your business' across a packed shop. For my mother, if anyone, let alone a scandal-monger like Eileen Henshaw, aired her private affairs in public it was a crime punishable by death. She'd have been knitting a noose if she'd heard Eileen spouting her venom at me.

'Can you tell your mother please, Paul, that she's overdue six weeks now with her papers and if she doesn't pay by the end of this week we'll have to cancel her *Echo*. It's getting beyond a joke. Tell her I'm not a charity.'

Oh, the shame of it all. Ground, open up and swallow me, let the Tardis appear and whisk me away to another dimension where there are no mothers who make their kids go into shops because they owe money and are too embarrassed to go in themselves. Oh please, baby Jesus, let Eileen Henshaw fall on her own bacon slicer and have her forked tongue sliced from her wicked mouth and thrown to the dogs in the street. In short, I was mortified. My only satisfaction was the knowledge that my mother would go apeshit when I related this message to her with a few exaggerations for inflammatory effect, thrown in to stoke her furnace.

'Cheeky cow, who does she think she is, shouting me business all over the bloody shop? I'll give her six weeks.'

She'd dip into either the rent money or one of the Prudential Club books that were hidden against burglars underneath the sofa cushion and pay up, worrying about how she'd balance the books later on.

'Here, give her this,' she'd hiss, pushing the precious pound into my hand. 'That's the club money short now, so when the Rediffusion man calls don't answer the door.' We rented a television from Rediffusion, everyone in Birkenhead did.

Reluctantly I shuffled off, dragging my feet, dreading the humiliation that I was bound to endure at the hands of Eileen Henshaw.

'Tell her to stuff her bloody *Echo*' was my mother's Parthian shot as I slunk out of the back door. I'd hang about outside the shop, trying to appear casual, waiting until it was empty of customers and it was safe to go in. Typically, as soon as I opened the door ten people appeared from nowhere and followed me in.

'Don't tell me your mother's finally decided to pay her bill!' Eileen would shriek in mock surprise, looking around the shop at her audience and clapping her hands to her face. 'This is a great day for the Henshaws, we'll be able to shut up shop and go on holiday to Spain with the proceeds from your mother's paper bill.' With what she probably considered a refined laugh, the sort she imagined one heard in smart drawing rooms all over Heswall, she tore the tickets out of the big red order book that recorded the names of who owed what and when.

Her husband George came in from the living quarters behind the shop. He always wore a white overall with a pencil in his top pocket as well as a permanent scowl. He took his profession very seriously and that's why I was so surprised at what came next.

'You've had experience as a paper lad, haven't you?' he said, plonking a large freshly cooked ham on the counter. He prided himself on his boiled ham. 'Do you want a temporary job?'

Eileen's eyebrows shot up into her hairline along with her voice. 'What sort of a job?' she shrieked at her husband, picking bits off his ham like a carrion crow.

'We need a paper lad for a few weeks,' he said, moving the ham away from the claws of his wife and to the safety of the refrigerated glass-fronted counter. 'Do you have any better ideas? We're desperate, we can't afford to be fussy, there's no one else unless he wants to get up and do it.' Here George Henshaw inclined his head towards the back room, where the child prodigal sat stuffing his face with an Arctic roll and watching the telly.

Eileen bristled and in no uncertain terms told her husband that no child of hers was going to walk the streets of Tranmere with a bag of newspapers weighing four times his own body weight, twice a day in all sorts of weather, and if anybody dared to think that she would be party to such a thing then they didn't know her. 'And besides,' she added, 'he's far too busy with his homework to deliver papers.'

She glanced into the back room to where the prodigal, now replete, lay sprawled out on the sofa preparing for a long session of children's telly and quickly closed the door. She turned and looked at me over the counter as if she were forced to buy a diseased slave at the market and then, shaking her head in disgust, enquired grandly if I had any references.

'Don't talk daft, woman,' her husband snapped. 'We only want him for a few weeks until the regular lad gets back. What do you want references for? Get those papers marked up, he can start now.' Child labour laws meant nothing to George.

And so, until Eileen sacked me a week later for missing a Sunday morning when instead of dragging a sack of Sunday papers around the streets I went to Wales with the Legion of Mary like the good Catholic lad I was, I became the Henshaws' paper boy. My mother reckoned I was sacked because the

Henshaws were Protestants and it served me right for working for them. The paper round covered quite a large area, from Old Chester Road to Church Road, which meant a lot of steep hills with two sacks of heavy *Echo*s.

Eileen marked the papers up with the names and numbers of the various streets, admonishing me all the while to pay attention and put the right *Echo* in the right letter box, and not to be late in the morning. The papers were then packed into two large canvas bags and lowered over each shoulder. I literally staggered off under the weight and out into the night. I didn't care, I was earning half a crown a week.

Two hours later I reeled home and into the kitchen.

'Where the bloody hell have you been?' my mother said. 'Your father's been worried sick and your tea's ruined.'

'I've got a job,' I explained.

'A job? A job? What sort of job? Do you hear this, Paddy, he says he's got a job?'

'I'm delivering papers for Henshaw's,' I said proudly, 'half a crown a week.'

My mother stopped stirring gravy and stared at me as if I'd just admitted that it was me who had shopped Anne Frank.

'Papers?' she exclaimed, screwing her face up and raising her voice ten octaves. 'Papers! Henshaw's? Half a crown? Are you listening to this, Paddy?' she shouted into the front room, fanning herself with a tea towel. 'Delivering papers for Henshaw's, how could you?' she asked. 'Mother of God!'

She couldn't have been less pleased if I'd announced that I was joining the Ku Klux Klan. I'd thought she'd be delighted, but there was no telling what the reaction would be when it came to my mother. She used to accuse me of being contrary and unpredictable – well, Mother, who did I inherit that from? What's in the bitch comes out in the pup, to quote Aunty Chris.

My dad came out from the front room. 'What's going on?'

'He's only gone and got a job with Henshaw's delivering papers, that's what,' she said in the voice of a woman betrayed. Glaring at me, she asked, 'What were you thinking?'

'Now, Molly . . .' My dad, forever the bearer of oil for troubled waters, pointed out that it would do me no harm, was only for three weeks and it would earn me some pocket money.

'Fair play to you,' he said to me over his shoulder as he returned to his front-room sanctum to read his *Echo* in peace.

'Working for that bitch,' my mother said, shaking her head angrily. 'Well, tell her nowt, do you hear me? Nowt. She's a nosey cow, that one, and I don't want her knowing my business.'

I said nowt the morning that Tina, the owner of the barking Alsatian, came into the shop to ask if she could use the phone. She explained that hers was out of order, the phone box by the flats had been vandalized and she had to ring the vet as a matter of urgency, or words to that effect. Eileen loved this. She could play Lady Bountiful and offer succour to one of her flock, plus she got the gossip first-hand.

'I hope it's nothing serious,' she asked, brightening up and opening the counter flap so Tina could 'come through'. She stood listening at the open door while Tina made her call in the back room, and repeated everything she heard to her willing audience of customers. 'Oh, she got up this morning and the dog was dead in the yard . . . stone cold by the outside lavatory . . . doesn't know when it died, some time in the night . . . Oh my God, she thinks it's been poisoned by someone!'

I kept my head down and loaded the morning papers into my sack, hoping nobody would notice the deep red flush on my face.

Tina finished her phone call and stood behind the counter. Eileen, aware that she held the stage, turned her expression into one of grave concern and put a solicitous arm around Tina's shoulders.

'Here's the money for the phone call, Mrs Henshaw,' Tina said in a small voice.

'I wouldn't hear of it, love, put it away,' Ma Henshaw said, full of the milk of human kindness as she pushed the coppers back into the pathetic Tina's hands. 'You put it back in your purse, love. You poor thing, I can't believe that someone round here would poison a dog.'

Her voice trembling, more from the attention she was receiving than from the death of the dog, Tina said, 'Oh, I can, Mrs Henshaw. They hated my dog, especially that lot at the back of us.'

I was turning deep purple and could feel Tina's eyes boring into me.

'I'll be off then, Mrs Henshaw,' I shouted and got out of the shop quicker than a rabbit with a ferret down its hole.

As I walked the streets on my round I questioned whether my mother was capable of poisoning a dog. Surely not, I told myself, not my mother, not a dog . . . My round took a little longer that morning as I mulled over the facts and sifted the evidence.

When I got home I came straight to the point.

'The dog in the end house is dead. Did you poison it?'

If she did then she deserved Best Actress at the Oscars. She lowered the *Birkenhead News* that she was reading and stared at me, shocked and disbelieving.

'How dare you talk to me like that!' she said. 'And don't even think of saying anything to your father. Get yourself down to confession and tell the priest what you've just accused your mother of, wicked little swine.' And tut-tutting to herself she went back to reading her paper.

I've often wondered if she really did have anything to do with the sad demise of the hound. I wonder if she . . . no, I think I'll let sleeping dogs lie. That's not the image I have of her in my mind. Time has softened her.

34

On warm summer afternoons when the garden was looking its best my mum would make herself a cup of tea and, grabbing her library book, would sit contented at last, on a foldaway chair in her beautiful little garden admiring the fruits of her labour. I can picture her now, surrounded by her magnificent roses, legs crossed, swinging her foot contentedly in time to the music coming from the radio inside the house.

'Is that you, Paul? What do you want for your tea?'

CHAPTER THREE

MY MOTHER COULD BE A BIT OF A SNOB, PARTICULARLY when it came to holidays. We never went to Blackpool, which is surprising really considering the proximity to home. I never got a chance to sample the delights of the Fun House or have my picture taken at the top of the Tower until I was in my twenties and worked a club there. My mother thought Blackpool was common. It *was* common. We never went to Butlins either, another magical place I was desperate to visit. That was common as well. I'd watch the commercials on our telly and drool at the images of holidaymakers having the time of their lives courtesy of Billy Butlin. And there was the added bonus that once you got inside the camp you could avail yourself of every single amusement at no extra charge. I couldn't get over that. Apart from Disneyland, which was in America and therefore out of the question, Butlins was my ultimate goal.

'Mam, can we go to Butlins?' I'd plead.

'Butlins!' she'd scream, raising her eyebrows, in the same tone of voice that the Beadle used on Oliver when he asked for more. 'Good God, I'd rather die.' She'd have hated the enforced joviality and feared that at any moment she might be coerced into participating in a game, just as I would now. I'd lock myself in my chalet and take to my bed, burying myself under the blankets.

Taking to your bed is a family trait, inbred in all of us. When the going gets tough and a safe haven is sought from the afflictions of the world, we take to our beds. Safe in the dark, it's the perfect environment to mull things over and find a solution to the problem that's been aggravating those vulnerable nerves. You can wallow self-indulgently and allow all those petty grievances that have lurked, festering, in the dark corners of your mind to grow out of all proportion and blossom into visions of revenge and retribution. Preferably violent.

'Me nerves are bad' signals a malaise peculiar to some women and gay men in the Merseyside region. If not treated fairly quickly, the disease can degenerate into a more debilitating condition known as 'Me nerves are hanging out'. The cures range from excessive intake of nicotine, caffeine, antidepressants and strong drink to flinging the dinner up the wall and taking to your bed. My mother was a great advocate of the bed cure and frequently took it when she felt she'd been pushed to the limit, with the addition of a little Valium 'to take the edge off'. During my difficult teen years, when I drove her up the wall she'd frequently declare, 'Right, that's it,' pulling off her overall and flinging it on the sofa, 'I'm taking to me bed. You can all bloody well get on with it,' emphasizing the 'all', drawing it out and using a sweep of her arm for dramatic effect.

I don't know who the 'all' were as there was only me and her in the house. Slamming the door behind her so that the crucifix above it shook, she'd make the ascent upstairs, banging her foot down hard on each step with all the ferocity of a mountain troll in a Wagnerian opera. The entire house trembled as she crashed about in her bedroom above me.

Minutes later she would be back out on the landing shouting down the stairs. 'And you needn't think you're sitting up all night smoking your bloody head off and watching television using all MY electricity!'

I'd turn the telly up to drown her out.

'D'ya think I'm made of money?' she'd rant. 'If the leccy goes, that's it, I haven't got any change for the meter so you'll have to sit in the dark.' Slam!

'That's her closing the bedroom door then.'

Thump, Thump, Thump, THUMP!

'That's her going back to bed. Give her five minutes and she'll be out again,' I'd mutter to myself.

Sure enough, she'd be out again, declaiming from her landing pulpit in a voice that could've given the Revd Ian Paisley a run for his money. 'And you can just pack your bags and sling your hook, you wicked little swine, making me take the Lord's name in vain when you know I've just been to confession.' Slam!

After a period of time – you never could tell just how long she'd confine herself to barracks; it could be a matter of hours or a couple of days – her temper would burn itself out and she would leave her mountain eyrie to come back downstairs and rinse her face in the bathroom sink.

'I'm going to tell Father Lennon about you,' she'd sniff piously, popping her teeth in. 'You'll roast in hell for what you've done to your poor mother. What do you want for your tea?'

A frequent threat she made – and as a teenager I'd pray she'd carry it out but I knew she never would – was to cry, 'I'm off,' as in 'Right, that's it, I'm off,' usually to the Isle of Man. She'd done it many years before when she was a teenager herself and was working as a tweeny for the Mulligans, a wealthy family in the prosperous district of Oxton. A tweeny was a maid of all work, a slavey who toiled day and night above and below stairs; between floors, hence the abbreviation 'tweeny'.

She'd heard that girls were earning good money and enjoying a better lifestyle working as chambermaids in the many boarding houses on the Isle of Man. To add to that, the weekly turnover of punters meant the prospect of generous tips. Oh yes, there were chamber pots of gold under every bed in every boarding house, waiting to be claimed by a girl who didn't mind a bit of hard work in the Isle of Man. A girl could have a bit of fun as well, being by the seaside with its many interesting diversions.

Only a labour camp could be worse than life in the watchful employ of the parsimonious Mrs Mulligan. The hours were long and the work physically exhausting. Mrs Mulligan was a tight-fisted tyrant who expected miracles for the pittance of a wage she paid and treated her staff like galley slaves. She gave my mother a length of cheap material as a Christmas present so that she could make herself a new afternoon dress for her duties in the parlour as she'd noticed that the one she was wearing was looking a little 'frayed at the edges'. I'm surprised that it wasn't hanging off her back in rags judging by the amount of work she was expected to do. Her day started at 6 a.m. and finished when the last member of the Mulligan household had gone to bed.

After a year of this misery my mother finally rebelled and persuaded her friend Nora, the cook, who was equally disgruntled with life serving the Mulligans, to go with her to the promised land that was the Isle of Man. Together they escaped out of the kitchen window, leaving their miserable employer high and dry in the middle of a dinner party upstairs. Afterwards my mother always wondered what had happened when Madam rang the bell for the main course to be served and then, when nobody answered, excused herself to her waiting guests and went in search of 'that wretched Savage', only to find that the bird had flown the coop.

Once or twice, for our annual holiday we graced a boarding house in my mother's old stamping ground in Douglas, Isle of Man, that went by the predictable title of Seaview. A big brass gong hanging in the hall was rung punctually at mealtimes and it had 'a very nice class of residents'. One of the chamber-maids, a sexy Cornish girl named Grace who always managed to look like she'd just fallen out of bed, gave me a box of pastel crayons and a sketchbook and taught me how to use them. I drew endless pictures of the little castle on the rock that sat out in the bay and then hung listlessly around the landings, hoping to bump into the lovely Grace so that I could show her my etchings. A patient girl, she would sit on the stairs sucking on the end of her pencil, pretending to be deep in concentration as she cast an approving eye over my attempts to capture the delights of the Isle of Man as seen from the bay window of Seaview's television lounge. If she was in the mood she'd let me put my hand inside her blouse and have a feel.

'Only a little one, mind,' she would purr, teasingly un-buttoning her blouse. 'I don't want you getting me pregnant now, do I?'

Since I didn't relish the responsibility of becoming a father at the tender age of nine I made sure that I didn't linger longer than recommended. I hope my dad gave her a decent tip; I'm sure he did because he always tipped more than he could afford as he liked people to think that he had a few bob. Grace made a nine-year-old boy very happy. Not only did she teach me to sketch with pastels, she also cleared up a few questions I had concerning the female anatomy.

I was crazy for the Isle of Man when I was a boy. It ticked all the boxes and suited every nine-year-old's requirements. I thought it was rather chic, with a whiff of Monte Carlo about it – not that I'd ever been to the South of France. The Isle of Man had palm trees and a casino and I'd seen these on an episode of *The Saint*, so they made Douglas an extremely glamorous location. I wouldn't have been the least surprised if Roger Moore had turned up at the door of Seaview in his white dinner jacket, eyebrow raised, enquiring after a room.

We took coach trips to various parts of the island, driving

over fairy bridges and shouting out as we went, 'Good morning, little people, and how are you today?' to the fairies who lived under the bridges, because, as the driver explained, if we didn't the unpredictable fairy folk might put a curse on us. My mother would mutter under her breath that they needn't bother as she was cursed enough, thank you very much, and continue to suck contentedly on a boiled sweet and stare out of the window at the scenery. Headscarves bearing images of the Laxey Wheel and other notable landmarks of the Isle of Man would be brought back as souvenirs, together with 'amusing' ashtrays and boxes of fudge. On the crowded beach my dad sat in a deckchair wearing a shirt and tie while my mum poured tea from a flask and handed out fish-paste sandwiches from the meagre packed lunch provided by the hotel. Giggling girls with beehives and skirts that stuck out strolled down the prom, their arms linked as leery lads with Brylcreemed quiffs trailed behind them making inane remarks. Cheery pensioners sat on benches contentedly licking ice-cream cones and watching the world go by. These images were unconsciously absorbed and would re-emerge much later on when I was creating a world for Lily Savage to live in. I believe that comedy is formed in childhood and fortunately for me I had a wealth of memories to draw from.

On one of the rare occasions when my mother and Rose Long, our neighbour, were on speaking terms, Rose graciously consented to rent out to my mother, at a reasonable rate, her much-envied static caravan in Talacre, North Wales, for a week in July. I can only recall going there once, when I was about four. I got a fat lip from my cousin Maureen when I ran round a corner and banged into her head on. I remember so well the horrors of a hand-knitted pair of bathing trunks, highly impractical but, for reasons better known to parents in the fifties and early sixties, de rigueur for children on a beach.

My mother had knitted mine and they grew heavier and heavier with each trip into the sea as they gathered a mountain of wet sand in the crotch. As the day went on they would sag and swing between your legs obscenely, forcing you to swagger as you walked across the beach with your legs bowed – much to the merriment of the grown-ups.

Rose Long was a permatanned peroxide blonde, who wore open-toed sandals that revealed toenails painted blood red. She had a bit of a mouth on her, did Rose, and was usually at loggerheads with most of the women in the neighbourhood. 'A dyed-headed bitch' was how my mother dismissed her. It didn't help that she was a member of the Orange Lodge and grew orange lilies in her front garden either. On 12 July, the day that the Lodge marched through Birkenhead and then over the Mersey on the ferry boat to Liverpool to catch the train to Southport for their annual bash, Rose Long would open her windows and play a pipe and drum band's loud and rousing version of 'The Sash Me Father Wore' on her radiogram.

This inflammatory act would ignite my mother's Irish Catholic blood, bringing it dangerously up to boiling point. Thankfully her dignity and the fact that a doorstep confrontation would mean 'making a show of herself in front of the neighbours' prevented her from marching round to Rose Long's and letting her have it. She remained on the sofa and silently fumed, cursing inwardly as she furiously knitted, the knitting needles going like the clappers as she conjured up all manner of foul but deeply satisfying ways to put paid to the hated Rose.

Aunty Chris had no such qualms. She wasn't going to sit there and ignore the gauntlet that her hated enemy had thrown down. Impervious to my mother's pleas of 'Don't, Chris, the neighbours!' she would open the front-room windows, drag the Dansette out to the middle of the room and play a track from one of my dad's favourite albums, *Tommy*

Makem And The Clancy Brothers, Live At Carnegie Hall.

> Up the short line,
> Down the long rope,
> To Hell with King Billy,
> And God bless the Pope.

Not to be outdone, Rose Long would turn the volume up to full on her radiogram and take herself out on to her front step to treat the residents of the Grove, our household in particular, to a rousing version of 'The Sash'.

'"My father wore it as a youth in bygone days of yore,"' she'd croak, marching up and down on the spot, clapping her hands in time to the music, '"And on the 12th I love to wear the sash my father wore."'

'Right, that's it, Molly,' Aunty Chris would say, marching into the garden. 'She's asking for it. I'm going to let that lemon-pelting bitch have it.'

I was out of that house behind her faster than catshit on lino to get a ringside seat, ignoring my mother's squeals of 'Get back in here, you!'

'I'm surprised that a good Orangewoman like yourself isn't off to Southport,' Aunty Chris would shout over the hedge, her arms folded defiantly across her chest as she squared up for a bout of verbal. 'You used to go, didn't you? Spent all day in the alehouse getting rotten drunk while your kids sat outside on the step.'

Rose Long thrived on doorstep altercations. They were her lifeblood. Aunty Chris was a worthy adversary for her to get her talons into.

'Is that right?' replied Rose, slowly bringing her hands to her hips and cocking her head to one side in the traditional stance adopted when responding to a provocative remark. 'Well, it's a damn sight better than her in there,' she spat, referring to my mother, 'starving her kids all day and night just so they can have a bit of bread shoved down their throats by a bloody priest in the morning.'

' "Keep thy tongue from evil and thy lips from speaking guile," Rose Long,' Aunty Chris replied, pursing her lips and raising her eyes piously to the heavens. She wasn't a church-going woman but she did have a smattering of useful biblical quotes at her disposal for when the occasion demanded it.

'You what?' mocked Rose.

'Psalm 34, verse 13,' she came back smartly, having heard it from the nuns on numerous occasions. 'You should ask your Michael to look it up for you in the Holy Bible next time he's in church.' There was a hint of menace in her voice at the mention of Michael. Rose's son would these days have been tagged and asboed at birth. 'Never out of church, is he?' she went on, picking an imaginary thread off the sleeve of her blouse. 'He should be on the altar, your Michael. Oh, but then he was, wasn't he?' She looked Rose Long straight in the eye as she stuck the knife in. 'He was on the altar of St Joseph's – nicking the bloody candlesticks, the thieving little bastard.' This statement was an outrageous lie, and Aunty Chris knew it, but it was guaranteed to light Rose's blue touch paper and send her off like a rocket.

Rose Long's nostrils flared and her voice went down a couple of octaves. 'You're a fine one to call anyone a bastard,' she hissed, starting to play dirty. 'At least our Michael knows who his father is . . . unlike your John.'

Bedroom windows in houses up and down the Grove began to open and the occupants, hidden from view behind their nets, hung on every word.

'And at least I've got a husband,' said Rose, head in the air, preening like an arrogant parrot.

'Jesus, I'd be happy to die an old maid rather than have to share a bed with the likes of your George, the scrawny-arsed rat,' sneered Aunty Chris.

Rage escaped from Rose like the air from a fast-deflating balloon. 'You want to look at your own,' she spluttered, pointing her finger accusingly at me. 'He's like an old woman, that child, the way he hangs round adults. You don't want him growing up funny.'

'Pecu or ha ha?' Aunty Chris said through clenched teeth, tapping her foot dangerously.

'You know full well what I mean . . . one of them.' Rose put her hand on her hip and minced up and down the path blowing kisses.

'One of what, Rose?' said Aunty Chris, flicking the butt of her cigarette into the hedge.

Although my mother, listening to this exchange from behind the front-room curtains, thought fighting in the street with neighbours was beneath her dignity, she wasn't letting Rose get away with that one. Smiling sweetly, she came out into the garden and proceeded to give Rose a history lesson.

'Did you know that King Billy of Orange was a homosexual?' she said matter-of-factly, emphasizing the *homo* and drawing it out. I'd never heard her say that word before and neither had Aunty Chris, judging by the surprised look on her face.

'Oh, didn't you know that, Rose?' she continued, going in for the kill. 'Yes, he was an 'omo-sex-ua-l and that's the reason why you lot are called "Orange" – it's because you're named after a bloody fruit, you foul-mouthed, bleach-headed, dirty-minded, slack-jawed owld cow, and if you don't want me to come over there and slap that big orange gob of yours shut I suggest you get in and turn that shite off.' And with an 'In, you two,' she swept us into the house and slammed the door, leaving Rose speechless.

It's not hard to see where Lily Savage learned her trade. This colourful vernacular was stored away for future reference and came in very handy when a heckler in the audience chanced his arm.

*

When my mum wasn't feudin' with Rose they generally got along quite nicely. Relationships had broken down during the war years when my dad, exempt from conscription as an Irish citizen, joined the air force and went to war. He could have got himself a 'safe' job in Lever's or Cammell Laird's, a job considered essential war work, and made himself useful in that way. It galled my mother that her husband was away fighting the Hun while Rose Long's cowardly George slept soundly in his nice warm bed. It was a grievance that she bore for the rest of her life.

Holly Grove was perilously close to Cammell Laird's, which, as a shipbuilding company, was a prime target for the German bombers. My mother refused to get in the Anderson shelter in the back yard during the air raids, choosing instead to remain in her bed. My dad had built the Anderson, a small underground bunker with bunk beds either side. The roof was made of sheets of corrugated iron, buried under a mountain of earth on which my mother grew tomato plants and sweet peas.

A cockroach had crawled up her leg one night in the shelter during a heavy raid while she was pregnant with my sister Sheila. She ran back into the house screaming, preferring to dodge shrapnel rather than share a bed with a cockroach. Curiously enough, my sister has a cockroach-shaped birthmark on her thigh, a tiny thing, in exactly the same place my mother felt the creature crawl over her. (I'm afraid you'll just have to take my word for it unless I can persuade my sister to roll her tights down and bare her leg on television.)

Holly Grove was crawling with cockroaches during the war. They'd crawl up and down in between the wall and the wallpaper, 'big as your fist', attracted by the homemade adhesive of flour and water. She'd lie in bed, her babies beside her, watching the 'cockies' in the shadows and listening out for the doodlebugs during some of the worst air raids over Merseyside. *Dum dum, dum de dum, de dum.* The doodlebugs were easily identified by the noise they made. She lay in the dark not daring to breathe, waiting for the engine to cut out. When it did she would begin slowly counting as the doodlebug dropped, whistling, from the sky. Counting aloud in the dark was a mantra to soothe and calm her, helping her to hold her nerve as the evil thing fell, indiscriminately seeking out a target.

'One . . . two . . . three . . . Please don't let it be us, God.'

God must have heard her prayers because it never was. The church at the back of the house took a direct hit, as did many houses in the area. Number 23's windows were frequently blown in and my mother was often without food, water and gas. Rats and cockroaches abounded, yet as well as looking after two very young children she managed to hold down two jobs, as an auxiliary nurse in St Cath's and as a cleaner in a private house. When she spoke about her experiences during the war, she was dismissive. She never considered herself brave in any way. Yet she dodged bombs on a daily basis; air raids became a way of life. She ate whalemeat and spam and made cakes with dried egg and carrots. She stood patiently in never-ending queues and, like millions of other women, shrugged her shoulders and got on with it.

While Hitler waged war in the skies, my mother fought many a battle on the terra firma of Holly Grove, usually with Rose Long. My mother wasn't the only one at daggers drawn with Rose, most of Birkenhead was. To coin a phrase, Rose Long could cause trouble in an empty house.

Winnie Eatock, who lived next door to the wood yard at the bottom of the Grove, blamed Rose for bringing on a miscarriage after a verbal spat with her in the street.

'She murdered my baby!' she'd shout pitifully from her

back-yard step whenever Rose, defiant and looking to cause trouble, walked past her house. 'Murderer!' she'd scream until her husband came and gently led poor Winnie back indoors.

Another of the neighbours, Mrs Docherty, put Rose's front-room windows in with a brick one drunken night after hearing that Rose had accused her of 'going with Yanks' while her husband Jimmy was at sea. Mrs Dock, as she was known, always looked a bit grubby – 'like a bed in a flophouse' was how my mother described her. She rarely washed her face but just applied another load of paint over the previous night's. Her sister Kitty, effortlessly glamorous even after a long shift in the munitions factory, was the antithesis of her.

Mrs Dock would persuade my aunty Chris to set her hair for her in a victory roll on the nights she went out lindy-hopping with the Yanks, bribing her with nylon stockings and American cigarettes. Aunty Chris wasn't keen on the idea of being Mrs Dock's personal hairdresser as she'd once discovered a family of lice setting up house in her neighbour's less-than-savoury barnet. But Aunty Chris was a devoted worshipper at the church of St Nicotine and she would've sold a kidney for one whiff of a ciggie, and both of them for a packet of ten. Cigs were a luxury, hard to come by in the war, so she turned a blind eye to Mrs Dock's little infestation, hoping that the strong setting lotion would kill or at the very least stun the lice. As she got her comb out and proceeded to tease Mrs Dock's rat's tails into a passable resemblance to Anne Shelton's lovely locks, she'd say, 'Beggars can't be choosers, especially when they haven't got a pot to piss in or a window to chuck it out of.'

Aunty Chris locked horns with Rose Long nearly every week. They hated each other. After getting wind of a vicious bit of gossip that Rose had spread around about her, Aunty Chris stormed into Rose's house all guns blazing, dragged her out of the kitchen and into the back entry by the 'black roots of her bleached 'ead' and knocked one of her teeth out. No wonder my dad joined up: it was probably a lot safer as a rear gunner in the air force than it was getting caught in the crossfire of the harpies who reigned over Holly Grove.

CHAPTER FOUR

MY MUM MET MY DAD AT AN IRISH DANCE IN BIRKENHEAD. Like thousands of other young Irishmen and women before him, Patrick Grady had arrived in Liverpool on the boat from Dublin looking to make a new life. He was a handsome fellow, tall and slim with wavy red hair and a jaunty smile. He could whistle through his teeth, beat a tune out by snapping his fingers on the back of his hand and charm the birds out of the trees.

My dad's father, also Patrick, had died of a heart attack when he was only thirty years old. I have a copy of his obituary from the local paper of 1912:

It is with feelings of deep regret that we have to announce the sudden and unexpected death of Mr Patrick Grady, Glinsk, when just in the prime of life. The deceased was ailing for some time in the month of November but seemed to have quite recovered from the attack, as he was working up till the day he died. He went to bed on Monday night in his usual health and at six o'clock on the Tuesday morning, as he showed signs of uneasiness, his wife spoke to him. He was unable to answer her and passed away in a few minutes.

The deceased was a member of the Pollocks Estates Committee and was on the committee of the Kilbegnet branch of the United Irish League. He was an honest, straightforward and earnest worker in both. His death has come under very sad circumstances. His principal desire from the time the sale of the Pollock Estates was first spoken about was to see the poor people taken from their miserable patches of bad land and settled on the rich lands of Glinsk. He was the first to migrate and got a good holding and nice house with offices, and was getting on very well and improving it daily.

He was liked by everybody for his very kind disposition; he was a most obliging neighbour, a good son and a kind husband. He leaves a mother, a wife and two little children to mourn his loss.

The funeral was by far the largest witnessed in this district for years past.

The remains were borne to Kilbegnet burial ground, a distance of over three miles, by twenty-four young men wearing white sashes. To his sorrowing mother, wife and little children we offer our deepest sympathy. May he rest in peace.

The United Irish League was a nationalist political party that campaigned for the fair distribution of land to relieve the plight of the peasant farmer. Its founder, William O'Brien, fought for the right of the tenant farmer to purchase his own land. The lads in white sashes who bore the coffin no doubt belonged to the UIL.

My grandfather Patrick Grady had married Bridget Brittain, better known as Biddy. They had two daughters and a son. Mary, nicknamed Mayo, was the first to arrive in November 1908, followed by Sarah-Ann or Sadie a year later. My grandfather never saw his son Patrick. The widow Grady was two months pregnant on that bitterly cold morning in January when she stood by the graveside and buried her young husband. She gave birth to Patrick seven months later, on 26 July 1912, with her mother-in-law acting as midwife.

After my grandfather died Biddy Brittain took stock. She

was still young, an elegant woman who carried her height well, with blue eyes, pale skin and a glossy mane of thick red hair swept up into a bun on the top of her proud head. She had the farm registered in her name and with the help of her late husband's brother, James Grady, she managed to run it and raise her family.

It was a time of political unrest for Ireland. The Easter Rising had taken place in Dublin in 1916 and the cells of Kilmainham Gaol were full of patriots, the walls in the execution yard stained with their blood. By 1920 the first of the hated Black and Tans had marched into Glinsk, their orders to bring English law to the filthy peasants and to 'make Ireland a hell for Rebels to live in'. There was a saying in England's courtrooms at the time that you had two choices: go to prison, or join the Black and Tans and go to Ireland. The Tans were paid ten shillings a day with full board and lodging, a good enough incentive for the scum of England's gaols and the unemployed veterans of the First World War to head for Ireland.

Any sign of Rebel activity and the Tans carried out brutal reprisals, torturing and killing innocent civilians. House raids, supposedly looking for arms, were frequent, and when a gang of drunken Tans raided my grandmother's house, they dragged my great-grandmother, a frail old lady, from her chair and hit her with a rifle butt. During one house raid they rounded up all the men, my great-uncle James included, and took them off in the dead of night on the back of a lorry. They released James three days later but the others weren't so lucky: they were shot.

My father, running barefoot across the fields, was frequently shot at. When I was a young boy spending my summers on the farm in Ireland, I sometimes used to take my shoes off and run across the fields pretending that the Black and Tans were using me for target practice. I wanted to get a feel of what it might have been like. I didn't get very far, as the stubble from where the corn had been cut was murder on the bare feet.

The Tans abused the local women in the street. They would jeer at them, asking lewd and inappropriate questions when they attempted to cross the border and get past the many roadblocks. Biddy Brittain would clutch the basket of eggs that she was taking to a sick friend closer to her side, pulling her shawl around her and lowering her head as she passed through the checkpoint, impervious to the lecherous stares and crude catcalls of the Tans as she went about her real business. If the Tans had bothered to search her, not only would they have discovered a few dead chickens and geese hidden inside the folds of her long woollen skirt, they just might have found a couple of rifles as well, according to my dad that is.

When my father was thirteen, Biddy cashed in her life insurance and emigrated to America with her two daughters. My father, who didn't want to leave Ireland, was left behind in the care of Uncle James. Biddy sailed for America from Liverpool on the *Franconia*. She was a superb seamstress and would have made sure that she and her daughters were suitably dressed for the voyage. With fabric bought at the draper's in Galway and inspiration provided by a ladies' fashion magazine, she boarded the *Franconia* elegantly attired, her daughters hurrying behind her, self-conscious in their new matching dresses and with large velvet bows pinned to the back of their hair.

One would think a farmer's widow would've travelled steerage like the rest of the immigrants. Biddy opted for a stateroom and travelled to America in first-class luxury. Mary, the elder daughter, rarely ventured on deck as she suffered from violent seasickness but Biddy and Sadie had a wonderful time.

The *Franconia* had been at sea for less than two years. She was the pride of Cunard's fleet. The opulent interior of this beautiful single-stacker boasted elegant garden lounges, a health spa, a smoking room decorated in the fifteenth-century Venetian style and tastefully furnished cabins. Each evening Biddy and her daughter would descend the staircase into the first-class dining room and feast like empresses amid the crystal chandeliers and snowy white linen. They docked at New York at the ship's pier and, as befitted their status as first-class passengers, they were spared the indignities of Ellis Island. When, years later, she was teased about her humble Irish roots, Biddy's daughter, my aunty Mary, would answer grandly, 'I didn't arrive in this country via Ellis Island, you know. I arrived first class.'

New York in 1925 was a vast construction site, a place of prohibition, bath-tub gin, organized crime and jazz babes. The Empire State Building had yet to be built, *No, No, Nanette* was packing them in at the Globe Theater and President Calvin Coolidge was in office. The Americans were still recovering from the abominations of the First World War. It was also an era of disenchantment.

Biddy was certainly disillusioned with America. She lived in the Bronx with a relative of Uncle James's, a woman named Annie Duane. Annie was a jolly character of prodigious proportions, who had one eye and a fondness for a drop of 'the holy water' – whisky. She added the words 'Christ on the Cross' to everything she said. 'Would you like a drop of tea, Christ on the Cross?' she would ask cheerily, proffering a cup of black, sickly sweet liquid to her disdainful houseguest. Biddy would survey the claustrophobic, overcrowded, cockroach-infested kitchen adorned with religious icons and inhabited by this Cyclops and her blasphemous tongue, and regret ever leaving Ballincurry.

'Would you not ever consider remarrying, Biddy, Christ on the Cross?' Annie enquired, lowering her voice so the girls wouldn't overhear such a delicate topic of conversation.

Biddy's eyebrows shot up to her hairline. 'Not at all,

especially to one of these Americans. Why, there isn't a good man amongst them. New York is nothing but a city of heathens and whores.' Only yesterday, hadn't she taken the girls to the Picture Palace to see Ramon Novarro in *Ben-Hur* and an animated short called *Felix the Cat* and been called a 'snooty broad' by a 'big, uncouth pig' of a man who had approached her in the street? And hadn't she had to walk past a theatre with pictures of naked women outside, and run, her hands over the eyes of her two impressionable daughters in case they saw these trollops parading in little more than their underwear for everyone to see? Jesus, this country was no place for a decent God-fearing woman.

After living in America for less than a year Biddy booked her passage home to Ireland, sailing once again on the *Franconia*. She took Sadie with her, while Mary elected to stay and eventually married an Italian, Joe Schillaci. (That set the cat among the pigeons – but that's another story.)

Biddy died from cancer on 16 November 1932. The house that this independent woman had reared her family in is still there. The upper floors have long collapsed and the building stands empty, providing shelter still but only for the animal feed and farm machinery that's stored there. The family who own the property built themselves a bigger, more comfortable home next door.

My dad took me to see his birthplace on one of our many trips 'home'. An animated old lady with wild hair and an apron that she kept taking on and off made a great fuss of us. She rushed around, chattering excitedly, making strong black tea and carving huge slabs of fruit cake, while an old man sat smoking a pipe and spitting contentedly into a great open turf fire. To my young eyes it was a dirty, primitive hovel. To my dad it was home. 'I was born up there,' he said sadly, pointing up the stairs to a bedroom.

He showed me where he'd carved his name in the back of a

barn door when he was a boy. As he ran his finger over the old letters that spelt out the word 'Pakie', a tear rolled down his cheek. He hadn't been a rural hoodie in his youth, carving out racial abuse on farm outhouses – the name was an abbreviation of Patrick. It was what my dad was called by his family in Ireland: 'Cousin Pakie'. My mum called him Paddy. I was used to seeing my dad cry in Ireland. As soon as he stepped off the boat he turned into a maudlin romantic, as did everyone else he ran into while he was over there.

He loved Ireland with a passion. He loved the people. He had always hoped that one day he would go back there, but my mother didn't share his sentiments. She'd felt that some of my father's family had objected to him marrying an English girl (as indeed they had when his sister Mary married an Italian) so she had been more than a little apprehensive about meeting them.

At the end of the war my dad took his bride and two children home to meet the folks. It must have been a culture shock for my mother. She felt as if she'd stepped back in time. They stayed with my uncle James and aunty Bridget Grady and their numerous offspring in their two-bedroomed farmhouse. She'd been to Ireland before to stay with her father's family in Dundalk, County Louth, but it was nothing like this. This was rural Ireland or, as she put it, 'the bogs'.

The plumbing, or rather the lack of it, horrified her. Not only was there no toilet inside the house but there wasn't one outside either. You simply went over to a patch of ground just beyond the apple trees and did what you had to do, using a collection of dock leaves and a handful of grass to wipe up afterwards.

I think my mum was constipated for the entire time she was in Ireland. It wasn't until the sixties that the house had a bathroom and toilet built. The tap in the scullery supplied rainwater collected in a big tank outside the house and this water was used for washing. Drinking water was collected each day in a bucket from a natural spring in one of the fields and kept cool in the tiny dairy alongside the big bowls of yellow milk. My mum liked the countryside; she liked it from the top of a bus though. She found the silence eerie, the cows and other farm animals unnerving. I can just hear her moaning to my dad in the bedroom with the sloping roof and tiny window that they shared with my brother and sister.

'Let's go home, Paddy,' she'd plead, sat perched on the end of the bed staring out of the window in her best Blanche DuBois manner. 'I can't stand it, all this mud and cowshit, chickens running in and out of the house and, worst of all, no toilet! I can't get over it,' she'd say, getting up and making herself busy tidying the room and combing my brother's hair. 'No toilet! At least we had a lav down the back yard in Lowther Street. I've never known anything like it, it's like the Dark Ages.'

My dad, trying to pacify her, wouldn't have stood a chance. She was warming to her theme.

'And they don't like me. I can tell. It's because I'm English,' she'd moan and the tears would fill her eyes. 'Let's go home, please! I hate it here.'

My brother Brendan, who was four at the time, went straight downstairs and repeated most of what he'd just heard to Aunty Bridget, who was in the kitchen making soda bread.

'Did she now?' she said, waving a floury hand at my brother. 'Well, you can tell ya mammy that if she doesn't like it then she knows where the road is.'

They didn't exactly get off to a good start.

Aunty Bridget was a sensible, no-nonsense countrywoman. She could be quite a formidable lady and extremely brusque when dealing with fools, but she was also sensitive enough to realize that this young woman who had lived through some of the worst air raids during the war was like a fish out of water in rural Ireland. My mother was uncomfortable in these strange new surroundings and suddenly shy among the many unfamiliar faces, and she'd got it into her head that they didn't approve of her. She felt excluded at the big family gatherings.

Bridget, who had an endless supply of fresh eggs, milk, cream and butter at her disposal, discovered that my mum liked to cook. Apples and pears hung from the trees in abundance. On the land grew potatoes, onions, beans and enormous green cabbages. There was pork, beef and chicken, as much as you could want. My mum, who hadn't seen an egg in years and was still under the parsimonious yoke of rationing back home in Birkenhead, set about demolishing this food mountain.

With Bridget's encouragement she produced sponge cakes filled with freshly whipped cream, soufflés light as a feather, scones, apple pies, biscuits, luxuriant egg custards and rich and creamy rice puddings by the score. She baked from morning till night. My mum was a wonderful cook and was delighted to be able to show off her skills, particularly since she had this infinite well of culinary riches to draw from. She secretly basked in the praise heaped upon her by the Grady family and she slowly thawed and began to blossom. Whatever my mother said about Ireland – and she had a lot to say on the matter, all of it contradictory – she and Aunty Bridget shared a lifelong affection for each other.

My dad was born into good farming stock. Hadn't his father fought for the right of the working man to farm his own land? But my dad had no aptitude for tilling the land. His heart wasn't in it. Years later he would reminisce about growing up in Ireland, telling of how they would take the donkey and cart down to the bogs and bring home the turf to provide fuel. He would paint dreamy pictures of cutting the hay on balmy summer afternoons and building golden haystacks until, exhausted, they would collapse on top of the haycart and enjoy a supper of freshly baked bread with great hunks of cheese and onion washed down with a bottle of porter. These were very sociable occasions, armies of family and neighbours turning out en masse. That was what he really missed about Ireland. What he enjoyed was the craic, the good company and all that goes with it. The physical labour was a necessary evil, tolerated if it meant good times with family and friends.

In his teens he was a drummer in an Irish show group, playing popular standards such as 'The Black Velvet Band' at dances and carnivals in villages and towns. I remember seeing a photograph of him many years ago; the photo has long since vanished but the image of him sat behind a drum kit, his hair and shirt soaking wet with sweat, eyeing up the line of drinks on top of the piano, is imprinted on my memory. Playing in the band broke the monotony of farming.

One morning he woke to find a note from his sister Sadie. She'd packed her bags and emigrated to England. That was probably the final straw for my dad, alone in the house, with the daunting task of running a farm on his own before him. He could see no future for himself in Ballincurry. He felt he was a burden to his uncle James, who had his own family and farm to look after, and so, like his sisters before him, he decided to take the boat to Liverpool.

He put the farm up for sale, though it wasn't until July 1946 that it was finally auctioned off for the grand sum of £885. My dad got £432 1s 9d, Sadie £50 and Mary £10, with the rest going on legal fees. Hopefully Uncle James benefited from the sale; that good man certainly deserved it as without his sensibility and guiding hand over the years the farm would have gone under long before.

The year after my dad received his share of the farm my mum inherited £104 14s on the death of her father. This meant that between them they had £536 15s 9d, nothing by today's standards but a small fortune back in the forties. They blew every penny. When you've been used to a life of poverty, common sense can go out the window when an unexpected windfall comes your way. I'm surprised that they didn't invest in some property – they had the perfect opportunity to buy a house – but they didn't, preferring instead to continue to rent Holly Grove. They ended up doing so for the rest of their lives, something my mum deeply regretted in later years.

'That money just slipped through our fingers like fairy gold,' she said reflectively. 'But we were young and stupid and we'd had enough of scrimping and saving and wearing the same dress, so we went mad and enjoyed ourselves.' They certainly did that. They celebrated on a grand scale, sharing their good fortune with family and friends. My brother and sister were kitted out with a complete set of new clothes; Mum and Aunty Chris, able to indulge their fantasies for once, spent a fortune on the New Look, a style introduced by Christian Dior in the spring of 1947, adding a couple of fox furs for a touch of film star glamour and, in Aunty Chris's case, a pillbox hat with a veil that she would blow smoke through à la Marlene Dietrich. My dad, always a snappy dresser and recently demobbed from the air force, treated himself to a new wardrobe as well: bespoke suits, shoes, overcoats and trilbies, so he cut a dash when he went for a drink to St Laurence's club. On a Saturday night the walls of Holly Grove would shake, the windows vibrate, only this time not from the effect of German bombs but from the racket as my mum and dad partied into the night. They went on a glorious spending spree – and who could blame them? After the misery and austerity of the war years, this influx of cash gave them a chance to live it up.

Back in 1936, Paddy was green to the gills on that morning when he dragged his case down the gangplank and on to the landing stage at Liverpool pierhead. The Dublin-to-Liverpool run is a notoriously rough crossing and my dad was no sailor. His one and only suit was crumpled and creased. He'd tried to get a good night's sleep on the deck of the lurching vessel, curled up underneath his overcoat for warmth, resting his head on his folded cap, one arm flung across a battered suitcase held together with string and a belt. Its contents were pitiful: a few shirts, a change of underwear, a sweater, a pair of trousers, his prayer book and a couple of pounds of bacon and sausage wrapped in newspaper to keep him going when he got to 'heathen England'.

The landing stage was teeming with people, mostly immigrants like himself. Thankful to be back on dry land, he stood for a moment to catch his breath and acclimatize himself to his new surroundings. He was still rolling slightly from the motion of the ship. Jesus, he was feeling rough; his eyes burned from lack of sleep, he ached all over and for a moment he thought he was going to throw up. A good few pints of Guinness and numerous shots of whiskey had been taken in Dublin and on board the boat as he bade farewell to the owld country. Little did he know that he would soon be bidding farewell to his surname, for when war broke out and he joined the RAF a careless government official mistakenly added an 'O' as a prefix on his identity papers and we've remained O'Grady to this day.

Lighting a Sweet Afton to calm his churning stomach, he looked about to find a place to get a cup of tea and something to eat. The pierhead had plenty of cafés to choose from. He found a hatch in the wall of a dilapidated hut and ordered a cup of tea and a couple of rashers on toast.

'D'ya mean a bacon sarnie, paddy?' the ferocious-looking woman behind the counter barked in her unfamiliar Scouse twang. He'd changed his Irish punts for English currency in the bank in Dublin and counted out the unfamiliar pennies and farthings on the counter. ' 'Urry up, will ya,' urged the woman impatiently, 'I haven't got all bloody day.'

'Now just hold on there, missus, and take a breath. I'm just off the boat from Dublin,' said my dad in his easy way.

'Bloody micks,' spat the woman. 'Place is crawling with them. Here's your tea.'

Feeling better after his breakfast, he rinsed his face and hands in the public fountain, dampened down his unruly hair, took out his cap and put it on. He weighed up his situation. He had a couple of bob in his pocket, a local contact and the promise of a job as a navvy on a building site. His sister was living over in Birkenhead along with a smattering of cousins, so he wasn't entirely alone. What was his problem? Wasn't this what he'd left the farm for? Wasn't this what he wanted? A fresh start? Maybe he'd even meet a decent girl and fall in love.

'C'mon, Pakie, get yourself on that boat to Birkenhead,' he told himself, suddenly optimistic as he joined the crowds fighting their way up the gangplank of the Mersey ferry.

He found lodgings with a Mr and Mrs Fawcett, a couple known as 'Old Ned' and 'Ma Fawcett'. They had two sons called William and Harold, both merchant seamen. Harold had married my mother's sister Anne, so my dad would already have been a familiar face through his friendship with Harold when he approached my mother in that dance hall and asked her politely if she'd like to 'get up'. Before the end of the night my mother would be coyly asking him if he'd like to 'come round for his tea'.

Her father, Mick Savage, approved of this relationship. Wasn't Paddy a good Irishman who brought a drop of whiskey with him when he came calling? They had a genuine affection for each other. For my dad, Mick was a reminder of home.

My mum and dad's courtship took place in dance halls and picture palaces and the front parlour of Mick Savage's house, 29 Lowther Street. My dad was enchanted by this pretty young woman. She was unlike her sisters. She'd never stand at the top of the entry and wolf-whistle like her sister Chrissie did. Sometimes she could be aloof and detached, preoccupied with her own thoughts.

When they were alone together he would tease her and sing to her his Irish songs, charming her with his Gaelic magic. Whenever they were separated for any length of time they kept the torch burning in the many love letters that they wrote to each other. As war loomed over the country, my dad asked Mick Savage if he could have his eldest daughter's hand in marriage.

'By all means, Paddy,' he replied, delighted, 'take the hell-cat off me hands and good luck to you.'

They were married on 10 February 1940 at St Laurence's Church. War against Germany had been declared six months earlier and rationing was in force. A wedding dress required an impossible amount of coupons so my mother was married in a smart velvet hat with a veil and her three-quarter-length Persian lamb coat. My dad wore his navy blue suit that was a little short in the sleeves. The wedding breakfast was held in Lowther Street.

Poor Ma Fawcett, my dad's landlady, was to die in agony from stomach cancer. Ned, her husband, out of his mind with worry, refused to give her the pain-relieving medication prescribed by the hospital as he was convinced that it was slowly killing her.

After Ma Fawcett died, Ned went into a decline. Unable to cope without Ma by his side, he took his own life. Draping his dead wife's coat over his head, he sat in front of the gas fire and inhaled the deadly fumes, slumping forward as the gas took effect and splitting his skull open on the corner of the hearth. It was my aunty Chris who found him lying dead on the parlour floor.

To a Catholic family, the unspeakable act of taking one's

own life meant violating one of the commandments: Thou Shalt Not Kill. Suicide was a mortal sin and your soul was condemned for all eternity, cursed to roast in the fires of Hell. Old Ned's death was never spoken about again. In the early sixties, suicide was still a criminal offence. The family were shocked and shamed into silence, the matter closed, the subject taboo.

CHAPTER FIVE

M Y MUM, BORN IN 1916, WAS THE ELDEST OF THE SAVAGE girls. Two years later Anne was born, followed by Christine. My maternal grandparents, Michael and Anne Savage, had married in 1914 on the same day that King George V and Queen Mary made a royal visit to Birkenhead to open the new entrance to Bidston Hill. This wouldn't have impressed Grandad Savage, who wasn't a royalist. He was an irascible Irishman and if the tragic death of his young wife softened him he certainly didn't show it.

My mother would tell me the story of her mother's death in the melodramatic style of Charles Dickens relating the death of *Oliver Twist*'s Nancy on his American tour. Lowering her voice to a suitably sombre tone, she would conjure up a vision of backstreet Birkenhead and all its poverty-stricken misery. Open sewers, workhouses, means testing, rickets, the whole kit and caboodle. The way she told it made it sound like one of Catherine Cookson's grimmer sagas – only sadly her tale was true.

I didn't really find out how grim it was until the Winter of Discontent in '79, a truly foul winter. (I know I'm jumping the gun here but what of it?) I was back living at home, skint and down on my luck again. The pipes in the loft had burst, as they always did at this time of year, flooding the bedrooms. Outside a blizzard raged, and the volume of snow and ferocity of the wind brought down the power lines and cut off the electricity. Birkenhead came to a standstill. My mother and I sat in the front room of Holly Grove wrapped in a duvet, the sofa pulled close to the gas fire for warmth. Apart from the fire, the only light in the room came from a couple of votive candles in little blue plastic containers that she'd brought back from Lourdes and was loath to use.

She kept the candles in her bedroom drawer among her smalls, along with other holy relics that she'd been given as gifts or had brought home as souvenirs from her travels to the various shrines that a peripatetic Virgin Mary had appeared at some time or other. Wherever Mary had appeared, my mother and the Union of Catholic Mothers would follow. Coaches bearing this horde of devoted groupies would sweep into any town in the UK that had a shrine to the great lady: Walsingham, Pantasa, Cardigan and Doncaster.

The women would descend on these towns and their shrines gripped by a frenzy of religious fervour, lighting candles, praying at grottoes, flirting with priests, singing hymns with gusto and then inevitably rounding off the session before they had their sit-down tea by doing the Stations of the Cross. This involved staggering up a hill barefoot, clutching rosary beads to bosoms and stopping to say a decade of the rosary at allocated points, each representing Jesus's journey to Mount Calvary and his crucifixion. This act sorted out the women from the girls and only the truly devout endeavoured to face the stony climb without the protection of their sandals. But the St Joseph's, Birkenhead, branch of the Union of Catholic Mothers were hard. Without hesitation and regardless of age, physical condition and capability, these game girls would whip off their shoes and stockings and, hanging on to each other for grim death, would slowly make the ascent up the hill, puffing and blowing, in a long unsteady line. From an aerial view they must have looked like a crimplene snake.

My mother loved these excursions. When the Mothers announced at one of their regular meetings that a trip to Lourdes was on the cards and that any ladies wishing to go should put their name down, she was first in line to sign up, as ecstatic as a kid who has just been told that this year's school trip is to Euro-Disney. The package included one night in Paris and by all accounts they had a ball. They stayed up late, drank wine with their meals and went to see the show at the Folies-Bergère. My mother thought this was spectacular, although a few members of the party didn't share her enthusiasm. 'Some of the Mothers weren't very amused. You should have seen Elsie's face when those girls came traipsing across the stage with their dirty great big you-know-whats hanging out.'

Lourdes was a big hit even though it looked nothing like the Lourdes of the movie *Song of Bernadette*. My mother loved that film. Gladys Cooper playing a cynical and embittered old nun, jealous and doubtful of Bernadette, played by Jennifer Jones, could'nt understand why the Virgin Mary chose to appear to an ignorant peasant girl and not to her, a faithful servant of the Church. After months of being an utter bitch to her, the old nun finally discovers the tubercular ulcer on Bernadette's knee and slowly realizes that she must be a true saint to endure such agony without complaining. Relenting of her cruel ways, the nun becomes the dying girl's devoted nurse – and this bit always reduced my mother to tears. 'See, she did see her, you wicked old bitch,' she would mutter to the telly as she blew her nose noisily.

She hated the commercial side of Lourdes, with all the shops selling religious tat. Yet when I came home from work the day she returned from Lourdes I found her pouring liquid from a five-litre plastic container into a plastic bottle fashioned in the shape of the Virgin Mary. On Mary's head was a little blue plastic crown which you unscrewed when you needed to gain access to her contents.

At first I thought that she'd gone into the business of boot-leg gin and was distributing her bath-tub concoction inside plastic Our Ladies.

'It's holy water,' she explained as she gingerly poured the precious liquid into the funnel sticking out of another Virgin Mary's head.

I looked around the table. There were at least forty of these bottles lined up neatly in regimented rows.

'Some people would kill for a bottle of this,' she said, nodding knowingly towards the bottles. 'It's the real McCoy, you know, none of your muck. This stuff would cure anything.'

She had an unswerving belief in the power of Lourdes water and these bottles with their magical contents would be handed out to those she considered to be deserving individuals. She was also rather fond of splashing it liberally around the house to dispel any evil that might have crept in. On New Year's Eve the house and its occupants usually got a good soaking.

If I came home from a club in Liverpool in the wee small hours of 1 January worse the wear for cider, she would be waiting and I would be greeted with a cup of holy water flung all over me. When my cousin Tricia was a young girl she had an unfortunate outbreak of warts on her face. Nothing would shift them until finally her skin was bathed in Lourdes water. They vanished overnight – positive proof for my mother and, indeed, the rest of the family of the miraculous healing properties of the waters of Lourdes. My aunty Bridget in Ireland swore by it and she often had a bottle handy in case a cow fell ill. I still have a bottle to this day, the holy water inside now a murky shade of green. I wonder if holy water goes off? Or like a fine wine does it improve with age? Answers on a postcard, please.

My mother never tired of telling how, after a dip in the waters of Lourdes, she came out 'dry as a bone'.

'You put this linen shift on and stand on a step that leads into the pool,' she would recall, 'and then these two nuns standing waist-deep in the waters, great big beefy nuns with hard faces and dirty big 'ands like shovels, get hold of you and throw you in it – backwards, head and all, casual as you like, without saying a bloody word to you. It was a bit of a shock.'

Pausing momentarily to allow time for this startling act of aggression on the part of two daughters of the Church to sink in, she would pick up the thread.

'They're very rough-handed, these nuns,' she said knowingly. 'I think they're Dutch. They were dragging the lame and dying alike out of their wheelchairs and chucking them into the pool as if they were a bundle of dirty washing. Still, they had a smile on their poor faces as they hit the water,' she added, fondly recalling the experience. 'It's ice cold, that water. I'm surprised some of them didn't drop dead from the shock of it. Anyway, when the nuns throw you out on to the other side,' she went on, and I had an image of the nuns hurling her out of the grotto and over the heads of the wailing pilgrims as if she were a body surfer at a Led Zeppelin concert, 'you're as dry as a bone! No need to dry yourself with a towel, which was just as well since I didn't happen to have one on me.'

The house was full of souvenirs carted back home after each charabanc trip with the Mothers. Over the years she amassed quite a collection of holy medals, mass cards and candles. Assorted chalk statues were dotted about the house; on the mantelpiece in my parents' bedroom sat a large plaster image of St Bernadette praying at the feet of the Virgin Mary at the grotto in Lourdes, complete with a little plastic font that was meant to hold holy water but was home to a shirt button and a safety pin for years instead. In the back of the statue was a music box which, when wound up, played 'Ave Maria'. The statues that were damaged or broken she couldn't bring herself to throw out. Instead she kept chipped and decapitated effigies of St Jude, the Virgin Mary and various other saints in a Co-op carrier bag at the bottom of her wardrobe.

Without doubt her pride and joy was a medal of St Bernadette that had been blessed by the Pope. She kept this wrapped inside a lace handkerchief and tucked away in her knicker drawer to preserve the power that His Holiness had infused into the medal by his touch. According to my mother, in the ecclesiastical pecking order there was God and then there was the Pope. She had a china plate of Pope Paul brought back from Rome by one of the Mothers who had made the envied pilgrimage to the Holy City and this had pride of place on the front-room wall, along with plates depicting previous popes she hadn't had the heart to take down after they'd died.

She'd stood for hours in the street to see Pope John Paul II as he drove past in the Popemobile when he made his papal visit to Liverpool. She said he nodded at her and went around for weeks afterwards like an excited teenager who'd just seen McFly.

On that night in 1979, my mother reached up from the sofa to examine the travel alarm clock on the mantelpiece.

'Half six,' she sighed, slumping back down and gathering the duvet around her. 'Isn't this weather bloody torture?'

We sat in silence listening to the tick of the clock while the freezing wind howled through the letter box and around the house. Suddenly she was up on her feet again.

'I knew there was something I wanted to ask you,' she muttered as she bent over the mantelpiece to rummage among the ornaments, squinting in the half-light. 'What's this?' She turned to face me, one hand clutching her bedjacket around her shoulders and the other holding up a lump of dope. 'I found it on your bedroom floor. It's not dogshit and it's

certainly not an Oxo cube or a bit of chocolate, so what is it?'
She sniffed the dope suspiciously.

I nearly died. It was a chunk of black Lebanese that somebody had given me to nibble on at a party and I'd forgotten to
give it back, whether by accident or by design I really can't
recall. Either way I was'nt particularly interested in it as I had
a puritanical attitude to drugs at the time. It must have fallen
out of my jeans pocket. I could hear the blood pounding in my
ears and feel my face flushing a guilty red. Thank God the
room was in semi-darkness and she couldn't see me clearly.

'I dunno,' I said airily, playing for time. 'Give it here and let
me have a look.' I took the dope from her and pretended I'd
never seen it before, staring at it quizzically.

As she waited for an answer it dawned on me that there was
no reasonable explanation. I'd have to bite the bullet and tell
her the truth. I mean, surely she wouldn't throw me out on a
night like this into the cold, cold snow? Would she? I took
a deep breath. 'It's a lump of dope,' I said flatly, bracing myself
against the onslaught. 'Someone gave it to me at a party.'

'You mean mara-hadge-a-wana?' she shrieked, her voice
rising ten octaves. 'Mother of God, tell me please that you're
not a bloody drug addict,' she went on, panicking but bringing
her voice down to a whisper in case next door heard her. I
assured her that I wasn't and calmed her down.

'I'll flush it down the lav,' I lied, getting up to brave the
glacial wind blowing up the stairs and straight into the toilet at
the top.

She pulled me back. 'You will not, I want to have a good
look at it first. Pass me one of those candles.' She sat
examining the dope in the blue light of the votive candle. With
her hair uncombed and her multicoloured crocheted bedjacket
draped round her shoulders, surrounded by a crumpled duvet
and pages of newspaper, she could have passed for an elderly
hippy sizing up a ten-pound deal.

'What does it do?' she asked. 'Does it make you hallucinate? Do you go out of your mind and jump out of windows?'

She never ceased to amaze me. Instead of going berserk as I had anticipated, she seemed excited and genuinely interested in the lump of dope. I tried to explain.

'It sort of relaxes you, makes you feel mellow and calm, a bit like a Valium, I suppose,' I added craftily. She couldn't object if she thought it was on a par with something she had in plentiful supply in the kitchen cabinet.

'Can you eat it?'

Jesus, I wished she'd give up on the dope and go back to moaning about the weather. Liberal Mother made me nervous. I preferred Mrs Fire and Brimstone; at least then I knew where I stood.

'Some people smoke it, some people eat it . . . I think,' I said offhandedly. 'Listen to that wind! It's getting louder.' I rubbed my hands together and blew into them. 'I'll make a cup of tea, eh?' I got up from the sofa, desperately trying to get her off the subject of dope and back on to her normal track.

'Mmm,' she muttered absently, staring at the dope. She pursed her lips and tapped her chin. 'The thing is, you don't know where it's been, do you?' she said, suddenly looking up at me. 'I'm not eating something that's been up someone's bum.'

My sixty-seven-year-old mother, a pillar of the Union of Catholic Mothers, was considering eating hashish. This was too much. She didn't even smoke or drink.

'They bring it into the country up their bum,' she went on knowingly. 'They wrap it in a Durex first, then shove it up their bums. I read it in the *Echo*. I suppose they wash it before they sell it though.'

'Mother, it's not clotted cream toffees, it's dope. It's illegal!' I shouted, our roles suddenly reversing.

'Shh!' she hissed, flapping her hand at me. 'They'll hear you next door. Jesus tonight, it's only a tiny little lump,' she reasoned, holding the dope up, pleading its case. 'This much couldn't be illegal. Now get that kettle on and give this a good wash under the tap and we'll have a little bit.'

What the hell, I thought, taking the dope from her and heading for the kitchen, might as well make use of this unexpected turn of events and get stoned. I was in a turmoil as I stood shivering, waiting for the kettle to boil. It would be interesting to see my mother stoned but suppose it made her ill? Had an adverse affect? She might get out of her mind and lose control, even collapse. How would an ambulance get up the hill in this snow? She might die and I'd be trapped in the dark with her corpse. Found by the police sat on the sofa with my dead mother wrapped in a duvet. Oh my God, this is straight out of *Psycho*! I can see the headlines in the *Echo*: BIRKENHEAD MAN MURDERS MOTHER IN DRUG BINGE! My mind raced as I poured the boiling water into the teapot.

'Don't forget to give it a good rinse under the tap,' she called out cheerily from the front room. 'Give it a scrub with the nailbrush and a drop of Dettol.'

When I got back she was like an excited child, grinning wickedly at the thought of forbidden fruit.

I'd heated a knife and cut a few slivers from the lump and put them on a saucer. She sniffed it cautiously.

'Poo, it stinks,' she said. 'What do I do with it?'

'Take a bite,' I replied, feeling like the witch with Snow White. 'Swallow a bit with a cup of tea.'

'Have you had some?' she asked.

I'd cut myself a large slice in the kitchen and told her so.

'Go on then,' she said daringly after a moment's pause. 'Give us a bit. Thank God your father's not alive.'

She took the biggest sliver and, pulling an exaggerated face, she swallowed it down with a swig of tea. She sat for a moment. 'It hasn't worked,' she announced, disappointed. 'Give us another bit.'

'Hang on,' I said, growing nervous. 'You have to give it time to kick in.'

We sat in silence drinking our tea and listening to the maelstrom outside.

'Are you sure that was dope? Because nothing's happening to me. I think you've been done, mate.' She sat back in her corner of the sofa. 'Don't know what all the fuss is about.'

We continued drinking our tea. She ate another sliver and then another. I was beginning to panic.

Mine had kicked in, so why hadn't hers? She must have the constitution of a horse, I thought, keeping a careful eye on her as she stared into the hearth, smiling to herself, the glow from the gas fire reflected in her eyes, which had suddenly become suspiciously wide and shiny. The penny dropped. She was off her face.

'Are you OK?' I asked her tentatively.

'I was just thinking about our Chrissie,' she said dreamily, gazing into the gas jets, her thoughts lost in another time and place. 'It was a night like this when she ran away from the convent.'

She was definitely off her face. Aunty Chrissie a nun? She never went near a church apart from weddings and funerals.

'What was Aunty Chris doing in a convent?' I asked, laughing in disbelief.

'St Margaret's Convent in Rock Ferry,' she said. 'It was an orphanage, run by nuns. Wicked bitches they were, wicked.' She shook her head sadly. 'We were living with Aunty Poll, at least me and Chrissie were. Annie had gone back to Lowther Street to look after my dad. Chrissie was wild in those days, a wilful girl. Aunty Poll had her put into a home. I fancy another cup of tea.' She broke off to pick up her mug from on top of the library book lying on the floor that she was using as an occasional table.

'I'll make one in a minute,' I cried. 'Tell me what happened.'

'There's nowt to tell.' She ran her finger around the rim of the mug absently. 'Chrissie had been caught nicking a packet of sweets. She must have been about thirteen. Aunty Poll said she needed a bit of discipline as she was out of control, and she turned the poor bugger over to the nuns, putting her away in St Margaret's for a year. She ran away after six months and you wouldn't blame her; she was half starved and made to work in the laundry. The nuns crucified her. She had great purple welts across her back where they'd beaten her with a belt. And all for a packet of sweets,' she said bitterly. 'When she escaped she went straight to Lowther Street. She had no coat on, only a thin cotton dress and a bit of cardigan and on a night like this. I'm surprised she didn't catch pneumonia; but you know our Chris, hard as nails. Anyway, when me dad saw the state of her he didn't send her back, he kept her at home. He went up there and played merry hell with the Mother Superior and didn't speak to Aunty Poll for years.'

She thrust her mug at me and pleaded for another cup of tea.

'My mouth's as dry as Deuteronomy,' she said, smacking her lips as I braved the freezing kitchen once again, 'and make me a bit of toast and bring those biscuits in,' she added. 'I'm starving.'

Even though she refused to admit it she was well out of it. She lay back on the sofa luxuriantly and wrapped herself in the duvet. I groped my way around the dilapidated lean-to that insolently called itself a kitchen, attempting to make tea and toast by the light of a votive candle. My icy breath clouded the sliding glass door on the solitary cabinet that hung from the wall as I searched for a pot of jam. A mushroom that looked like shaving foam was growing up the side of it. It seemed unreal in the ghostly blue light.

I wish I had the money and the know-how to be able to do something with this place, I thought to myself guiltily. I had

visions of buying my mother a comfortable little house somewhere, one that had central heating and a fully fitted kitchen
with every appliance known to man instead of this freezing
shack that had Walt Disney fungi growing up the walls, but
since I was unemployed with no prospects in sight it was a case
of dream on.

As I buttered the toast I could hear her singing:

'I wish, I wish, I wish in vain,
I wish I was a maid again,
But a maid again I'll never be,
Till cherries grow on an apple tree.'

She had a thin, reedy, tuneless voice that normally made me
laugh. Not tonight though; as I stood stirring the tea I felt like
crying. Christ, I must be stoned.

'My mother used to sing that song,' she said, hauling herself
into an upright position as I came into the room and handed
her a plate of toast. 'It's about a girl who gets pregnant to a
butcher's boy and then hangs herself. It's an old Irish lament,
terrible maudlin.'

'Aren't they all?' I said, joining her on the sofa. 'Can I
have a piece of that toast, please, before you demolish the
lot.'

She sat perched on the end of the sofa, humming softly to
herself as she munched.

'D'you like this jam?' she asked. 'It's diabetic. It was going
half price in Boots so I bought a pot. There mustn't be much
call for it.'

We sat in silence, slurping tea. Why is there no call for
diabetic jam? I thought. My mind wandered. Weren't there any
diabetics who shopped at Boots? Or, if there were any, did they
have an aversion to strawberry jam? My mother's voice broke
this chain of thought.

'My poor mother,' she said tenderly to herself. 'She died in childbirth, you know.'

I did know. I'd heard it many times before and it looked like I was about to hear it again. She had me trapped, a captive audience. The stories my mother told about her childhood always left me feeling unsettled. A profound sadness hung around me as I tried to link the lonely little girl of her stories and my mother.

'It was a little boy,' she said sadly, settling back into the sofa. 'We called him James. He only lived for a week. A week after we'd buried my mother at Flaybrick Cemetery we were back up there with the baby. Four great black horses with black plumes on top of their heads there was, pulling the hearse. It must have cost my dad a fortune, money he didn't have.' She stared unblinking into the glow of the fire, momentarily in a trance, her eyes blazing like chip pans, recalling a memory of when as a little girl she had stood by an open grave on a bleak winter's morning listening to the rooks calling to each other over the branches of the bare trees, and the quiet sobbing of the mourners as the priest read out the final prayer. She gave a long sigh as she came back from her dream and continued with her reminiscences: 'I can see my mother now, lying in bed in the front parlour, her face white as a sheet and her lovely hair wringing with sweat.' She paused to take a sip of tea. 'She was only in her thirties, God help her. It was a complicated birth. The midwife told me dad to run for the doctor, but it was too late . . . Her heart gave out . . . When he got back she was gone . . . Before she died, Aunty Anne crawled into the bed with her. She must have only been five. Look after your dad, my mother said to her, and d'you know what? It was a dying wish that your aunty Anne kept till the day my dad died. Look after your dad . . .'

Her voice trailed off as she took another sip of her tea. 'Where was I? Oh yes, Annie and my dad. She was his favourite . . . When Annie cooked his dinner he always used to leave a little bit for her on the side of his plate.' She laughed to herself, nodding her head, enjoying some secret joke. 'She did everything for him, even after she got married. Harold had to move into Lowther Street because Annie wouldn't leave me dad.' She lapsed into silence again. A blast of icy wind blew through the entire house and the candles flickered.

Aunty Anne, known as Annie to the family but Nancy to her mates, fell in love with Harold Fawcett from the moment she first saw him serving on the altar of St Laurence's Church. There was a touch of the Edward G. Robinson about him. Determinedly she set about wooing him until eventually he cracked and took her to the pictures. They were both fans of American movies. Aunty Anne with her owl-like specs and hyena's laugh fancied herself as a Janet Gaynor type and saw Uncle Al as her Fredric March. Together they would quote their favourite scenes from the movies they'd seen when they were out courting. Aunty Anne, the eternal romantic, bagged her prince and walked down the aisle with him wearing an ivory satin dress from Guinea a Gown, a shop that specialized in wedding dresses at just over a quid, with her sisters trailing behind her as bridesmaids.

'I wonder why your dad never remarried?' I asked my mother.

'Because who the bloody hell is going to take on a man with three little children?' she replied incredulously, turning towards me. Her eyes were rolling around in her head like the clown outside the Blackpool Fun House. 'My dad couldn't look after us on his own. He was working shifts at Lever's, used to walk there and back every day to save money – it must be over ten miles. He had no choice but to farm us out among various relatives. Sister Martha looked after us first. She was a lovely girl but she was going into a convent and couldn't keep us, so we were passed on from pillar to post, to ever-increasing levels of poverty and neglect.' She shuddered, more from the gale force wind howling around us than the bitter memories. 'Two of my dad's cousins took Chrissie in. She was only a toddler. They'd have been locked up these days for cruelty. Aunty Poll went round and found her sat on the stone kitchen floor in a filthy vest sucking on a stale crust, her little body black and blue with bruises those wicked bastards had inflicted on her.'

Aunty Poll, my grandmother's sister, took the girls in and gave them a home. She wasn't an intentionally cruel woman but she was cold and unfeeling, a strict disciplinarian who firmly believed that to spare the rod was to spoil the child. Yet my mother had a fondness for her and spoke of her with respect, even though she'd put Chrissie into an orphanage and herself and Annie into domestic service. Maybe the years had softened her memories and any anger had long subsided, unlike the storm which was still raging outside.

We both slept downstairs that night as the damp, arctic bedrooms would have meant certain hypothermia. My mother slept on the sofa, me on cushions on the floor. During the course of the evening we had got through a loaf of bread, a pot of diabetic jam, half a packet of chocolate digestives, two fruit yoghurts, cheese on toast and a Battenberg, and she claimed that she wasn't stoned.

She slept soundly for eight hours, a smile on her lips. When she woke in the morning she complained that she hadn't managed to get a wink of sleep and that the sofa was 'agony'. She looked remarkably refreshed and relaxed as she stood at the window, a mug of coffee in hand, surveying the snowy landscape outside. 'Don't you dare tell anyone that you gave me drugs,' she said, blowing on the steaming coffee. 'Not a word to Annie and Chrissie, and if I catch you bringing drugs into this house again I'm calling the police.' She took a sip of the scalding coffee and then turned to look at me, trying to suppress the laughter in her voice. 'Do you hear me, my lad?'

'Yes, Mother,' I said, 'your secret life as a dope fiend is safe with me.'

CHAPTER SIX

AUNTY ANNE LOVED A GOOD HYMN, AS THE RESIDENTS OF Lowther Street could readily testify.

' "So-well of my Save-eeour sancti-fy my brrreast," ' she sang out lustily in her ear-piercing screech as she set about sweeping the house through from back to front. Aunty Chrissie, sitting at the kitchen table reading the paper, winced.

'Give it a bloody rest, will you?' she shouted over the din, picking her fag up from its resting place in a saucer and taking a drag. 'Jesus tonight, anybody walking past will think we're being raped by the Russians.'

Chrissie's abuse fell on deaf ears. Aunty Anne carried on with her concert regardless; she was used to Chrissie's slings and arrows. '"Guard and defend me from the foe malign,"' she howled in a glass-shattering soprano that was so high-pitched, only bats and the local dogs could make out the lyrics. She was attacking the hall, or 'the lobby' as it was known, banging the brush against the skirting board as she sought out every last speck of dirt and dust before sweeping the lot into the street and swilling it away with a bucket of soapy water.

While she was at it she'd give the brass trim that ran along the edge of the doorstep a 'good rub' with a bit of Brasso, greeting passing neighbours cheerily as she knelt on the door mat and went at the trimming hammer and tongs.

'Hello, Mrs Duff . . . Just off to get your paper? . . . Mind yourself then, love . . . "Jesu dulcis memoriaaa!"' she screeched.

'Is there any need for that?' said Chrissie, raising her eyebrows and picking a bit of tobacco off her bottom lip. 'Talk about a one-note friggin' canary.'

A dirty step was the hallmark of a slovenly housewife, as was a pair of grubby net curtains hanging at your window. 'Have you seen the colour of that one's nets?' was a damning question heard during many a doorstep bitchfest. Aunty Anne's nets were beyond reproach; when not hanging in the window of the parlour they could be found steeping in the kitchen sink with a bag of Dolly Blue for company. The parlour was forbidden territory, used only on special occasions. A smell of lavender polish hung in the air, the floor was covered with blue shiny lino; against one wall stood a piano that nobody in the family could play, but a piano was an essential addition to the décor in most working-class parlours.

Vera Lalley, Aunty Chrissie's friend who lived further up the street, had the reputation of being 'better than Winifred Atwell' in the pubs and parlours of Birkenhead. She was indeed an accomplished pianist, self-taught and able to play any tune by ear, as she never tired of telling people, and after a few whiskies and brown ales would happily sit down at the piano and give an impromptu concert. She was very popular at parties, and as long as it meant 'free ale' Vera would pull up a chair and oblige with a few tunes.

In the middle of the room, arranged in a semicircle round the fireplace, was a 1940s three-piece suite covered in fading grey leather, piped round the edge with a red trim. It had smooth rounded arms ideal for sliding down, which if you were caught meant a dig in the back from one of Aunty Anne's arthritic knuckles followed by a 'Gerrowt an' play!' In the corner, in the spot where the bed that my grandmother had died in had been, stood a Dansette record player, leaning drunkenly to one side as it balanced on four wobbly 'screw-in' black legs, lurching dangerously close to a table under the window where the obligatory aspidistra, an unhealthy specimen with dull, leathery leaves, sat hunched in its pot like a depressed vulture.

All the residents of Number 29 Lowther Street, with the exception of Aunty Anne and my cousin Maureen who was too young to smoke, smoked like chimneys. Aunty Chris could kipper a net curtain just by walking past it. She was an inveterate smoker, never without an Embassy hanging out of the corner of her mouth. Her dressing-gown pocket was full of half-smoked cigarettes, or 'dockers' as she called them, handy for hard times when she ran out.

Smoke permeated the whole of the house, and although the parlour was only ever used for 'best' somehow the smoke managed to curl under the door and through the keyhole and get at Aunty Annie's nets, dulling their pristine whiteness with a nicotine tinge. This was the house the Savage sisters had been born in: end of terrace, three bedrooms, kitchen, parlour, no bathroom, and the lavatory outside at the bottom of the yard; a house similar to the many other back-to-backs built for the working classes in industrial Birkenhead in the early 1900s.

It was a mainly matriarchal society as most of the men were away at sea for long periods of time. My uncle Harold was a master baker and confectioner for the Cunard Line. My cousins John and Mickey were stewards, and all three could be away from home for as long as six months to a year, depending on the trip. Annie ran the household, keeping a tight rein on the purse strings. If towards the middle of the week she found herself short she could always rely on a bit of tick from Johnstone's, a corner shop in Bentinck Street that at best could be described as Dickensian.

When the tray in Ma Johnstone's window wasn't displaying an array of dubious-looking pies and pasties, her big black cat liked to stretch out in it, washing its paws and basking in the sun like a feline Amsterdam hooker, pawing the window coquettishly at passing trade. Ma Johnstone's enormous bacon slicer stood in the middle of the marble counter, where she'd slice raw bacon and cooked meats interchangeably, her only gesture towards food hygiene consisting of a cursory wipe round the blade with a grimy finger to pick up any stray bits of meat. These tasty titbits she would suck on as she squinted at the scales before announcing that your purchase was either 'just under' or 'just over'.

Across the road from Ma's was the Co-op, and next door to that was Barney's the barber, who would put a plank across his chair so his younger customers were the right height for him when he cut their hair. Not that he actually cut it: he favoured the National Service style, shaving it all off at the back and sides with a pair of electric clippers, and then slapping a dollop of Brylcreem on what little hair was left on the top, parting it severely down one side and combing it flat across your head. Sometimes he singed the ends of his customers' hair with a lit wax taper. As I sat on the bench waiting my turn I wanted nothing more than to have my hair singed, but this peculiar practice apparently wasn't performed on little boys, or so Barney explained, only on the men. God, I couldn't wait to grow up and have my hair singed, spit in the spittoon by the door, and buy a packet of something called Durex, whatever they were.

Nicky Clarke's Barney's certainly wasn't. The air was thick with the smell of brilliantine, sweat and cigarettes. A haze of yellow smog hung low in the room, a few postcards were pinned around the mirror and a small blue neon sign advertising the mystifying Durex sat on a shelf above it next to a radio that was kept permanently tuned in to the racing. A long queue of men waited patiently on a bench against the wall for a haircut, sucking on their pencils and scratching their heads as they studied the racing form in the back of their newspapers. As he cut your hair Barney would work the room with the confidence of a Las Vegas lounge act, wisecracking with the customers and offering racing tips.

Like most barbers of that time, Barney's was strictly men only. Women only ever entered the shop either to collect their offspring or to drop them off, and they seldom hung around. The presence of a woman in this male bastion made the customers feel uncomfortable and slightly resentful. The shop would go quiet whenever a mother dropped her child off, Barney's lone voice telling her to 'Come back in twenty minutes, madam, and he'll be a new man.' He was right. I must have unconsciously absorbed some of the testosterone-drenched atmosphere after a visit to Barney's, as on being picked up I would lower my voice to a growl and swagger slowly around the house, legs bowed like a cowboy, causing Aunty Chris to comment, 'Just got off your horse, John Wayne? Or have you just shit yourself?'

When I was six my mother went into hospital to have an operation. She had an overactive thyroid. All I can recall is being held up to a window outside the hospital ward and seeing her in bed with a row of metal clamps à la Frankenstein's monster across her throat. During her time in the Birkenhead General Hospital and then later on, while she was convalescing at the small hospital in the grounds of Arrowe Park, I was packed off to stay with the aunties in Lowther Street.

Through my six-year-old eyes the house appeared huge. When I sat on the bottom step of the stairs, the long narrow lobby leading to the front door stretched endlessly before me. Above me, the dark upper recesses of the cavernous stairwell seemed cathedral-like and forbidding. The upstairs landing was a place of terror after dark: the ideal setting for Sweeney Todd, the Demon Barber of Fleet Street, to lurk, razor in hand, ready to slit an unsuspecting boy's throat as he made his way to bed in the gloom.

Ever since I'd seen a wax model of Mr Todd dispatching one of his customers at the Tower Waxworks in New Brighton I'd lived in terror of him. I've heard people say that the Childcatcher from *Chitty Chitty Bang Bang* was the stuff of their childhood nightmares, but Sweeney Todd was my personal bogeyman, hiding behind the door of every wardrobe and lurking underneath the bed, biding his time until that moment when the landing light was turned off and he could silently creep out from the shadows and pounce on his prey.

In the big cupboard at the end of the landing – a cupboard whose door had the unsettling habit of slowly swinging open of its own accord – my cousin Maureen and I once swore that we saw a face. A tiny, childlike face, glowing like phosphorescence and mouthing silent words at us as it bobbed up and down along the shelf. Perhaps it was a trick of the light or just the imagination of two impressionable children winding themselves up in the dark, but at the time it was very real and down the years I've never forgotten the experience, imaginary or otherwise.

Aunty Chris, pleasantly pissed after a night out with the Lord Exmouth's ladies' darts team and trying to placate me after I'd charged down the stairs three at a time and run screaming into the kitchen, told me that it was a fairy. 'A little lost fairy,' she said dreamily, stroking my hair. 'A little lost fairy who's had her head ripped off and is going around the house looking for it.' If this was meant to comfort me then she wasn't doing a very good job. As far as I was concerned there was only one person capable of severing a fairy's head from her shoulders in cold blood, and that was Sweeney Todd. He'd struck again, claiming yet another victim, slashing her fairy neck with his cut-throat razor and then packing her off to be made into meat pies, and all on my aunty Annie's landing under the grown-ups' very noses. The cheek of the man.

I slept in between my aunty and Uncle Al that night. They didn't mind, as I was by no means the only member of the family to seek refuge in their bed in the middle of the night. The house was reputed to be haunted, and a silent visitor once shook Aunty Chris's shoulder as she lay in bed reading, causing her to wake the best part of the street with her screams. She ran from the room and jumped in between Annie and Harold in their bed. A photograph taken in the back yard had revealed the mysterious face of a woman hidden in the ivy that grew up the side of the house, and you could sometimes hear footsteps in the hall if you were in on your own and the house was silent – not that that was a common occurrence. Lowther Street was lively, to say the least. It always seemed to be a hive of activity; Holly Grove was quiet in comparison.

Our house was considered to be posher than Lowther Street for the sole reason that we had a garden and indoor plumbing. Higher Tranmere was thought a better neighbourhood than downtown Birkenhead. Lowther Street was 'rough'. At home there were only a handful of kids of my age to play with but Lowther Street and the surrounding area were teeming with kids. Packs of them roamed the streets all day like young wolves, only returning to their respective dens when the she-wolf called them.

'PAUL, GERRIN FOR YOUR TEA!'

'What have you been up to, buggerlugs?'

'Playing.'

As well as tribes of kids to play with Aunty Annie had a cat, a great ginger monster called Jinksy who conveniently gave birth to her litter of kittens in the outside lav, enabling Aunty Anne to flush them down the pan with the minimum of fuss while my cousin Maureen and I hid in the bedroom and covered our ears. Nowadays the RSPCA would quite rightly take action, but in the early sixties nobody round us dreamed of having their cat spayed. They couldn't afford it, for one thing, and a quick drowning seemed a more humane alternative to allowing litters of unwanted and feral kittens to haunt the back alleys of the neighbourhood.

Uncle Harold once returned from a trip abroad with a bushbaby. These were the days before quarantine and sailors frequently brought animals back to homes ill prepared for a menagerie of exotic pets. At first glance the bushbaby seemed to be a docile little chap as he lay curled up in shredded newspaper at the bottom of a box.

'Isn't he lovely,' cooed Aunty Anne, prodding the unconscious critter gently with her finger. 'And isn't he well behaved? Put him on the sideboard.' The bushbaby slept all through the day and showed no sign of waking up.

'Maybe he's hibernating,' Aunty Anne said, peering into the box. 'Anyway, he's as good as gold.'

Aunty Chris, eyeing the animal dubiously, was less confident. 'It's a bloody rat,' she said dismissively. 'Sling it out.'

That night, while the rest of the house slept, the nocturnal bushbaby came to life and decided, as bushbabies do, to go in search of food. The noise it made woke the house, if not the whole street. As Aunty Anne entered the room and switched on the light, the startled bushbaby, who had been sitting on the pulley full of washing which hung from the ceiling over the fireplace, leaped at her.

It ripped off her glasses and climbed on to her head, and then, clinging on for dear life to the rollers wound tightly in her hair, shat down the back of her dressing gown. Aunty Anne let out a scream that would have rivalled Cammell Laird's siren. In shock, the bushbaby hurled itself on to the mantelpiece, bringing down the clock and a brass camel.

'Jesus Christ, me clock,' Aunty Chris screamed from behind

the safety of Uncle Harold's back. 'I smoked like a bloody chimney to get enough Embassy coupons for that. Grab hold of that animal before it wrecks the gaff.'

As the bushbaby leaped across the room from mantelpiece to curtains it emptied the seemingly endless contents of its bowels with gay abandon, oblivious of the hysteria it was creating.

'Quick, throw a towel over it, Harold,' shouted Aunty Chris, more than a hint of panic in her voice as she watched it fling itself towards half a bottle of milk that sat on the table. But before Uncle Harold could act, Aunty Anne, who had been momentarily stunned by the loss of her spectacles and the unfamiliar sensation of something warm running slowly down the back of her neck, sprang into action. Pulling off her dressing gown, she threw it over the bushbaby and brought it down on to the sofa in a spectacular rugby tackle.

'Christ, she's nifty when she wants to be,' said Aunty Chris admiringly. 'Now let's get that whoring thing back in its box and clear this shite up.'

Before Uncle Harold secured the lid of the box with Sellotape Aunty Anne threw in half a banana. 'Shame really that it's not housetrained,' she said sadly. 'It had lovely big eyes.'

The next day the bushbaby was taken to a pet shop in the market, where it was transferred to a cage and later sold to a wealthy and elderly lady who lived in refined squalor in a large house in Oxton and wouldn't, as Aunty Anne said later, object to a bit of shit up her walls.

It was no hardship for me to decamp to Lowther Street while my mother recovered from her operation. My father was more upset than I was at seeing his family split up, but with his missus in hospital, my brother and sister at work and himself on nights at Shell in Ellesmere Port there was no other option but for me to stay with the aunties.

*

Aunty Chrissie was a clippie on the buses. She liked to look, as she put it, immaculate. She never appeared in public without perfectly coiffed hair, a full face of slap and her clothing nothing less than perfection. There was no running to the shop or the betting office in slippers and rollers for Aunty Chris – forget that for a game of soldiers. She didn't greet her public until she was properly painted and shod. Just like my father, she liked to create the impression that she 'had a few bob' and would step out in style in her set of Birkenhead market pearls and camel coat. She loved 'putting on the dog', as she called it.

Her dark navy conductress's uniform could easily have been mistaken for the work of a bespoke tailor. She'd taken it home and altered it herself, nipping it in at the waist and shortening the sleeves of the jacket so that her shirt cuffs showed. Each night she'd press it neatly with a warm iron and a damp tea towel so that the fabric didn't shine, taking her fag out of her mouth for a moment to spit on the iron before leaning on it to create a razor's edge seam down the front of the trousers. She wore a clean white shirt every day and tied her Birkenhead Corporation Transport tie in a smart Windsor knot. She suited this masculine attire; it made her look sexy and she knew it. Slung over each shoulder and across her chest, two leather straps carried her money bag and ticket machine. I thought she looked like a gunslinger as she stood at Woodside terminus pulling on her leather gloves, ticket machine casually dangling on her hip as she chatted to her driver, Bill Casey. They leaned against the wheel of a stationary 79 sharing a quick last-minute fag while they waited for the signal from the inspector to pull out for the long haul to Prenton and beyond.

I'd show her off to my mates as we caught the bus from Woodside on our way home from school. They were in awe of her. They'd been well primed before actually meeting her in the flesh, and warned that while on the one hand she might tell us all to bugger off, on the other, and depending on her mood, she just might give us a roll of unused bus tickets and a couple of pennies. Aunty Chris could be capricious. They soon learned that politeness and plenty of flattery usually got results.

'Doesn't your aunty look like *I Love Lucy*?' they'd say within her earshot, but casually so as not to seem as if they were 'crawling'. Actually, when she had her curly hair dyed red she did resemble Lucille Ball a little. I, and most of the men who travelled on her bus, preferred her when she was a blonde.

'Some feller on the bus today said I looked like Marlene Dietrich,' she'd say when she came home from another long shift, proudly pulling her 'Marlene Dietrich' face in the mirror, a spot of gurning that involved sucking her cheeks in, closing her eyes slowly till she could barely see, and letting her fag hang from the corner of her mouth. 'They all say it,' she'd add confidently through barely moving lips in case she should drop the fag or disturb the death's head mask she was creating in the mirror and thereby spoil the illusion.

The family good-naturedly humoured her, but standing under the stairs on the 79 bus in her tailored uniform with her beautiful cheekbones and sly smile, draped lazily against the partition, one hand on the bell, the other in her trouser pocket, she unwittingly conjured up an image that certainly was evocative of Marlene. Her bus was known as Marlene's Bus by the regulars of the 79 route, or, if she was going through her 'fiery red' stage, Lucy's Bus. Either way she didn't mind and secretly, although she was loath to admit it, she enjoyed the attention.

Aunty Chris didn't like men or strong drink. If offered the latter she would distort her face into a grimace of disapproval. 'Certainly not,' she'd snap, and turning the offender to stone with a withering glare would add with a shudder, 'I never touch the stuff. Get it out o' me bloody sight, and you with it, bloody reprobate.' She hated drunks, and would bang and crash about the house to show her displeasure if Uncle Harold and the cousins came home from the pub slightly intoxicated, or 'reeking the house out with ale' as she put it.

She hadn't always been so disapproving, not by a long shot. In her day Aunty Chris could have drunk Uncle Harold and the entire merchant navy under the table and still got up at six in the morning and worked a fourteen-hour shift. She was known on the streets of Birkenhead in her teen years as a bit of a wild one. She had after all been in a home for delinquent girls and was so bad that even the nuns with their fearsome reputation had not been able to control her. Aunty Chris said the nuns who ran that home made the female guards at Ravensbrück look 'soft'. Mind you, she said that about any woman in authority. The blonde woman who worked behind the counter at the Birkenhead General Post Office was known as Irma Grese because she once told Aunty Chris off for filling out a form incorrectly. She never went to that woman's counter if she could avoid it after that.

'Don't go in that queue,' she'd say, raising her voice ever so slightly so it was audible to the staff behind the counter, in particular her nemesis, 'you'll only get spoken to like you were a bloody fool.' And then, 'It's just as well she's behind glass,' she'd add conversationally to whoever was listening. 'She puts me in mind of a trout.'

Men who appeared pushy were known as 'Little Hitlers'. There were a couple of Little Hitlers working as inspectors on the buses. There was even a Himmler on the 60 route. Aunty Chris didn't like being told what to do by people she didn't think much of, and she made her feelings known and didn't care who heard her. Many a passenger who overstepped the mark was silenced with a withering look and the quick wrist action that followed as she turned the handle warningly on her ticket machine.

'She's got a mouth like a bee's arse, that woman,' one passenger who had been on the receiving end of a stinging retort was heard to remark.

*

I've frequently been asked over the years who Lily Savage was based on and I've always answered that it was no one in particular and she was just a figment of my imagination. The truth, I realize now, is that Lily owes a lot to the women I encountered in my childhood. Characteristics and attitudes were observed and absorbed, Aunty Chris's in particular, and they provided the roots and compost for the Lily that would germinate and grow later on.

Sometimes when I was pounding on the slap or teasing the fringe of the wig I would catch a glimpse of Aunty Chris in myself in the dressing-room mirror. I would notice myself adopting one of her mannerisms as I went through the ritual of getting Lily on. Years of being around Aunty Chris as she got ready for work meant that I unconsciously absorbed her actions as she slapped up. A fag hanging dangerously out of the corner of my mouth as I sprayed a gallon of hair lacquer over the coiffure, one eye closed against the rising spiral of smoke – here she was, coming back to haunt me in the mirror of a pub dressing room.

'How're you doing, Aunty Chris? Nice to see you again.'

Aunty Chrissie had a complicated beauty routine that she went through unfailingly every morning at the kitchen table.

Before she applied the warpaint she'd have what she called a 'good wash'. Since Lowther Street had no bathroom she'd carry a washing-up bowl of warm water up to the privacy of her bedroom and spend a leisurely half-hour 'bathing'. 'I don't wish to be disturbed while I'm having a wash,' she'd announce primly as she made her way up the stairs carrying her bowl, wearing an enormous pale pink housecoat from Brentford Nylons and a head full of rollers. They all had these house-coats, in a variety of lurid colours. Full length, quilted and made of nylon, they were lined with something that made them stick out. My mum and my aunties would glide round the kitchen looking like Daleks when they had them on. If Aunty Chris was running late she made do with 'a quick swill' that involved little more than a brief wipe-over with a flannel at the kitchen sink, but she never short-changed herself when it came to the maquillage. She could put it on in five minutes if necessary, but preferred to take her time. Having to rush her beauty routine always put her in a foul mood.

She never used soap on her face and would only splash the tiniest amount of water on to it, preferring to use a dollop of cold cream from the enormous pot of Nivea that sat on her bedside cabinet to clean that sacred area. She'd ladle it on, massaging it in until it had all but vanished apart from a slimy sheen across the skin. She'd throw her head back and slap her throat and jawline vigorously to 'tighten up the skin'. After sitting for a while to recover from this bout of self-abuse she would then remove what was left of the sheen, very gently, with a tissue, and spray a fine mist of rosewater and witch hazel from a plastic bottle all over her face. While she waited for this concoction to dry she'd take a sip of tea, light up a fag and use the momentary lapse in proceedings to peruse the racing pages of the *Daily Mirror*, blowing smoke rings out of the corner of her mouth as she studied the form with the critical eye of an old pro.

Satisfied that she had dragged the last available gasp out of her Embassy and found a couple of horses that looked promising, she would resume the ritual. A tiny dab of Ponds to moisturize, followed by a light application of Max Factor's Hi Fi foundation from a grubby-looking tube, which transformed her death-white complexion to a rosy hue worthy of any principal boy in the Empire panto. She sealed this with a light pressing of face powder using a decrepit powder puff, pulverized into a flat grey pad from constant use over the years. This she'd wipe over the compressed crème powder in an ancient compact that had no lid and pat across her face, pausing to enquire of Aunty Anne, scrubbing shirt collars on the draining board like a woman possessed, if there was 'any tea going in that pot. I'm parched here.'

'If you want tea then get off your arse and make it yourself.'

'I can't.'

'Why not?'

'I'm getting ready for work.'

'Oh . . .' and then, after a while, 'I'll put the kettle on in a minute.'

It could have been the back room of a geisha house. The importance of observing the ceremony, the skill and concentration required to paint the naked face into a flawless mask, was recognized and respected in Lowther Street as in any Japanese tea house. As the maid washed the clothes and made the tea the geisha painted her lovely face. Horses would be discussed as they waited for the kettle to boil. Aunty Chris favoured Lester Piggott. She was devoted to him and would back any horse that he was riding. Aunty Anne could always be persuaded to bet on a horse if it had a name that she thought might be lucky.

'There's a horse running in the one ten, Chrissie, called Half a Mo,' she would say, raising her glasses so she could get her face closer to the page of the paper and focus on the small print.

'What's the odds?'

'Fifty to one.'

'It's a bloody nag,' Aunty Chris would exclaim as she examined her paint job approvingly in the small mirror with the plastic frame that was propped up, as always, against the wicker hair tidy. The tools of her trade. 'Don't waste your money, woman.'

Ignoring her, Aunty Anne continued to stare myopically at the newspaper. 'You see, I've saved half a custard slice for our Mo,' she said reasonably, tapping her top set of dentures with her biro, 'and this Half a Mo might be a lucky omen . . . a sign . . . half a custard slice for Mo . . . Half a Mo . . . don't you think?' She put her glasses on and picked up her purse from the table. 'I'm going to put half a crown on it.'

'I hope there isn't a horse called Bloody Halfwit running,' Chrissie drawled, pencilling in two butterfly antennae for eyebrows. 'She'll be destitute come teatime if there is.' She started to laugh, making little grunting sounds and sending short bursts of smoke shooting out of each nostril.

'You're going to kill yourself if you don't pack those things up,' Aunty Anne said disapprovingly. Apart from the odd one at Christmas for a treat, like my mother she'd never smoked. 'And I'm still backing that horse, regardless to what you think.'

Adopting a suitably martyred air, she went in search of something to write her bet out on. Aunty Chris couldn't resist the odd smart one-liner and Aunty Anne accepted her role as stooge to her sister's Top Banana – up to a point, because at the end of the day it was Annie who wore the trousers.

'You've been titivating yourself for the best part of an hour now,' she said. 'Get your skates on or you'll be late for work.'

'Christ tonight,' Chrissie exclaimed, rooting in her make-up bag, 'look at the bleedin' time.' She produced a small bottle of black eyeliner and expertly painted it round her eyes, swiped a bit of blue eyeshadow across the lids and then dabbed a dot of black powder into her sockets and blended it into the blue with the tip of her little finger. Time for another fag. She lit it and sat back in her chair, examining her reflection in the mirror as if she was scrutinizing the ceiling of the Sistine Chapel for cracks. Dipping into her make-up bag again she opened a little black box containing block mascara and spat on it with gusto, mixing it into an inky puddle with the tiny brush provided, which was remarkably similar to the one that was supposed to be used for brushing fluff off the needle of the Dansette.

I opened this box once, to see what this magical black stuff that transformed pale, stubby eyelashes into a sweeping set worthy of Bambi actually looked like, but hurriedly closed it, appalled at the peculiar stench, which was due, no doubt, to the accumulation of years of nicotine-laced spit.

Peering into the little mirror inside the lid, she applied the black gunk carefully to her eyelashes. You weren't supposed to talk to her during this tricky operation as it spoiled her concentration and might make her flick a bit of the mascara on to her cheek – and then she'd vent her frustration on the offender with the kind of language that set Aunty Anne tut-tutting. I always wondered why she found it physically impossible to perform this task with her mouth closed. She sat combing on the mascara like a giant goldfish, her mouth set in a perfect O.

'I'm running across to the bookies,' Aunty Anne said, coming in from the kitchen. 'D'ya want me to put a bet on for you?'

'Yurgh,' Aunty Chris grunted, flicking the tips of her eyelashes with the brush. They were sticky with beads of mascara, one of which was threatening to drop on to her face if she didn't act fast.

'Well, come on,' Annie said impatiently, 'they'll be under starter's orders if you don't get a move on.'

'Urgh, uh, urgh.' The sound Aunty Chris made in the back of her throat as a response to her sister's urging could be loosely translated as 'What's your bloody hurry, woman? Can't you see I'm at a critical stage in the proceedings and if you hurry me this blob could fall on my freshly made-up face, ruining the entire effect?' She caught the offending blob with an adroit swipe from the tip of a tissue and transferred it to the saucer of ash and cigarette stubs that was already beginning to overflow on to the table.

'I wish you'd use a bloody ashtray,' Aunty Anne muttered, lifting the cup and saucer and taking it into the kitchen. 'It's a disgusting habit, this,' she said, tipping the stubs into the bin and tutting. 'Bloody disgusting.'

In the absence of the saucer Aunty Chris balanced her fag on the end of the table. The line of burn marks that pitted the table top, and her bedside cabinet, bore testament to the many cigarettes that had rested there previously.

'Put two bob each way on Lucky Jim,' she said, taking the money from her purse. 'And two bob to win on Saffron Sunset. Give us a rub of your hump for luck and then get a bloody move on, it's nearly five past.' When it came to bets Aunty Chris liked to leave it till she was right at the wire.

Grabbing the money from the table and checking to see that it was the correct amount as she ran down the hall, Aunty Anne was off at the pace of a whippet to catch the ten past one race.

'I hope her 'orse is as fast,' Aunty Chris said, watching her go as she started to take out her rollers. Unlike the application of her make-up, this operation was completed at high speed. As each roller came out it was deftly thrown into the wicker hair tidy. Then she attacked the tight blonde rolls with a brush, backcombing bits here and there until she had teased her coiffure into the required shape, finishing it off with a tail comb, using the end to twist and curl the tips.

Satisfied with her crowning glory, she lit another fag and let it hang from her lip as she proceeded to empty half a can of lacquer on to her hair. It was a miracle she never went up in flames as, one eye closed, she filled the room with the poisonous fumes of Belair, the tip of her fag glowing ominously as it caught the occasional tail end of a prolonged and heavy burst. Next she'd go down the back yard to avail herself of the outside lav, and after a 'quick pee' she'd go upstairs to dress, reappearing minutes later in her conductress's uniform, looking, as she liked to say, 'immaculate'.

'I'll just make that 22 down to the ferry,' she'd say, fixing her tie in the mirror over the fireplace. 'If the Pools man calls, me coupon's behind the clock.' She dabbed her cheeks carefully with a spot of rouge from an old-fashioned cardboard pot. A little of that stuff went a long way. In the pot it was a vivid scarlet, but applied carefully it gave her cheeks a rosy blush.

The last thing she did was put her lipstick on. This involved a lot of smacking of lips and dipping back and forth into the mirror so she could judge if it was going on evenly. When she was sure the crimson coating on her lips was perfect she would blot them against what looked like a cigarette paper. A squirt of My Sin behind the ears and on her wrists and she was off to catch the bus to the Woodside terminus to start her two-till-ten shift.

Being on the buses and therefore in the public eye was akin to show business, according to Aunty Chris. She wouldn't dream of going to work with unpressed trousers, unpolished shoes and less than perfect make-up, and neither would the other clippies who rode and ruled on the Birkenhead Corporation buses. They were a smart lot, both in appearance and in attitude, and were admired and respected by the passengers. Without doubt, though, Aunty Chris was the pride of the fleet. She ran a tight ship, or rather bus, and passengers felt safe on her route. She was scrupulously honest. If she let anyone off their fare, for whatever reason, she would make it up with her own money. Sometimes she let me ring the bell. One ring for stop, two for go, and three for keep moving, we're full up.

I regret the passing of the clippie and the conductor as I do the Routemaster buses. When Ken Livingstone phased them out and replaced them with the impractical and cumbersome bendy bus in London it was as if he had removed a vital lyric from a favourite song. There was something very reassuring and nostalgically romantic about a London bus, lights ablaze, going slowly over Tower Bridge on a winter's evening. Made you want to get home for your tea.

*

When war broke out Aunty Chris was nineteen. She joined the ATS (Auxiliary Territorial Service) and was stationed in Norfolk, where she trained to be a height and range finder for the men who worked the ack-ack guns. Having the sharp eye of an accomplished darts player she found this no problem, and she was invariably right on target. Occasionally she got to fire the shells herself, even though it was considered a man's job, and proved herself to be more than competent, earning herself the moniker 'Never Miss Chris'. She was fearless and quite a sight, apparently, blasting enemy aircraft out of the sky during a heavy raid, her face fully made up as always, the ubiquitous fag hanging out of the corner of her mouth.

There were plenty of US army and airforce bases in Norfolk and Aunty Chris was very popular with the 'Yanks' at the dances. She never ran out of Woodbines and stockings and although she appeared to be the archetypal good-time girl it was mostly bluff. She was nowhere near as world-weary and experienced as she painted herself, and in reality she was rather naive.

However, in the words of the music-hall song, 'Only a glass of champagne, but it drove a young girl into sin,' though in Aunty Chris's case it is more likely to have been a couple of Guinness. For as D-Day approached, when she was on a boat about to leave for France, the results of a routine medical disclosed that she was three months pregnant.

She was discharged and sent home, but fearing her father's reaction to the news she turned up on the doorstep of 23 Holly Grove instead of Lowther Street.

It wasn't good news for a single, working-class, Catholic girl to find herself pregnant in those days. It could mean a life sentence in the Magdalen laundry, a cruel institution for single mothers run by an unholy army of nuns who forcibly removed the newborn babies from their mothers and gave them up for adoption. The traumatized girls were left to a lifetime of slavery under a brutal regime in the laundry as a penance for their sins.

Being a Catholic, however lapsed, meant an abortion was out of the question; besides, Aunty Chris had heard too many horror stories about desperate young women who had visited Fat Pat Murphy, a backstreet abortionist in Rock Ferry, and ended up bleeding to death in agony, to even consider termination. No, she intended to have her child and bring him up as a single mother, a brave decision to make back then. The hard part was going to be keeping it secret from her father and the neighbours. My mother was angry but sympathetic; she knew that underneath her younger sister's tough veneer lay a vulnerable girl with little knowledge and experience of men. She vowed to 'track down the bastard responsible for this' but got no help from Aunty Chris, who was unwilling to give any information as to the identity and whereabouts of the father. She simply refused to discuss it, throwing a strop if the matter was mentioned and 'taking to her bed'.

There were rumours, of course. She was, as they say, the talk of the washhouse: she'd had one too many at a party for her birthday and got carried away with a 'Yank'; she'd fallen in love with an officer; there were even dark hints that her condition could be the result of a rape. My dad, on leave from France, went down to Norfolk to see if he could glean any information around the camps, but came home none the wiser. The identity of her child's father was never disclosed. The subject was taboo. She never spoke of it over the years, and took her secret with her to the grave.

A suitable explanation was concocted to explain Aunty Chris's reappearance. She'd been discharged from the ATS due to poor eyesight and she was living at Holly Grove to keep my ma company and help with the kids while my dad was at war. This would do at least for the time being; when Chrissie's pregnancy really started to show they'd have to come up with something else. It wasn't an easy pairing. Both women were volatile to say the least, and there were as many explosions inside Holly Grove as there were in the skies above it. Chrissie teamed up with Vera Lalley again and went back to work as a clippie on the buses, and when she could no longer conceal the fact that she was pregnant she hid herself away from the prying eyes of her passengers and colleagues in a Chinese laundry. Working six days a week from seven in the morning till eight at night meant she was out of sight. The laundry was opposite the brewery in Oxton Road, which meant that as well as the long hours she had a fair distance to walk. Her job was to iron the stiff shirt collars with an array of flat irons, heated by a cast-iron range, hunched over an ironing board for thirteen hours a day: back-breaking work for which she earned two pounds ten a week.

She went into labour during an air raid. There was a shelter in the brewery but she chose to walk home and take her chances rather than risk giving birth in the shelter. It was a particularly heavy raid but somehow she made it back to Holly Grove, screaming with every twinge on the way. There had been a direct hit on a street at the back of the house and my mother was able to get her into one of the ambulances that had turned up, slipping her own wedding ring on to her sister's finger on the way to the hospital and registering her as Mrs Savage to avoid the stigma of single motherhood. Aunty Chris gave birth to a boy, whom she called John, in Grange Mount Hospital, her screams drowned out by the noise of the bombs falling outside.

John was hidden in Holly Grove. Aunty Chris went to work for Littlewoods Pools and if anybody asked who the baby belonged to my mother would say she was minding him for a friend. A deeply suspicious Rose Long refused to swallow this story, having guessed the truth a while back. She went about the neighbourhood painting Aunty Chris as a slut, until Aunty Chris got to hear the tales she was spreading and 'dragged her out of the house by her bleached blonde 'ead'. On one of his rare visits to Holly Grove, their father was told that the child wriggling on the mat belonged to one of the neighbours.

Eventually my dad, home on leave, took the little boy down to Lowther Street and introduced him to his grandfather. Our grandfather's reaction was to go out and buy him a set of clothes from O'Kell's in Exmouth Street. He was saddened that Chrissie had thought she couldn't come to him for help, but said no more about it, welcoming John into the family and defying any outsiders to ask embarrassing questions about the boy's parentage.

After that, Aunty Chris didn't last long at Holly Grove. Like my ma she had an explosive temper and the two frequently clashed. The front door was hanging off its hinges because of the number of times it was slammed shut as one of the women 'banged out'. Eventually Aunty Chris, after a particularly vicious row, banged out of the house for good and went back to Lowther Street. Aunty Anne had just given birth to my cousin Tricia, and as well as her young son Michael, she had her irascible old father to care for. Nevertheless, she found room for her sister and nephew and there they stayed.

It was a busy house. Annie and Harold had three kids in all, with Maureen, the youngest, only a few years older than me. She came on holiday to Ireland with us and we spent hours together in the front of a bus whenever our mothers fancied 'a little spin out', as they put it.

Our Mo, as she is known, had a friend who would call for her by putting her lips through an open knothole in the back-yard door. In the vernacular of the day, this friend was said to be 'a bit daft'.

'Is your Mooreeen in?'

'No, love, she's out.' Aunty Chris, filing her nails on the back-yard step, would answer the melancholy voice booming out from the disembodied lips at the bottom of the door. 'Who shall I say called?'

Tricia, Mo's older sister, had an auburn beehive that defied gravity. She was never seen without her best mate Maeve, whose name I was to borrow years later for Lily's confirmation name. Tricia – I'm sure she'd deny it today but I could swear that I saw her doing it – used to practise her jiving technique, in the absence of a partner, by tying a stocking to the door-knob.

The eldest, Mickey, had that heady something that could only be described as a whiff of Hollywood glamour. He was a merchant sailor, tall, blond and handsome, the absolute apple of the family's eye. He was engaged to be married to a girl he'd met in Hong Kong but he was killed in a car crash on bonfire night, just before his twenty-fifth birthday, five minutes from home on his way back from a three-month trip to the Far East.

It was my first encounter with death. The family were devastated. They seemed to visibly shrink before me, the life essence sucked out of them, going slowly about their lives like hollow-eyed spectres. Bonfire night was never really celebrated after that. On the anniversary of Mickey's death it seemed disrespectful to be waving sparklers about or throwing bangers under the outside toilet door, guaranteed to give the unsuspecting occupant a heart attack. My dad never approved of bonfire night anyway, always taking care to remind me that it was the effigy of a Catholic that was being burned on the fire.

CHAPTER SEVEN

MY DAD HAD ATTENDED A LITTLE COUNTRY SCHOOL IN Glinsk, and although he had left by the time he was thirteen to work on the farm he said that his schooling had been excellent. He was certainly very clever. He had a good head for figures, wrote in a beautiful copperplate hand and held extremely strong and unshakable opinions about nearly everything in life. He taught me to read. By the time I was four I was able to read my copy of *TV Comic* from cover to cover. In a way this went against me when I started school.

My first school was St Joseph's, a Catholic primary in a road that went by the Blytonesque name of Dingle Dell, but was actually a row of extremely run-down houses that had probably once been grand but had long been converted into bedsits. My teacher, Miss Bolger, thought she had a child prodigy on her hands when she heard me rattle through the entire Janet and John series in ten minutes flat and then proceed to read out a hefty chunk from a *Reader's Digest*. Consequently, she left me to it, giving her time and attention to the slower pupils in the class of thirty-five kids.

I was more than happy to sit at the back of the class during arithmetic lessons and mouth my way through the two times table. I didn't have a clue about any of it, and had no interest in figures. They might as well have been hieroglyphics.

It wasn't until I'd been there over a year that Miss Bolger twigged that I had no idea what two times two meant. 'Paul must apply himself and catch up with his arithmetic,' she had the nerve to write on my school report. It was her bloody fault that I was behind in the first place, and it's thanks to her that I've been catching up ever since. You should see me trying to work out my bank statements, VAT and tax bills. It's no wonder I've had heart attacks. Maths is a complete mystery to me. Everything about it eludes me. Logarithms, algebra, fractions – they could be some sort of alien language for all I know.

I sweated and fidgeted my way through every single maths lesson as I went through school, dreading being asked a question or, even worse, told to come out to the front of the class to work out the sum on the blackboard. Blind panic would grip me as I took the piece of chalk and faced the board, all eyes upon me, everyone waiting to see what answer I would come up with. I'd stare blankly at the incomprehensible figures before me, and try to resist the overpowering urge to scrawl something obscene across the board and then make a run for it. Nowadays I would be recognized as 'dyslexic with figures', but back in the 1960s I was classed as just plain thick.

'There are moments that you remember all your life . . .' So go the opening lyrics of a song from the movie *Yentl*. I love that film, and I ain't ashamed to stand up and admit it. I saw it nearly every day for a month when I was working in a club called Madame Arthur's in Copenhagen. One of the regulars at Madame Arthur's worked in the box office of a little cinema just round the corner from the club, and he let me in each afternoon for free. His name was Jens, and like me he was a big Barbra fan. No, he was more than a fan – he was a crazed obsessive. He lived and breathed Barbra Streisand twenty-four hours a day. She was his purpose in life – the reason why he got up in the morning. Well, as you can imagine, it got a bit wearing after a while. I mean, I'm a big fan of the woman myself but I don't bang on about her all bloody day. Nor is every conceivable inch of wall space in my flat adorned with photos and posters of her.

I don't stand in front of the mirror on the wardrobe door and throw my arms about dramatically as I mime to the words of 'Don't Rain On My Parade' either. (Well, not all the time – only occasionally, like when I'm feeling cheesed off or slightly drunk. You should try it yourself some time. It can be quite energizing, a bit like a workout. You can also march round the kitchen to 'Before The Parade Passes By' from *Hello, Dolly!* if you're up to it, using the mop as your baton, but be careful of the light fittings. *Hello, Dolly!* is not one of her best films. She's too young to play Dolly Levi, and— Oh, God, I'm beginning to sound like Jens.)

I will confess to knowing all the words to 'Pappa Can You Hear Me', but then so would you if you'd sat through *Yentl* every day for a month. It was either that or rot in the freezing garret that the management of Madame Arthur's provided in the way of accommodation for visiting acts: two tiny rooms in the roof of a crumbling building that had formerly been a wartime brothel. A slum, basically, but they thought it was perfectly adequate for two struggling drag queens in the middle of a freezing Danish winter. We worked each night in the club, and slept all day; there was very little to do out of doors that was warm and cheap. Jens was a godsend. I got to keep warm and see La Streisand for free, even if it did mean listening to his endless eulogies of his goddess.

But I'm digressing badly here. All I wanted to say was that those opening lyrics – 'There are moments that you remember all your life', in case you'd forgotten – apply to my first day at St Joseph's. It's a memory imprinted on my mind. I can see myself now, hanging on to the hem of my mother's coat as she chatted to another mother called Celia Mooney, whose little boy Franny was also starting school that day. He stared at me indifferently from behind his mother's back, a pale, delicate child with buck teeth and ginger hair.

'Go and sit down with Paul,' said Mrs Mooney, dragging Franny forward by the arm and virtually swinging him into a seat behind a double desk. 'He can be your little friend.' She beckoned me to come and sit down next to him. 'Come on, chuckles,' she called out cheerily, 'sit here next to our Franny. You two can be little pals, can't you?' She stood back and put her head to one side, considering. 'Ah, God love them, look at them, they could almost be brothers, couldn't they?' she said fondly to my mother. 'They've got the same colouring.'

My mother forced a nervous laugh. The snob in her would rather I sat next to another boy. A posh boy, not one that looked as though he'd been dressed by the parish. She also sent up a silent prayer that no one in their right mind would ever mistake Franny for her own flesh and blood. My hair was reddish brown; Franny's was the colour of a glass of carrot juice. 'Yes,' she said faintly to a beaming Celia Mooney, her tone lacking any conviction whatsoever, 'brothers . . .' Her voice tailed off into thin air.

The mothers were told to leave. Miss Bolger was ushering them out with a forced grin frozen on her face. 'Say goodbye to your mummies, children,' she shouted over the mothers' heads, setting half the kids off into a frenzy of hysterics. My mother gave me a sad little smile and one last wave as she left the room and I could feel the muscles in the back of my throat beginning to contract. Suddenly I felt overwhelmed by my new surroundings and I was unsure of what to say to Franny.

'Are you going to cry?' I asked him, feeling my bottom lip beginning to wobble dangerously.

'What for?' he asked scornfully, pulling a bag of sports

mixtures out of his pocket, his sharp little eyes darting suspiciously round the class as he hid it from view under the desk. 'I ain't scared of her.' He nodded towards Miss Bolger, who was bashing lumps out of her desk with the wooden back of the duster she used to clean the blackboard with in a futile attempt to gain the attention of the class. 'It's only school. D'ya wanna sweet?' Franny might have looked like a nervous little mouse on the outside but inside he was as hard as nails. A born survivor.

We sat sucking happily on our sports mixtures and looked about us, giving the room the once-over.

The infants' classroom was a prefabricated building, separate from the main school. Light and airy, it had a frieze of the alphabet running the length of one wall and a Wendy house stuffed full of interesting things like a pretend cooker complete with tiny pots and pans and a plastic tea set in the corner. I was itching to get in there and set up house but Miss Bolger, an irascible little woman driven to the brink of insanity by a life-time of teaching infants, thought otherwise. The Wendy house was strictly out of bounds and instead she said we should sit at our desks and make something 'nice' out of the big lump of blue plasticine that sat, hard as a rock, on a slate in front of us. The sound of thirty-five kids smashing rock-hard lumps of plasticine on slate was enough to set Miss Bolger off with her duster again.

'Quietly children, QUIETLY!' she shrieked, making more noise than the entire school put together as she laid into her desk once more. 'The boy or girl who makes the best model out of their plasticine can come up to my desk and take a sweet, only one, mind, from the sweet tin as a prize.'

'Balls to her,' said Franny. 'I've got me own.'

Around mid-morning Miss Bolger told us to line up and collect our bottles of milk from a crate by the door. I hated milk then, especially milk that had sat outside in the sun all morning before being brought in by two bigger lads from the main school.

'Take one bottle each, children, and then return to your desks . . . quietly,' said the Bolger, clapping her hands. I looked at the little bottle of milk as if it were poison. Franny sat sucking his through a straw, swinging his legs contentedly and humming to himself.

'You gonna drink your milk?' he asked. I'd rather have drunk the contents of the spittoon in Barney's, but before I could answer him the Bolger appeared before me.

'Do I spy a little boy who doesn't want to drink his lovely milk?' she asked in a saccharine-laced voice, bending down to get a better look at the ungrateful child before her. I didn't like her being so close. Her breath smelt of peppermints and her cold eyes belied her tone.

I didn't think her question merited a verbal answer so I kept my eyes averted from hers and just nodded.

'Oh, but you must,' she said, a hint of threat beginning to creep into her voice. 'Little boys who don't drink their milk won't grow up to be big and strong, will they?' She pushed a straw through the foil cap and offered the bottle to me. 'Come on, drink it up,' she said firmly. 'There are little black babies out in Africa who never see milk from one day to the next and here's a naughty little boy like you refusing to drink his.'

Lucky them, I thought as I sat on my hands and shook my head defiantly, my lips tightly sealed.

I became obsessed with these little black babies as I progressed through St Joseph's. There was a scheme, popular in all Catholic junior schools at the time, called the Good Shepherd. You were encouraged to contribute a penny or two out of your pocket money to this fund, and at the end of term the child who had given the most got to name a baby in Africa and have tea with the bishop. Fiercely competitive, I'd cadge a penny from someone every day to hand in to the Bolger to make sure

I was always top of the league. Apart from the occasional group of sailors at Woodside ferry ('Don't stare, Paul'), the only other black person I was aware of at the time was Chamois Davies, a wiry little guy who wore a camel coat and a fedora, so named because he sold chamois leathers off the back of a handcart in Birkenhead Market.

Come the day of reckoning, the pennies were counted and the bearer of the Good Shepherd title, the child who had collected the most money, was none other than Paul James O'Grady. Oh, I basked in the glory and gave long and careful thought to the name of my black baby. Eventually I came up with Twizzle, after the puppet on the telly. It was explained to me that this was highly unsuitable and wouldn't I be better off choosing the name of a saint? I settled on Michael, boring but safe, and no doubt a huge relief for some poor kid out in Africa.

Tea with the bishop was akin to meeting royalty, better even. My mother washed, scrubbed and polished me to within an inch of my life, dressing me in my Sunday best clothes. With the winners from the other classes at school, I had jelly and orange juice and a huge fuss was made of me. I floated home in a beatific state, much to my brother's amusement.

'What did the bishop have to say to you then?'

'He said I could kiss his ring.'

Total collapse of brother.

The Bolger was a no-nonsense woman. She it was who broke the earth-shattering news to me that Father Christmas didn't exist. It was quite a shock. There was no counselling before or after, no gentle preparation for such devastating news. She just came out with it, as blunt as a widow's knife, telling me that all along the bearer of the pillowcase at the bottom of my bed had been my dad. I sit here today and think what a bitch, and I can still taste that warm milk as she forced it on me.

113

'Don't be silly and open your mouth,' she said, her patience deserting her as she prised my lips open and pushed the straw in. 'Drink your milk.' I could hear Franny sucking air noisily through his straw as he drained every last drop out of his bottle. I could smell the disgusting stuff. My mouth grew dry and I could feel my stomach beginning to rise in revolt. I closed my mouth tighter and shook my head fiercely.

'DRINK YOUR MILK!' the Bolger roared, losing it completely. She pulled the straw out of the bottle and forced the milk down me. The inevitable happened: I threw up all over her suede shoes. Her cheeks burned red and for a moment I thought she was going to hit me.

'Francis Mooney,' she said, trying to hide the fury in her voice, 'take this . . . take Paul O'Grady to the lavatory, will you?'

'I can't, Mrs,' said Franny nonchalantly, chewing on his straw.

'It's Miss, Francis, not Mrs, and why can't you go with Paul to the lavatory?' she asked, her face by now a vivid scarlet.

'Cos I don't know where it is, that's why.'

The Bolger marched us to the classroom door and out into the playground. When she raised her arm up into the air, I thought she was going to lash out at us. So did Franny, judging by the way he winced and covered his head with his hands. She didn't hit us, although she probably felt like killing us, especially me. Instead she was pointing across the yard to the boys' toilet block. 'Over there,' she said. 'The boys' lavatories are over there, and don't be all day about it.' She turned on her heel and marched back into the classroom, leaving us alone in the yard.

'D'ya wanna poo?' asked Franny casually as we walked towards the toilet block.

'No I don't,' I replied with all the dignity a five-year-old can muster.

'Well, d'ya wanna wee then?'

'No, I don't think so.'

'Well why did she send us to the lav, then?'

'Dunno.'

Even if I had wanted to go, the sight of the boys' lav would have given me instant constipation. I was as anally retentive as my mother when it came to using strange lavatories and these were grim to say the least, housed in an old brick lean-to and stinking to high heaven of disinfectant and pee. Only a case of severe dysentery would've induced me to use this cesspit.

We stood there staring up at the sky, unsure of what to do, while the gurgling water ran down the decrepit urinals. Franny, having no piss-elegant qualms about public lavs, kicked the door of the solitary lock-up open, strolled in and sat himself down on the toilet seat. He rummaged in his pocket for his bag of sweets.

'D'ya want one?' he asked, shoving a couple in his mouth.

'No thanks,' I said, breathing through my mouth, trying to avoid the smell. How Franny could even contemplate eating anything in a lav was beyond me. But then Franny was a species I'd never come across before.

'I'm going to have a poo,' he announced in a matter-of-fact way, jumping off the seat and dropping his trousers. I didn't know where to put myself. I'd never seen anyone poo before. In our house we always closed the door, and here was Franny looking as if he was about to haemorrhage as he sat there, grunting loudly, straining to 'do one'. His knuckles were white as he gripped the lav seat, his face slowly turning purple with the sheer effort of it all. Suddenly there was a loud plop and Franny exhaled loudly, letting out a grateful sigh of relief. He jumped from the seat, his colour returning to normal, and turned to peer into the pan.

'Cor,' he said in amazement. ''Ave a look at this . . . it's massive.'

Curious as I was, I was spared the experience by the arrival of the Bolger.

'What are you boys up to?' she demanded, wrinkling her nose, her gentility offended by the smell of the place.

'Franny's having a poo,' I offered helpfully, pointing to Franny, who by now was wiping his bum on one of the hard sheets of Bronco hanging on a bit of string from a nail in the wall, totally unabashed by the presence of an audience.

'I don't need to know what he's doing, thank you very much,' said the Bolger, turning her face away and holding the handkerchief she kept up the sleeve of her cardigan close to her nose. 'Just hurry along and get back to class . . . and quickly!'

'All right, Mrs,' Franny sang out cheerfully, pulling his pants up and rushing past her with me in close pursuit. I didn't want to be left alone in the boys' lav with someone as scary as the Bolger.

'It's Miss not Mrs,' the Bolger shouted after us. 'And come back here this instant, Francis Mooney, and pull that chain and rinse your hands under the tap.' But we pretended not to hear her and carried on running to the comparative safety of the classroom, leaving the Bolger to deal with the problem of Franny's gargantuan turd.

At dinner time we were marched two by two up the road to the hall of the Tranmere Methodist Church. I didn't know what a Methodist was, but I was sure they weren't Catholics and a slight niggle of anxiety lurked in the back of my mind that I'd probably go straight to hell for entering such an unholy and alien temple. Wait till I tell my mother about this, I thought. She won't be pleased at all. I eyed the Bolger suspiciously as she herded us into the hall, counting our heads and barking instructions as we trooped past her.

'. . . sixteen, seventeen, eighteen . . . Stop that, Edward Kelly, and walk properly . . . nineteen, twenty . . . I hope that's not a sweet you're putting in your mouth, Francis Mooney . . . twenty-one . . .' Aunty Chris would call her a right Irma Grese if she ever came across her, I said to myself.

The inside of the hall was dark and foreboding. Whenever I watch David Lean's harrowing adaptation of *Oliver Twist* and it comes to the scene where Oliver and the miserable orphans line up for their gruel in that cold, bleak workhouse I think of the Tranmere Methodist Church Hall. Like the Dickensian workhouse of the film, the hall had bare brick walls and long trestle tables with benches for us to sit on. We even had a Mr Bumble in the shape of an enormous woman with an angry florid face, her blonde hair severely dragged back into a mean little bun, and a starched white apron pulled taut across her ample bosom.

Seeing this woman years later, I could hardly believe that the apple-cheeked sweet little old lady who smiled gently to herself as she made her way to church was once the stuff of my night-mares. Back then she was as terrifying as a rogue bull elephant as she stood behind the counter, her face scarlet with rage, viciously smashing a ladle of alarming proportions on the counter's metal surface. Banging assorted implements on hard surfaces with a heavy hand seemed to be the preferred method of terrorizing little children into petrified silence, but after a while you got used to it and no longer found it quite so frightening. Instead, you learned to live with it as part of the soundtrack of school life.

'Silence,' the she-monster roared, her great booming voice reverberating around the hall. 'And sit yourselves down smartish, or there will be no dinner. Do you hear me? No dinner!' She emphasized her point by hammering her ladle on the counter again.

The children in the know chorused 'Yes Miss McGregor' and sat down smartish. We infants, ignorant of the protocol of school dinners, gathered together in a confused huddle, some of us starting to cry. I could feel my throat muscles beginning to tighten again as I came out in sympathy, and fought back the tears.

'Don't start grizzling and whingeing, children,' the Bolger said in a voice that was not unkind, shepherding us together and sitting us down at one of the vacant tables. I found myself with Franny on one side and a strange-looking kid who was known as Plug on the other. I've no idea what his real name was; he'd earned his unfortunate moniker because of his uncanny resemblance to one of the Bash Street Kids in the *Beano*. Poor old Plug certainly wasn't the prettiest puppy in the litter. Tall and skinny with ears like the FA Cup, he had protruding teeth and a really bad turn in his right eye for starters. He was the kind of kid that caused my mother to coo 'Ah, God love him' under her breath and press a couple of pennies into his hand whenever she saw him hanging around the school gates waiting hopefully for someone to remember to come and pick him up after school. Plug was always the last to be claimed. 'Don't worry, love,' my mother would shout (she always spoke to Plug as if he were deaf), 'your mam will be here soon . . . the dilatory bitch,' she'd add sadly to herself under her breath, turning to look up the street for Plug's errant parent. Plug's mum would eventually appear, tall and gangly like her offspring, loping down the street, her mouth open and a vacant expression on her face, absently wiping her nose. Permanent nose drip ran, if you'll pardon the lame pun, in the Plug family. Plug's nose ran like the proverbial glass-blower's arse.

'Wipe your nose, child,' the Bolger snapped as Plug sat blowing a snot bubble out of his right nostril. 'Where is your handkerchief, for heaven's sake?'

Plug, slow and adenoidal, looked up balefully. 'Haven't got one,' he said, one eye fixed on the Bolger, the other staring at the ceiling.

'Well tell your mother to give you one in future,' she said, handing Plug a paper tissue from the supply she kept in her pocket for such emergencies as blowing noses, wiping sticky hands and removing vomit from suede shoes. Shuddering, she moved quickly down the table and pretended to busy herself with a small child at the end so she didn't have to watch.

'Yes, Miss Bolger,' chanted Plug, wiping his nose on the back of his sleeve and shoving the tissue in the top of his sock.

Once everyone was seated and had finally calmed down the Bolger gave the frightening woman, whom we now knew as Miss McGregor, a curt nod. This was the signal for Miss McGregor's minions to spring into action and remove the lids from the great boiling urns. The rising steam was caught in the solitary shaft of sunlight that struggled to make its way into the hall through the big leaded window high up in the wall above Miss McGregor's head. It looked like hell's very own kitchen and the McGregor woman the devil herself, surrounded as she was by curls of rising steam. So this was what Methodists were like.

'Line up,' shouted Miss McGregor, eyeing our table. 'Little ones first.' Open-mouthed with fear, we dutifully lined up and filed past the counter clutching our plates, on to which unsmiling women slapped the unappealing fare. The thin watery discharge that called itself gravy was doled out by Miss McGregor herself, who stood at the end of the counter, her crimson face shiny with sweat, one hand on the ladle, the other on her ample hip, dribbling the brownish liquid over our food as parsimoniously as if it were her own lifeblood.

When every child had its food and was seated again, the Bolger said grace. As I sat with head bowed and hands clenched in prayer, listening to Plug sniffing and burbling next to me, I opened one eye and took a sneaky peek at my first school dinner. My heart froze. It was a piece of liver. Filthy, stinking liver sat there sniggering at me on the plate, with a pair of cold, grey, waxen boiled potatoes, a trickle of cold gravy staining their sides, for company, and a flaccid mound of the ubiquitous vegetable common to all school dinners of a certain era – overcooked, limp, wet cabbage. I could've heaved again.

There was no way that these Methodists were going to get me to swallow one mouthful of this disgusting fodder and that was that. Fortunately, Franny would eat everything and anything that was put before him, and as he was always hungry it was no hardship for him to devour another piece of liver that I'd deftly flicked off my plate and on to his. Franny got two school meals a day for quite some time as I passed him the food I didn't like, which was just about everything, until eventually, to my annoyance, the Bolger caught up with me and separated us, banishing Franny to another table. Luckily, though, there was still Plug. Like his predecessor Franny, Plug turned down nothing that was edible and was happy to take over the role of human dustbin.

Once a week we were given a dish of gooseberries floating in a sea of thin, anaemic-looking cold custard for dessert. The first time this happened I sat staring mournfully at mine, wondering if I should try it. I picked up my spoon and took a small mouthful. Not bad. I might try some more, I thought, and popped another couple of gooseberries into my mouth. It was then that I made the mistake of looking at Plug. From his right nostril he was blowing a gigantic snot bubble, a horrific, quickly expanding monster, emerald green and glistening in the light and not unlike the gooseberry I was chewing at that very moment. It looked like one of the glass snot bubbles I used to buy from the Wizard's Den, a joke shop in Moorfields over in Liverpool. I loved that shop – every penny I had was spent on phoney dog turds, stink bombs and magic tricks that I never quite got the hang of. Plug's bubble of snot would put theirs to shame. The gooseberry in my mouth suddenly became harder to chew, and virtually impossible to swallow. It was growing in my mouth, clammy and gooey, expanding along with Plug's nasal balloon. After a quick bout of projectile vomiting I was ushered off to the toilet block by that woman on the edge of a nervous breakdown known as Miss Bolger and cleaned up none too gently. Plug, unfazed, wiped his nose on the back of his hand and carried on eating his gooseberries. I've never been able to look at one since. What little appetite I had was finished off by school dinners.

I was picky when it came to food, and I still am. I see it now as I saw it then, as a necessary evil, although I've got better with age and can now actually sit down in a restaraunt and eat a meal, providing it's served quickly and the food hasn't been messed around with. I can't bear food that's been artfully arranged on the plate. Nouvelle Cuisine. I sit and look at this nonsense and wonder if the chef's hands were clean as he fiddled endlessly with the two tiny lamb chops, the half-dozen mangetout and the minuscule dollop of mashed spud 'drizzled' with a rosemary jus displayed before me. Leave it alone. Just fling it out of the pan and serve it up. It's food. If you want something to play with, then buy a bloody puppet. I appreciate that presentation is important, but you've got to admit that some of these cooks get a bit carried away with their fanciful endeavours to ensure that your meat and two veg arrives looking less like food and more like a display in Tate Modern. I don't want to sit there looking at it. After an initial couple of words of appreciation I want to 'wire in'.

Nor do I want to hang around a restaurant for hours and starve through forty-minute waits between courses, at the mercy of over-attentive waiters fussing around, folding napkins, pouring water and, in the good old days when a fag could be enjoyed after a meal, endlessly emptying ashtrays. Surprisingly enough I can pour my own water and fold my

121

own napkin. I can even use cutlery, so I don't need assistance just yet. There's plenty of time for that, if by some chance I live to a ripe old age and find myself being 'cared for' in my twilight years in some bleak council nursing home. I've made a living will. Inside a rather large Jiffy bag is a pillow with a note attached to it. It reads: *In the event of the said Paul O'Grady ever being found writing his name on his bedroom wall with his faeces please put pillow over his face and hold down until he stops kicking.*

I'm not scared of dying, not in the least. After two heart attacks I suppose I've come pretty close, although I have to admit I've nothing profound to say about either experience other than that it's thanks to the skill of the cardiologists, nurses and the much-maligned NHS that I'm alive to tell the tale today.

When I had the first heart attack I died in the ambulance on the way to the hospital. I'd like to oblige and reveal that before I was resuscitated I saw a long tunnel with an angel bathed in light at the end of it but I didn't, or at least if I did I don't remember. Which seems unlikely as I'm sure I'd remember seeing such an interesting Ziegfeld Follies production as that. No, much as I would love to say it happened, the heavens did not put on a celestial light show for my arrival at the pearly gates that night in the ambulance. Heaven, and I'm assuming it was heaven and not downstairs, was obviously invite-only that night and I was an unwelcome gatecrasher who was turned away. Maybe it's true when they say your time is up or it isn't; mine obviously wasn't. All I can recall as I re-entered the land of the living is the paramedic shoving fizzy aspirins down my throat. Hardly something to crow about on *Desert Island Discs.*

It's not the actual dying, the final croak, that bothers me, it's the speed of it. Will it come quickly? And will I know anything

Don't look now…!

Top, from left: Owld Ned, my mum in the middle and Aunty Anne, Moreton Shore.

Bottom left: My dad with his sisters Sadie (left) and Mary (right), with Uncle James in the middle.

Bottom: My dad in his RAF uniform.

Top: Gran and Grandad [sa]vage.

Bottom right, from [lef]t: Aunty Anne (left, [cr]oss-legged), Aunty [Pol]l (centre) with Mum [be]side her, Aunty Chris [cr]oss-legged, right) and [tw]o Fawcett cousins. The [pu]dding-basin styles are [th]e result of Aunty Poll's [ha]irdressing skill.

Bottom: My mum, aged [fo]urteen. She paid for [th]is photograph from [he]r first wage packet in [do]mestic service.

Opposite, top: Mum and Dad on their wedding day (left) and courting (right).

Opposite, bottom: Dad, Chrissie, Ma Fawcett in the middle and Anne (right), on another day out at Moreton Shore.

Below: Chrissie at Arrowe Park (left) and at Ma and Dad's wedding. I don't know who she's with.

My brother called me the Mekon when I was born because of the size of my head. Here's proof, with my sister Sheila.

Me in a lovely knitted outfit, with Mary next door.

Me at eighteen months.

Me aged eight.

Above: Holly Grove in the 1980s, the last time I saw it.

Below left: Sheila in her home-made frock, aged nineteen.

Below right: My first Holy Communion.

Aunty Chris, the Pride of Birkenhead Buses, and her driver, Bill Casey.

about it? Speaking from experience I'd favour a nice quick fatal heart attack over a long lingering death any day. I don't want to rot, slowly, before my loved ones' eyes. I'd rather make a quick exit.

I don't know how I've managed to digress like this and get on to the subject of death. It's not something I care to dwell on unless it's late at night and I'm sitting with a pal, maudlin drunk, recalling the friends we've buried. I seem to remember that I was banging on about restaurants and celebrity chefs. My favourite celebrity chef was a celebrated Edwardian cook by the name of Rosa Lewis, a true eccentric who ran the Cavendish Hotel in St James's and was the inspiration for the BBC series *The Duchess of Duke Street*. I follow her good advice. 'Potatoes are humble things,' she said. 'Serve them gently boiled with a little salt and pepper and a knob of butter.' It's not hard, is it? Good food simply cooked and served plain. Pretentious arrangements get on my nerves. Why go to the bother of cutting carrots into ridiculously thin slivers, calling them 'julienne' and then dishing them up balanced one on top of the other so that they look like a pile of loosely stacked miniature deckchairs? Is there something shameful about a carrot that I don't know about? Are they so socially unaccept-able in smart restaurants that they have to undergo drastic surgery before they can be presented at the table?

And while I'm sticking the boot in, why must chefs be such prima donnas? Is it the heat of the kitchen that brings these men's blood to boiling point, so that they're off into orbit effing and blinding and flinging pans because a sauce has curdled? You'd never catch Delia telling you to eff off out of the kitchen. Well, not on camera anyway. It's only cooking, after all. A piece of dead animal, some vegetables, fling 'em into a pan with a bit of water and cook over a low heat, adding herbs and seasoning as you go. As I said, it's not hard, so why all the bloody fuss?

*

Apparently when I was a baby I ate everything that was put in front of me. It was after a holiday with the Gradys on the farm in Ireland that I turned pernickety. How could I eat the roast chicken on the table when I'd seen it walking around the farm-yard that morning hale and hearty and minding its own business before my aunty Bridget caught it and wrung its neck? I'd seen my uncle James milk the cow, sitting ankle deep in cowshit on his milking stool in a cowshed swarming with flies, pulling on the cow's warty teats, expelling the milk into an old tin bucket, and now here it was in a glass in front of me on the kitchen table, warm and creamy. Ugh!

Visiting an elderly aunt I was given a 'nice big soft runny egg, freshly laid' to eat for my tea. The size of a pterodactyl's offering, I thought at the time, it smelt strong and gamey, its vile contents trickling slowly down the side of the shell like yellow emulsion. Unlike the rest of the clan this aunt had no truck with little boys who wasted 'God's good food'. Her name was Aunt Sabina and she said I couldn't get down from the table until I'd eaten it all. I sat there defiant in her front parlour listening to the big old clock on the wall chiming the hours, the hated duck egg untouched and congealing in front of me, until the cavalry came to the rescue in the form of my dad, back from the pub, to take me home to Aunty Bridget's.

Aunt Sabina said that I was a spoilt, wilful child and threatened to keep the egg in the pantry for me to eat on my next visit. Needless to say, I never went back and to this day I could no more eat a boiled egg than I could stand in Selfridges window bollock-naked.

I could go for days without food. I still can, although it's no longer something to be endured instead of enjoyed. At one time I would only eat three things: pancakes, roast potatoes and spinach. The only reason I'd touch spinach was because

124

my all-time hero, Popeye, ate it, but at least I was getting some vitamins inside me. It was my sister who solved the eating problem.

My mother was being driven slowly demented by my reluctance to eat. She tried the 'You're not leaving that table, my bucko, until every last bit on that bloody plate is cleared' routine, she tried coaxing me with tasty morsels, she tried pleading, cajoling and even praying to St Jude, the patron saint of lost causes – and by now she'd given me up for one.

My sister Sheila made a can of spinach out of an empty Radox Bath Salts pot. She rinsed it out and glued a crudely made label on the front that read *Popeye's Spinach*. Well, that was it. I'd eat anything, bar eggs, that was put into that Radox pot. Fish fingers, mashed spuds, baked beans, all squished together and then squeezed out of the pot à la Popeye straight into my mouth, while my sister stood behind me feeling my non-existent arm muscle and singing 'Na nana na na-na na' which, for the unenlightened, is the theme that was played in the Popeye cartoons when he was about to eat his spinach.

I realize now how lucky I was to have such a loving family. I thought then that every child had a family like mine and it came as a shock when I went to school and discovered otherwise.

CHAPTER EIGHT

M Y MOTHER WAS SMART AS A WHIP. WHEN I WAS GOING
through old papers in the box I found her school report
for 1927. Like her sisters, she attended St Laurence's School.
Of the three, Chrissie found it hard to sit still and was easily
bored, so 'the devil found work for idle hands' and she was
forever getting into trouble with the nuns. Annie liked the
cookery classes and would cheerfully turn out scones and rock
cakes which, if hurled with only a little force behind them,
could concuss a twenty-stone docker. Like Chrissie, she would
rather have been elsewhere. Not so my mother. She loved
school and couldn't get enough of it. When she wasn't in class
she could usually be found with her head buried in a book.
That term she had come top out of fifty-five pupils, was only
absent from school once and excelled in every subject the nuns
taught her including sports and games. In those days the latter
involved little more than skipping, or tucking your dress into
your knickers and playing two ball up against the playground
wall. Bored with these limited activities, my ambitious ma took
herself off to Livingstone Street baths and taught herself to
swim. Apparently she could have given Esther Williams a run
for her money, and she won all sorts of competitions. She
taught my sister and brother to swim, but by the time I came
along age had made her too self-conscious to appear in a

bathing costume in public and so she made do with a paddle, holding her dress a respectable half-inch above the knee so folk would be spared the sight of her varicose veins.

She had one of those 1950s swimsuits that could stand up on its own. It had enormous conical breasts, with deep, deep cups that could have provided accommodation for a pair of six-month-old twins. It was made of a rubberized fabric that smelt peculiar, and it covered the hips and ended just above the thigh. For as long as I could remember, it had lived in the bottom of the bathroom cupboard. I used to enjoy taking it out now and then and jumping on the huge tits from the end of the bath to see if I could collapse them. The lining had yellowed with age and I only ever saw her wear this relic once. For some reason she'd thrown caution to the wind and, varicose veins or not, had decided to take to the waters of the Mersey one Saturday afternoon while we were at New Brighton 'beach'.

She seemed to be enjoying herself, splashing about and floating on her back, until a dead dog, minus its fur, bumped into her. Needless to say she never went in that 'dirty, filthy, stinking sewer' again and neither did any of us. I would content myself with collecting some of the many used condoms, or 'tonkeys' as me and my mates called them, that littered the shore, picking them up on the end of a stick and putting them in my bucket. Occasionally I'd hang them from the ends of the handlebars on my bike. That went down well with the aunties.

'Molly!' Aunty Anne would shriek. 'That dirty little mare has got a couple of D U R E X trailing off his handlebars,' she'd say, spelling out the word Durex in the voice reserved for describing terminal diseases and unnatural practices.

My dad was terrified of water and never went near it if he could help it, which was unfortunate for him when he found himself taking part in the Normandy landings. He nearly died of fright as he made his way to shore from the boat. The other men swam but my dad walked on tiptoe holding his rifle high above his head, and silently thanked God that he was lanky. So I received no encouragement from my parents to learn how to swim and apart from one lesson from my sister at New Brighton baths I seemed doomed to remain on dry land.

I didn't really grasp the rudiments of swimming until I was way into my thirties, and even then it wasn't what you could call 'proper' swimming. I got over my fears after a lot of determined practice in shallow water, attempting, at first, just a very slow doggy-paddle. I progressed after a period of five years to slightly deeper water. At first I could only manage my slow crawl if my head was underwater; if I dared to raise it I sank like a stone. And as for speed and distance, well, think of a blind, geriatric, arthritic old turtle with three flippers missing and a lead weight attached to its neck struggling through the water and you'll be half right. It wasn't until fairly recently that I mastered the mystery that was swimming.

Now you can't get me out of the water. I love swimming and there's something very satisfying in the knowledge that I'm self-taught. I'm not half bad, I'm proud to tell you, but just in case Mark Spitz or Duncan Goodhew is reading this I'd better reassure them that I won't be inheriting their respective crowns just yet.

The first time I dared to take to the water was on Australia's Great Barrier Reef. I'd been working over there and had taken a trip to Queensland with my manager, Murphy, when the three-month tour of comedy festivals, some good, some lousy, had finally ended.

It was a glorious holiday. The weather was beautiful and we did everything from night-walking in the rainforest and riding across stretches of deserted beach to a trip on a cruiser out on to the reef. However, one thing I didn't do, couldn't do, was go in the ocean. I'd inherited my dad's hydrophobia; as far as we were concerned, the sea was something you stared at from the safety of the shore or sailed across to Ireland. That was fine. I loved the sea as long as I was on it and not in it and, just like my dad, I gave swimming pools a very wide berth; I was forever looking uneasily over my shoulder if I had to stand near one, expecting someone to rush up and push me in 'for a laugh'. Ha bloody ha.

But as I stood alone on the deck of that cruiser, jealously watching every last passenger on the boat swimming below me in the beautifully clear waters of the Great Barrier Reef, with its coral gardens and tropical fish, my guts ached with envy and I realized there and then that something had to be done. I had to get in there with them.

Armed with snorkel, mask and lifejacket, I gingerly climbed down the ladder at the side of the boat and tentatively lowered myself into the water. It was a while before I dared let go of the rung I was clinging on to, white-knuckled, in case I sank to the bottom. At last it dawned on me that the lifejacket actually served its purpose and made sinking impossible. I was in seventh heaven as I floated in the warm clear water by the side of the boat like a bit of old driftwood. It was ab-so-lutely fucking brilliant! I found myself singing 'Beautiful Briny' from Disney's *Bedknobs and Broomsticks*. Life didn't get better than this.

Gaining confidence, I gradually built up the courage to put the mask on, position the snorkel and lower my face cautiously into the water. It was a revelation. Fish of all shapes and sizes in every colour of the spectrum swam around and below me, quite unperturbed by my clumsy presence, darting swiftly through the coral like quick bursts and flashes of forked lighting. This was a world I'd never witnessed at first hand before, an uncharted and terrifying territory that I had conquered my fears to explore. Wasn't I just the cleverest person in the world! At that moment I could have climbed Everest if I'd chosen to.

I carefully started to move my arms and legs, and found to my delight that I could propel myself through the water. I was swimming! Oh, dear Mother of Christ, look at me, Paul O'Grady who can't add up, swimming. My heart sang with happiness. I was dipping under the water, moving faster and faster. This was bliss. Look at the fish, look at the shafts of sunlight shining from above through the arches of the pink coral. I was drunk with the beauty of it all.

And then, suddenly, my dream was shattered. Coming towards me in the water was something that struck terror into my heart. Not a shark or one of those killer jellyfish peculiar to Oz, but something far worse. Something that was more than capable of capsizing a neophyte swimmer like myself, something noisy and unpredictable, thrashing about and causing me to rock from side to side and lose what little control I had in that great, deep, suddenly once again terrifying water. It was a shoal of Japanese schoolchildren. I reared my head out of the water like the deadly Kraken of Norse mythology and lashed out with my arms and legs to try to disperse them. If the odd slap or kick helped to encourage them to change course then so be it. Finally, just to make sure that they got the message that this Portuguese man-of-war was not to be messed with, I spat out my snorkel and roared at the top of my lungs, 'FUCK OFF!'

To quote my mother, bad language is the riposte of the inarticulate. I fully realize this, but there are times when it does come in very handy, and that was one of them. I don't know if they understood me but they certainly moved away from me sharpish, like startled minnows in the path of a malevolent pike, shouting remarks in Japanese as they swam back to their boat. Apart from sushi and karaoke my Japanese is extremely limited, but I've a good idea that what they were saying was something along the lines of 'Piss off, you miserable old fart'.

To my surprise I was actually quite far out over the reef; the cruiser was a fair distance away. I also seemed to be the only person left in the water. I hadn't realized how long I'd been absorbed in my newly acquired skill. Someone was waving from the deck. It was Murphy. As I slowly propelled myself towards the boat I could see his expression change from one of anxiety to admiration. He helped me up from the ladder on to the deck.

'Well done,' he said, genuinely delighted that I'd taken the plunge. 'Although I'd ditch the yellow lifejacket if I were you,' he added. 'You looked a bit like a coeliac's turd the way you were floating in the water.'

My mother's headmistress, a kindly but firm old nun who went by the fearsome moniker of Mother Mary Cleophas, realized my mother's potential and encouraged her to work harder. She was more than delighted when my mum won a scholarship to Holt Hill Convent, the best Catholic girls' grammar school on the Wirral. It was not to be; Aunty Poll saw to that. She considered education a waste of time for a working-class girl. Circumstances such as my mother's didn't allow the luxury of further schooling and she couldn't expect to live on Aunty Poll's charity for ever. No, she must earn her keep. Education was for the upper classes; what use would it be to my mother? Far better she left school and went straight into a good, steady job in domestic service. Aunty Poll firmly believed that Jack was not as good as his master and would be far better off tugging his forelock and knowing his place in the social pecking order. Education filled a girl's head with dangerous nonsense and gave her ideas above her station, which always led to trouble.

Despite Mother Mary's pleading my mother's case, Aunty Poll stood firm and at the end of term my bitterly disappointed ma was packed off to a life in service. She was keen that the same fate should not befall me.

I did well at St Joseph's. Apart from arithmetic I was a fairly competent and enthusiastic scholar, according to my old school reports. I remember winning an Easter egg in a class raffle. I sat there willing it to be me as Miss Bolger drew a name from the cardboard box.

'And the winner is . . . Paul O'Grady.' An electric shock ran through me when she called out my name, although I was confident even before she did so that I had won the much-prized Cadbury's egg. I'd so arrogantly assured myself that it was mine for the taking that the gods looking down must have decided there and then that this attitude was something to be nipped in the bud. I've never won a bloody raffle since.

Although I enjoyed school I wasn't keen to let my parents think that. I told my mother that nobody would play with me and I used to stand alone in the school yard at playtime. She told me years later that she would come down to the school during the break and hide behind one of the pillars of the gate to watch me playing happily and loudly with a gang of kids. Why I said what I did I don't know. Yes I do. Who am I kidding? I was playing for the sympathy card, trying to get back into her good books after I'd run away on my first afternoon at school.

I'd reminded Miss Bolger that it was nearly time for *Watch with Mother*. Monday was Picture Book and I wasn't missing that for anything.

'*Watch with Mother*?' she said, blinking at me over the glasses hanging off the end of her sharp little nose. 'There's none of that here, dear. This is school. We don't watch television here, and besides, you're a big boy now. Time to put *Watch with Mother* away.'

Was she out of her mind? Time to put *Watch with Mother* away? I wasn't having any of that, and so when the Bolger wasn't looking I put my coat on and went home.

Franny didn't see me go. He didn't have a telly and was blissfully unaware of the potent pulling power of Andy Pandy and co. Besides, he was tired after eating two dinners, mine as well

133

as his own, plus the seconds he'd gone up for, so he had curled up in his seat and gone to sleep with his head on the desk like the dormouse.

When my absence was eventually noticed, a search party was sent out. Even the headmaster got in on the act and drove to my mother's to see if I was there. At the time my ma was being treated to the delights of a home perm by Mrs Long's daughter, Jean, who was training to be a hairdresser. ('Our Jean's training to be a beautician. She's going to get a job on the liners. You can go anywhere in the world if you know how to set hair.') She wasn't best pleased to meet my headmaster sitting as she was in the middle of the room on a kitchen chair in her bra, her eyes streaming from the smell of the ammonia, her hair in pin curls and papers, with only a plastic pacamac over her bare shoulders to conceal her modesty. On hearing the news my mother instantly panicked and ran out of the house to look for me, her pacamac flapping behind her, and her hair wound into tight pin curls so that her head resembled a plate of winkles. She wouldn't have looked out of place on a Blackpool hen night. All she needed was an L plate on her back. She hurtled up the back entry with the headmaster and Jean in hot pursuit, followed by half the neighbourhood, who had instantly picked up on the jungle tom-toms that something was amiss.

Meanwhile, I was enjoying the walk home. I'd crossed two main roads safely thanks to the Gospel According to Tufty of which I was a devoted disciple, being a fully paid-up member of the Tufty Club. (Look Right, Look Left, Look Right Again. I still do it today.) On arriving home to an empty house, I let myself in and settled down for my weekly dose of Vera McKechnie and her Picture Book.

It was Mary next door who discovered me and shouted up the entry 'I've found him!' causing a chain reaction of 'He's been found' around the back streets of Tranmere. My distraught mother returned home, supported bodily by a couple of neighbours, and flung herself on me with all the passion of Serafina from *The Rose Tattoo*.

'Oh, my Christ, I thought you'd been abducted,' she wailed, but her anguish quickly turned to anger when she remembered that she'd run across Holt Road in her bra and her home perm solution was probably rotting the hair from her scalp by the very roots. She shook me vigorously, like a maraca. 'You naughty, wicked child,' she shouted (she would probably have gone for a stronger and more colourful invective, but my head-master was there), 'don't you ever do that again, d'ya hear me? I nearly had a heart attack.'

Still, I got a ride back to school in the headmaster's car, a rare treat as no one we knew owned a car. I did my maraca impression all over again when I was deposited back into class. The Bolger gripped my shoulders, digging her bony fingers into me, and shook me violently, promising me that next time I tried any tricks it would be the cane. Nowadays if a teacher hit a small child with a wooden stick they'd end up in court – if the pupil hadn't got to them first and stabbed them. In 1960 it went unquestioned and was considered a perfectly acceptable way to discipline a child.

In all the time I was at St Joseph's I was only caned once and that was for hiding my underpants behind the radiator and stinking the class out after a sudden accident one day while playing with the ubiquitous blue (or rather, by now, grey) plasticine with Deirdre Walsh. The next school I attended, St Anselm's, Redcourt, was a very different story. It was a place where the teachers and Christian Brothers positively relished beating young boys with leather straps. Strappings were so frequent that they should have been part of the curriculum.

I was happy at St Joseph's and had progressed from the Bolger's class to the care of Miss Edwards, who wore lots of perfume and marked your work with an orange pencil. I was the class joker, a highly overused term that I'm loath to repeat, but since no other springs to mind it will have to suffice.

I'd make light of our group inoculations as we waited in our vests outside the school office, temporarily transformed into the doctor's surgery, by cracking gags and acting the fool, an approach to life's unpleasant moments adopted by various family members that I'd absorbed as I grew up. Uncle Al told me about a convicted killer who, as he was being strapped in to the electric chair, wisecracked and joked as if he were about to have a haircut instead of a few thousand volts. This was the attitude I admired and tried to emulate, and it has stood me in good stead on more than one occasion.

My school work was promising. I was no genius or 'child prodigal' like Eileen Henshaw's son, but I enjoyed learning and was enthusiastic about most subjects, and at this early stage my teachers held out great hopes for my passing the eleven-plus. So, encouraged by my school reports and prompted by an advertisement in the *Birkenhead News* for St Anselm's, Redcourt, a fee-paying preparatory school for boys between the ages of eight and eleven that had a record of getting boys through the eleven-plus and into the main college, my ambitious mother decided that I was to be taken out of St Joseph's and 'privately educated'. She couldn't wait to drop that little bombshell next time she was in Henshaw's buying two ounces of corned beef and a small loaf.

After sitting down and doing his sums, my father agreed that they could just about manage the school fees at a push, and applied for me to sit the entrance exam.

I thought that I wouldn't want to leave Joey's; it was an easy pace, I liked my teachers and I'd miss my friends, especially Franny, whom I'd grown very protective towards. We'd walk home from school together each day and I'd tell him stories.

Since we went our separate ways at the corner of Derby Road, these tales became a never-ending serial to be continued the next afternoon.

Franny was easy pickings for the school bullies. I always found the best approach, when Franny was in the grip of a headlock and having his scalp severely rubbed by Billy Boggins's knuckles, was to wade right in from behind and deliver a side punch to the assailant's face while jumping on to his back and dragging him to the floor. Once he was down it was wise to sit on him, stick two fingers up his nostrils and pull hard, then hope and pray that the Bolger would hear the commotion and abandon her break-time cup of tea and biscuit and come to the rescue.

Billy Boggins lived down the hill on Sydney Terrace and apart from his unpredictable bouts of violence we were good friends. His mother Pat was a good-natured, warm-hearted woman from Northern Ireland who was mad on the telly, in particular *Bewitched*. Kicking off her shoes, she'd sit on the sofa with her arms folded across her heavily pregnant belly, surrounded by kids, and roar laughing, even though she said it was sinful to believe in magic or witches as they were the work of the devil.

Franny wasn't keen on Billy. He was always a bag of nerves when the bigger boy was around, waiting for the moment when Billy would pounce and give him a knuckle-rub or, even worse, the dreaded Chinese burn. Billy couldn't help himself, though. He couldn't resist picking on Franny, whose size and colouring ('like a little ginger weed who's been grown in the dark' as Aunty Chris described him) attracted bullies like moths to a flame. He was often the butt of jokes and taunting in the playground, when his anger would slowly build up until, swearing at his tormentors through clenched teeth, he'd rush at them, pinching and kicking with the rage of a malevolent elf.

He lived with his parents and two brothers and sister above

a shop that sold gravestones. Franny's mum cleaned that shop and when we got the chance we'd sneak in and I'd wrap myself in a dust sheet and stand in the window next to one of the headstones, eyes downcast, hands joined in prayer, pretending to be an angel, while Franny stood by the door panicking in case his mum came down and caught us. Later on the premises were taken over by Servoheat, a company that sold heating appliances. Boilers and loft insulation didn't have the appeal that gravestones had and so we stopped playing there.

Franny's parents were strict. His dad was handy with the belt if the boys stepped out of line. I couldn't believe it when I called for Franny one Saturday morning and Mr Mooney told me that he couldn't come out until he'd finished his chores. Spoilt as I was, I'm ashamed to say that I never even made my own bed. I felt sorry for Franny, having to wash dishes and hoover, but Franny didn't seem to mind in the least and as soon as he was free we'd run for the Saturday morning kids' matinee at the ABC. If we didn't have the entrance fee we'd try to bunk in through a side door, but usually we'd begged and cadged the money from somewhere.

Inside, it was pandemonium. It was also slightly dangerous, since the kids in the balcony would pelt those in the stalls with sweets and bottles. They also had spitting competitions in which the aim was to see who could hawk up the biggest 'golly' and then score a direct hit on some unsuspecting child below. In view of this, it was a good idea to get there early and bag a seat somewhere near the front, out of the range of fire.

The one and only time I joined in the balcony kids' terrorist activities I got carried away and thought that instead of spitting it would be a hoot to pee over the edge. This proved to be a trickier manoeuvre than I'd anticipated, entailing standing on tiptoes and remembering to lean back so that the stream of wee would arc over the balcony instead of soaking me. I got caught in mid-flow by an angry usherette and frogmarched to the manager's office, where I was given a clip over the head and banned from attending ABC Minors for a month.

That cinema manager must have hated Saturday mornings. He had to get up on the stage before the film started and through gritted teeth welcome a horde of unsupervised kids with a cheery 'Hello ABC Minors!', only to be greeted with a deafening chorus of cheers, catcalls and whistling. If it was any of the kids' birthday they'd be invited up on to the stage and presented with a bag of sweets in front of the rest of us. I never got up; I would rather have died than walk down the aisle and up on to the stage and stand there in the spotlight, cheeks burning with shame, clutching a bag of sweets and cursing inwardly while everyone sang 'Happy Birthday'.

At last the lights would dim and the cinema would shake as we stamped our feet and cheered. The screen would spring into life and the words to the ABC Minors' anthem would appear, complete with a bouncing ball underneath each word, not that we needed prompting. We knew the song by heart and would sing along to the tune of 'Blaze Away':

'We are the boys and girls well known as
The minors of the ABC,
And every Saturday we line up
To see the films we like and
Shout aloud with glee.'

The programmes we liked usually began with a serial, inevitably an ancient print of Zorro that was scratched and blurred in places and had a tendency to jump on to the next scene at crucial moments. We'd boo when this happened and shout abuse up at the projectionist. An army of usherettes would then appear, scanning the rows of kids with their torches like prison officers looking for an escapee and trying to restore law and order with a few kind but firm words, like 'Sit down and shurrup, you little shit, or I'll kick yer arse and chuck you out!' The Zorro stories always ended on a cliffhanger with our hero dangling over a bottomless drop or trapped inside a burning building with half a ton of dynamite strapped to his chest. If you didn't manage to get in the next week to see the next instalment you hung around outside waiting for someone you knew to come out and tell you what happened.

The serial was followed by a few Disney cartoons and then came the main feature, always a hoary old black and white relic, but as long as it contained a degree of violence involving gangsters or cowboys and Indians and no kissing of heroines we didn't care and brought the house down cheering for the good guy and booing the villain. Afterwards we'd re-enact what we'd just seen on the screen in Mersey Park. If the day's offering had been a cowboy epic then we'd canter along the paths slapping our hips and holding up imaginary reins to show that we were riding a horse.

'Hurry up, you.'

'I can't.'

'Why?'

'Me 'orse has got an arrow in its hoof.'

If you got bored with running around the park and slapping your arse you could always stop dead in your tracks and hurl yourself to the ground. This implied that your horse had encountered a rattlesnake and, having reared up in fright, had thrown you. Bad luck if the Injuns caught you as you would be taken to their encampment and tied to a tree. No actual rope was used; you just sat on the grass with your arms behind you, wrapped round the tree. You wouldn't dream of moving from this position until one of your comrades sneaked up unseen by the Injuns and set you free by severing your invisible bonds with the deadly bowie knife he kept down his boot. To a passing observer it might have looked like an ordinary lolly-ice stick that had been shoved inside a grubby regulation grey school sock, but it wasn't. In our eyes it was a genuine, pearl-handled, ten-inch, razor-sharp bowie knife nestling inside a hand-tooled, custom-made, ass-kickin' cowboy boot, just like the movies.

St Anselm's, Redcourt, was a big redbrick building that had once been, before death duties crippled the gentry, a rather grand private house. Situated in a leafy road in elegant Oxton, it was considered one of the best boys' schools on the Wirral, and was run by the Christian Brothers, a body of mainly Irish men, who conducted themselves as if they were the SS of the Roman Catholic Church.

The day of the entrance exam, we were shown around the school by one of the Brothers, who had my mother eating out of his hand. 'We have a wide and varied curriculum,' he was saying. 'The arts, sciences, sports and languages plus the benefits of good strong religious education.'

My dad was nodding in agreement. He'd pulled all the stops out today and was wearing his best suit. My mother, who was almost unintelligible so strong was the half-crown voice she was putting on, was asking the Brother if it mattered that my maths was a little weak.

'Not at all,' the Brother reassured her, rubbing his hands and smiling at me. 'We'll soon knock him into shape.' I didn't realize he meant it literally.

Outside the classroom where we were to sit the exam was a lifesize statue of Our Lady complete with a plaster effigy of a suitably pious St Bernadette kneeling at her feet. It was set in a grotto in the wall adorned with gold stars and wouldn't have looked out of place at the pleasure beach in Blackpool. Nevertheless I dutifully blessed myself and said a quick Hail Mary for luck, prompted by a dig in the back from my dad. Our Lady must've been in a beneficent mood that day as I passed the entrance exam. Only by a hair's-breadth, but it was enough to convince my well-meaning parents that I was destined for a college education.

The list of requirements for a St Anselm's boy before he could set foot in the building was extensive. Apart from the school uniform (short trousers only), there were rugby, football, PE and cricket kits to buy, a satchel for books and a duffel bag for the sports kits. Everything had to be paid for: textbooks, writing materials, the works. I'm surprised they didn't charge for the toilet paper. Selfishly oblivious of the expense of it all, I spent a glorious day in Rostance's of Grange Road West shopping for this elaborate wardrobe, made financially possible by the weekly terms of the Provident Cheque Company. Perhaps blinded by the glamour of a royal blue blazer piped in yellow with matching cap, and a rugby kit with shiny boots destined to remain as pristine as the day they were bought, such was my total lack of enthusiasm on the pitch, I left St Joseph's without a backward glance and looked forward to joining the elite.

Religious education at St Joseph's had been a cosy affair. I liked the branch of Catholicism they taught there. The Bolger's account of the Nativity was enchanting and in my mind's eye the story ran like a Disney cartoon, prince and princess played by Joseph and Mary. The angel became the fairy godmother, Herod was a perfect substitute for the wicked queen, the Magi provided the magical effects and the shepherds and animals contributed the comedy relief. I was more than pissed off when I was chosen to play a sheep in my first nativity play. I wanted to be the Angel of the Lord, and instead I had to crawl around on all fours wearing my sister's white polo-neck jumper with the neck pulled up over the back of my head for a fleece and a black sock on each hand and foot for hooves. I didn't even try to upstage the rest of the cast by employing a bit of focus-pulling imaginary grass-munching or letting them have a couple of well-timed baas; instead I just mooched around in the background, bitterly disillusioned with showbiz.

I made my first confession and communion at St Joseph's, and thank God I did, for if the Brothers of St Anselm's had been instrumental in preparing a young child to search his conscience and confess his sins before partaking of a slice of Christ's body then the occasion would've rivalled the Inquisition. I couldn't wait to get in that confessional; it held all the mystery of a conjuror's box. First you had to examine your conscience – had you honoured your father and mother? Or taken the Lord's name in vain or coveted your neighbour's goods? I had no idea what coveted meant but it sounded sinful so I mentally ticked the box. We were told to write our sins down so that we would remember them come the day. I was forever leaving lists of sins around the house that my mother would find.

'What's all this? "I have coveted my neighbour's goods"? "I have been disobedient"? "I stole a penny off the mantelpiece"? Did you now, my lad? Well, you'd better tell the priest or you'll roast.' I did tell the priest, and on a slow week when I hadn't been particularly sinful I would invent some peccadilloes so he wouldn't feel I was wasting his time. The penance you received depended on the severity of your sin, and in my case it was usually half a dozen Hail Marys and Our Fathers and an Act of Contrition.

Nowadays I'd need a team of exorcists working through the night to hear my confession and my penance would probably be crucifixion. I haven't been to confession in years and nor can I see myself going in the foreseeable future, but back then I thought it was marvellous – confess your sins on a Saturday night and after holding back on any thoughts, words or actions that could be construed as sinful you took your communion with a clear conscience on the Sunday morning. Then, allowing a suitable space of time for the host to go down (God forbid you should chew it), you went straight out and started sinning again.

There were two types of sin: mortal and venial. A venial sin was nicking a penny off the mantelpiece. Mortal sin was a little more serious; you only earned this badge if you committed murder or missed mass. Newborn babies were scarred with the Original Sin of Adam and Eve and if they died before receiving the sacrament of baptism they went to a place called limbo. If you died with the stain of sin on your soul, having been unable to get a priest to your bedside to hear your last confession, then you were packed off to purgatory. This was only temporary, though – just until your soul had been purified and 'purged in the flames'. If you liked, you could help the dead on their way to their heavenly reward and spring them from purgatory by offering up a spiritual appeal in the form of prayers or in-dulgences, particularly during Lent. It felt good when, after a prolonged bout of chewing the altar rails – Aunty Chrissie's description of the devout at a heavy session of prayer – another tortured soul entered the pearly gates of heaven.

You only went straight up to heaven, bypassing the annoy-ance and inconvenience of a stopover in purgatory, if you were truly righteous. St Bernadette, the Holy Family and other A-listers of the Catholic stage held court there. On the gates stood St Peter, all beard and flowing white robes, beautifully backlit against the clouds, leaning on a marble lectern and idly flicking through the pages of a large tome that contained all the names of the worthy allowed to enter, a sort of celestial bouncer on the door of a very exclusive members-only club. Hell was for folk like Hitler, Rose Long and the Orange Lodge.

So, as you will have gathered, I had theology all sewn up and sorted out neatly into little compartments in my mind at an early age. I was ready for the big day, the most important day in a Catholic child's life, known in the trade as your First Holy Communion.

Along with all the other kids in the class, I took it very seriously. Father Doyle from St Joseph's Church came and spoke to us, stressing the importance of the occasion and heightening our growing excitement at the knowledge that we were finally getting to sample that little white wafer.

Oh, the magnificence and splendour of it all! The church packed to the rafters, ablaze with candles and alive with music as the church organist, working full steam ahead, blasted out a hymn to glory while I sailed majestically down the aisle with Clare McGrath, my communion partner and secret love, at my side.

My mother had knitted me my communion jumper, and she'd also made one for Franny while she was at it. Underneath this startlingly white garment I wore a Bri-nylon shirt and a red tie on elastic; a pair of grey shorts and knee-length socks completed the outfit. The pièce de résistance of this ensemble was emblazoned proudly across my chest: a shiny scarlet sash. This was my finest hour – Steve Zodiac, eat your heart out. With the beautiful Clare of the soft brown curls and rosy cheeks walking alongside me, resplendent in her scaled-down version of a bride's dress, complete with veil, her eyes modestly downcast, her tiny fingers encased in white lace gloves and wrapped around a prayer book, I thought we were possibly the most gorgeous sight on the face of Planet Earth. I tried to keep up the butch Prince Valiant act as I knelt at the altar but I was afraid my shaking would give me away as I trembled in anticipation of my first taste of God.

Would it taste salty like a crisp, or like a sherbet flying saucer, I wondered as Father Doyle lowered the wafer into my mouth. I closed my eyes respectfully and waited for an electric shock of divine energy to enter my body as the sacrament and I became one. It was a bit of an anti-climax. The wafer slid off my tongue and clung to the roof of my mouth until I scraped it off with the tip of my tongue, when it dissolved into mush and slid down my throat. No lights, no heavenly choirs, no pounding in the ears. Was this what I'd starved myself and missed supper and breakfast for? Surely there should be some slight indication from the physical body, a tremor at least, or better still blinding rays of light emanating from various parts to show that a spiritual earthquake had just taken place inside and I was now in a state of grace. Still, I wasn't going to be downhearted, and at the undoubted post-mortem back at school, when the recipients would excitedly discuss their experiences of swallowing the host, I'd hold my own with a completely fabricated but compelling story of flashing lights and divine interventions.

Apart from the sheer glory of it, making my First Holy Communion turned out to be a highly profitable occasion. I got a pound from Aunty Chris, a pen off my dad and a prayer book from my sister, and in every 'Congratulations on your First Holy Communion' card there was at least a ten-bob note. After the ceremony there was a party in the school hall with trestle tables laid out with orange juice, cakes, sandwiches and jelly, which was just as well since most of the kids were close to fainting from hunger, not having eaten since the night before. After the feast came the group photo and then individual shots of us standing, smiling shyly, on a wobbly table with a statue of the Virgin Mary peering over our shoulders. Living as I did in my protected and cloistered world, of which the majority of the inhabitants were of the Catholic persuasion, Catholicism felt like more than membership of an exclusive and superior club. I felt part of a large, secure and loving family, but my attitude to religion was about to change as I was introduced to some of the darker members of the Catholic brotherhood.

CHAPTER NINE

THE SUNDAY BEFORE I STARTED AT ST ANSELM'S I WAS ALLOWED to wear my new school uniform to church. My parents never went to Sunday mass together. My dad preferred St Joseph's while my ma was a worshipper at the altar of downtown St Werburgh's. Usually I went to St Joseph's with my dad, but this day was my mother's moment of glory and she paraded me around outside St Werburgh's like Madam Rose showing off Baby June. In response to Father Lennon's obvious delight at seeing me in my new school uniform, the hallowed badge of St Anselm's embroidered on my breast pocket, my mother went into the act.

'Yes, Father, he does look smart, and he'd better stay that way . . . or else.' She broke into peals of false merriment but the look in her eye said if I got that uniform dirty I was dead meat. 'He starts at St Anselm's in the morning,' she went on to explain, emphasizing the *St Anselm's* just in case anyone within a two-hundred-yard radius hadn't heard her. 'Yes, he passed the entrance exam; now all he has to do is work hard. You wouldn't believe the books he has to read . . .' and she was off. Brother Ennis, the headmaster, had sent a letter to my parents advising them of what was suitable for a St Anselm's boy in the way of reading matter.

All comics, with the exception of *Look and Learn*, a weekly magazine for children that was considered educational, were forbidden. The only comic strip deemed suitable to grace the pages of *Look and Learn* was Asterix the Gaul, which I hated, so I took myself off to Mersey Park to read my *Beano*, *Dandy* and *Beezer* in peace, hiding them, along with the stack of American comics Uncle Al and the cousins had brought back from sea, under the guinea pig's cage in the shed outside. I loved American comics, in particular Casper the Friendly Ghost and Archie and Jughead. The small ads at the back had me drooling. What wouldn't I have given for a pair of X-ray specs or a tank full of Sea Monkeys, but you needed to send dollars or a money order and had to have something called a zip code, all very frustrating to an eight-year-old on a mission.

Brother Ennis went on to advise that reading should be restricted to suitable works such as *Moby Dick*, *Ivanhoe*, *King Arthur and the Knights of the Round Table* and, of course, the Catechism. Consequently, to my horror, I received copies of those hated books for Christmas instead of the usual Popeye annual, Famous Five sagas and Borrowers stories.

Television was to be heavily restricted and censored by the parent, said the Gospel According to Brother Ennis. Instead of watching television the time could be spent more productively, quietly reading or studying.

No more *Avengers*? I rebelled against this outrage instantly. No more evenings wrapped in a towel after the Saturday night bath, glued to the telly, absorbing and memorizing every detail of the plot that was unfurling before me so I could re-enact it in my mind the next day on my way to church? It was my reason for living, my source of life. What were these Christian Brothers thinking? Didn't they have tellies? Hadn't they relished the sight of the glorious goddess that was Mrs Gale dressed head to toe in black leather beating ten bells of shite out of the villain's henchmen? I lived for *The Avengers*. John Steed with his bowler and brolly at the ready and his cavalier attitude to life, and Cathy Gale the ice-cool anthropologist who chucked men over her shoulder with a flick of her wrist, touched a nerve and started a lifelong love affair with the show. In the end my dad agreed that providing I'd done my homework I could watch *The Avengers* and a few selected children's programmes approved of by the Brothers, a rule that I'm glad to say was never really enforced.

My mother took me to school that first September morning in 1963, but not without paying a visit to Henshaw's first to show off her very own child prodigal.

'I see they've arrested that Christine Keeler for perjury,' Eileen said as we came into the shop, looking up from the *Daily Mirror* that was spread out before her on the counter.

'I'm not interested in the affairs of trollops,' my mother replied curtly. 'I'll just take a *Woman's Own*, please, something to read on the bus.'

'And where are you off to then?' Eileen asked, looking at me and pulling a face as if she'd just discovered dogshit on the floor.

'School,' my mother replied before I could speak. 'It's his first day of term . . . at St Anselm's College.' She savoured the words. 'It's two buses, you know, but worth the journey seeing how it's the best boys' school in Birkenhead.'

Eileen, resenting the implication that her own little darling's school might be somewhat inferior to the omnipotent St Anselm's, took the gloves off and unsheathed her claws.

'Isn't that a fee-paying school?' she asked, her face a picture of innocence.

'That's right,' my ma replied airily, as if money were no object.

'Then let's hope they don't have to wait as long for their money as I do for the paper bill,' Eileen crowed.

My mother remained cool in the face of such heavy gunfire.

149

'Oh, thanks for reminding me,' she said sweetly. 'I've had such a lot on my mind, what with Paul's new school, that I completely forgot about the trivial little things like the paper bill.'

Picking up a tin of marrowfat peas, she ran her gloved finger absently round the top, examining it for dust. 'Business must be bad if you're making such a fuss over a few coppers on a paper bill.'

She put the tin back and fastidiously rubbed her hands together, glancing pityingly around the tatty little shop as if she were in a refugee camp. 'I'd like to cancel the papers if you don't mind. To be honest they're not worth reading, the only thing you can believe in them these days is the date, and besides, that paper lad of yours is sooo dilatory, delivers them sooo late, we often get the *Echo* just as we're going to bed – that's if we get it at all.'

'It's nigh on impossible to find a paper lad who's reliable. You wouldn't believe the riff-raff and lazy little ne'er-do-wells I've had to deal with in the past,' Eileen sniped back venomously, looking straight at me.

'Never mind, it's only a back-street grocer's after all. We customers can't expect too much in the way of service, I suppose.' My mother spoke in a way that was meant to convey that she was used to regular and prompt deliveries from Fortnum's, her gay, tinkling laugh, however, laced with undertones of menace. Eileen gave a snort of disgust.

'What exactly is that?' my ma enquired politely, pointing to a lump of meat in the refrigerated cabinet.

'It's roast beef,' Eileen said curtly, still stunned from the assault on her shop. 'And your paper bill comes to more than a few coppers, it's eight bob actually.'

'It's a very funny colour of roast beef,' my mother went on, ignoring her and counting the change out of her purse on to the counter. 'If you don't mind me saying, it's got a sort of unnatural green tinge, a bit like a bluebottle's wing. Are you sure it's not off?'

'That beef' – Eileen's voice was beginning to shake – 'that beef, I'll have you know, has not only been cooked to perfection by my George but has also been properly hung.'

'Well, you want to watch your George doesn't end up being properly hung himself at Walton nick for selling dodgy meat and poisoning half the neighbourhood,' my mother replied. 'If the public health man saw the colour of that he'd close you down, and then where would we be?' she added, smiling kindly before making her exit, leaving Eileen to closely examine the accused under the fluorescent strip light, cursing my mother angrily to herself.

I think I was the only child that morning who went to school on the bus. All the other kids were dropped off by Mummy or Daddy in the car. I said goodbye to my ma at the gate and made my way into the building by the side entrance, as directed by a Christian Brother.

This part of the school had formerly been the kitchens of the great house but now, years later, had been reduced in rank to the cloakrooms. After hanging up our coats we shyly weighed each other up as we congregated to sit cross-legged on the floor of the large assembly hall, waiting to be allocated our classroom. Within minutes, one of the Brothers had dragged a boy up from the floor and given him a vicious slap with a leather strap across the back of his legs.

'No talking,' he barked, dangling the shocked victim by his arm as an angry welt developed across the back of the boy's leg, 'unless you want to feel the strap.'

As well as the Brothers there were a few lay teachers, notably Mr Smith, a stereotypical *Daily Mail* reader in cord trousers and highly polished brogues, whose well-worn strap hung from his belt and down the side of one hip, the end peeping out from beneath the hem of his tweed jacket. Another teacher who stands out in my memory was an effeminate bully. Highly unpredictable and prone to sudden outbursts of fury, he'd lay into boys who had displeased him with his strap, a terrifying and yet compelling spectacle to watch from the safety of your desk.

St Anselm's was a male-dominated society not at ease in the presence of women, which perhaps explains why there was only one woman on the teaching staff. This solitary female was called Miss McGee, known to every boy behind her back as 'Lulu'. She'd been at St Anselm's since the year dot, and expected everyone, Brothers included, to treat her as if she were royalty.

She was as miserable as sin. A grim woman whom I don't think I ever saw smile, she'd sit behind the grand piano picking away at the keys like a chicken in a talent show, her face set into a permanent sulk. There were fussy feminine touches about her: a lace handkerchief tucked under the watchstrap on her wrist, the overpowering smell of lily of the valley which made you sneeze if you got too close, and the seed pearls round her neck with which she toyed coquettishly when talking to any male in the school who wasn't wearing short trousers. Her cold and distant attitude towards the rest of us made it perfectly clear that she hated little boys, and unlike Miss Edwards and even the Bolger back at St Joseph's she was totally devoid of any warmth.

We dreaded Lulu's classes. Since her repertoire was severely limited, we spent most of the torturous hour practising endless rounds of scales, loo-loo-looing our way up and down the octaves, hence her nickname. After a session of this we'd launch into 'Hearts of Oak' or 'Kitty of Coleraine', the latter enabling us to infuriate her by singing 'as Kitty was stripping' instead of 'as Kitty was tripping'. 'Enunciate!' she would scream, glaring over the lid of the piano. 'And Paul O'Grady, go and stand at the back of the group. You're deafening me.' Each music lesson with Lulu ended with a rousing chorus of 'Rule Britannia', but the Kids from *Fame* we were not.

Once a week Lulu took us for elocution. The majority of the class were well spoken, and one or two were so frightfully affected that they sounded like juvenile Lord Haw-Haws. I was one of the flies in her eloquent ointment.

'Mary has fair hair.'

'Maireee 'as fer'rair.'

She cracked me in the end, though, and after months of weekly brainwashing sessions I became 'awfully posh'. My ma was ecstatic and would nearly wet herself with glee whenever someone remarked in the street how 'beautifully spoken' I was. My brother and cousins would send me up and sit on me and punch me. With hindsight I can't say I blame them; St Anselm's was turning me into a snotty, piss-elegant little snob.

The final straw for my brother was when I corrected him for saying budgie with an imperious 'It's not a budgie, it's a budgerigar' and he kicked me down the stairs.

'New boys form a line and follow me.' A bullet-headed, wiry little Irish Brother was showing us to our classroom; I stood in line waiting to go upstairs, uncomfortably aware out of the corner of my eye that the fat kid next to me was desperate to grab my attention. Ignoring him, I suddenly became engrossed in an uninspiring painting of a lake hanging on the wall, hoping that he'd get the hint and realize that I didn't want to be his little friend. Staring at the picture was a bad move; it gave Violet Elizabeth Bott a perfect opening line.

'I went there with my parents last year,' he said nonchalantly, as if we were gathered at a smart conversazione. 'It's an oil of Lake Como seen from the Villa Serbelloni on top of Monte San Primo. Have you been there?'

I opened my mouth to speak but all I could manage was a strangled 'ungh' sound which could have meant anything.

'My father is a doctor and very senior at British blood

transfusions,' the monster prattled on. 'What does your father do?'

'He works in oil.'

'Oh. Texas?'

'No, Ellesmere Port.'

Despite the fact that I had virtually nothing in common with most of these kids – our lifestyles were poles apart – I never felt underprivileged in any way. Quite the opposite, in fact. It didn't bother me that their folks picked them up from school in the car and that their summers were spent on the Italian riviera. My dad had a moped that didn't work and, providing she was on speaking terms with my mum, we rented Rose Long's caravan for a week in August or went to Ireland. Apart from being used as an occasional substitute for a punch bag by the Brothers, I was happy with my status quo.

The bullet-headed Brother was our form teacher. His name was Brother Kearney and he couldn't have been any older than his late twenties. At first I was prepared to like him as when he leaned over my desk to slap the boy in front of me across the head for talking he smelt reassuringly like my dad – a familiar whiff of whisky and cigarettes.

Brother Kearney was a man's man: he favoured the boys who were bright and competitive and excelled at sports. 'The emphasis in my class is on achievement,' he used to say. The boys who didn't come up to his high expectations he tortured. My inability to grasp even the basics of his arithmetic lessons unleashed the sadist in him. He would slowly drag me round the classroom by the hair of my temple, much to the Schadenfreude of the class, repeatedly asking a question that I had no answer to. Lifting me by the hair so I was forced to walk on tiptoes, he would twist it tighter and shout in my face, 'You're a cretin, O'Grady. What are ya?'

'A cretin, sir.'

'Now for the last time before I take the strap to ya – divide sixty-eight by nine and then multiply by two.'

You try working that out with the Marquis de Sade of the Christian Brotherhood tearing your scalp off with his bare hands. Enraged by my total incomprehension of anything mathematical, he would drag me to the front of the class, tell me to hold out my hand and hit me three or four times with his strap. The pain wasn't instantaneous. It kicked in as you walked back to your desk, head down, determined to stem the flow of tears dangerously welling up behind your eyes.

It was Brother Kearney who gave my mother her favourite quote about me. He was the one who said that I was 'born to trouble as the sparks fly upward'.

'Job, chapter five, verse seven,' my mother had replied, completely knocking the wind out of his sails.

My mother read her Bible and could quote chunks of it ad nauseam when the occasion warranted, but she had an aversion for the Bible-bashers who would knock on the front door at least once a week.

'You go to your church in peace and I'll go to mine,' she'd say to them. 'Just don't stand on my doorstep battering the door down to bloody well tell me about it.'

Every morning we took religious instruction. This involved learning the highly convoluted and seemingly meaningless answers to a series of cryptic questions set out in the Catechism.

'What is purgatory?'

One could say it was the perfect way to describe a day at St Anselm's, but fortunately I was able to answer: 'Purgatory is the state of those who die in God's friendship, assured of their eternal salvation, but still have need of purification,' etc., etc.

I didn't really understand what any of it meant at the time, but since my memory was sharp I was able to learn it fairly quickly and recite it parrot fashion. Those who failed to get the answers right were given the strap, so I was word perfect in the hated Catechism very quickly. I never questioned anything that we were taught in religious instruction. I'd learned that lesson when I'd innocently asked Brother Kearney what the Holy Ghost looked like.

I'd always imagined that it was the archetypal wailing white bedsheet complete with a couple of holes for eyes, a pair of wings and a halo. I was given the strap for being blasphemous and disrespectful so I never found out. I still think that the Holy Ghost looks like that. From that day I was a model Catholic child: we were to accept the doctrine of our Church without question and I never asked a single one.

Monday afternoon was devoted to sports and we'd hike across Oxton to the school playing fields at the end of Beryl Road in Noctorum. We played football or rugby regardless of the weather, although when I say 'play' I mean that I spent the duration of the game hanging around the edge of the pitch, managing to avoid any contact with the ball while pretending to look interested at the same time. I always returned to the changing room with my kit as gleaming white as when I'd left an hour earlier. The playing fields made way for a housing estate later on and I can't say I shed a tear.

In retrospect, I'd say that the three years I spent at St Anselm's were a waste of time and my parents' hard-earned money. I learned virtually nothing from the Brothers, apart perhaps from a degree of low cunning necessary for survival. Each Monday morning Brother Kearney would ask which mass we had attended the day before.

'Who went to seven o'clock mass then?' he'd ask. A couple of hands, each belonging to a goody-two-shoes of the class, would shoot up. Most of us went to the ten o'clock. 'Good,' Brother Kearney would say, smiling, preparing himself for the kill. 'Who didn't go to morning mass at all and went in the evening instead?' A few incredibly naive hands would go up. Kearney's mood would switch from benign little Brother to Chief Inquisitor. 'Come up front,' he would roar. 'Lazy boys who can't be bothered to get out of bed in the morning to attend holy mass need to be taught a lesson. Hands out.' And the bemused offenders would be given six of the best.

Honesty, as I soon discovered, was not the best policy when dealing with the Brothers. I quickly cottoned on to the fact that if you showed the slightest inclination towards joining the ranks of the Brotherhood when you grew up it gave you a bit of breathing space from the strappings. The thought that they might have made such a lasting impression on one of their charges that he wished to emulate them appealed to the Brothers' vast egos. Another recruit for the ranks of God's Army. Frankly, there was more chance of my joining the Royal Ballet, but I kept up the pretence for a while until Brother Kearney finally twigged that my intentions might not be that sincere and it was back to business as usual. There was no point my telling my mother that the Brothers were strap-happy and that the reason I couldn't hold my knife and fork properly was because my thumb and fingers were bruised and swollen from yet another vigorous strapping – she'd only have taken the Brothers' side. In her eyes they were good and saintly men of the cloth and therefore unable to do any wrong. If I did tell her that they'd hit me I'd usually get a slap across the head from her for 'obviously deserving it'.

I learned a lot about Greek mythology at St Anselm's, but not from a teacher, from my pal Szwelski. (It was the custom to call each other by your surnames.) His father owned the woodyard at the bottom of Holly Grove and we became 'bezzie mates'. We both hated the same people, which is always a strong bond in friendships, and his enthusiasm for the tales of the Cyclops and the Labours of Hercules infected me until I too became an addict. I must have read every book on Greek mythology that was available in Birkenhead Central Library.

Szwelski also shared my passion for *The Avengers*. Cathy Gale had moved on by then and had been replaced by the mind-boggling Emma Peel. We'd practise judo throws on each other in his back garden and sneak into his father's woodyard when it was closed via a small hole in the back fence that led on to the park. Szwelski played the dual roles of the Diabolical Mastermind and John Steed, while I of course took the part of Mrs Peel. He would tie me to a plank facing one of the very large and very real buzz saws and then switch on the circular saw. He had assured me that there was no chance of the blade's actually touching me, let alone cutting me in half, but it was a very nervous Mrs Peel who lay on that plank and I was always relieved when Szwelski eventually metamorphosed into John Steed. Then, after an energetic session throwing himself noisily around the woodyard to show that he was fighting off the Diabolical Mastermind, he would rescue me from the jaws of death.

We were also big fans of *The Man from UNCLE* and spent hours inventing secret codes to foil the enemy, the evil Thrush. We longed for the incredible gadgets that Napoleon and Ilya had at their disposal and made do instead with homemade versions concocted from things found lying around the house. ('Paul, have you seen my powder compact? And have you any idea where the aerial off the tranny is?') If I couldn't get a job on the buses or behind the counter of the dry cleaner's, which at the time were my chosen professions, I decided that a career as a secret agent was where my true destiny lay.

It was Szwelski's older sister Hannah who introduced me to classical music. I found her one day in the front room sobbing heavily into a tissue as she listened to Madam Butterfly belting out 'One Fine Day'. I joined her on the sofa and she explained the plot to me between sobs. Something on the lines of American sailor gets underage geisha pregnant and then dumps her, causing the heartbroken geisha to top herself. 'Typical bloody man,' Aunty Chris snorted with disgust when I related the sorry tale to her.

I was also introduced to one of the mysteries of the female

sex when I saw the unappealing sight of used sanitary towels at the back of the unlit fire, laid and awaiting a match, in the front-room grate. These we would poke and prod at with a stick, unrolling them and examining them for clues. We had no idea what they were or where the blood had come from; we just had an inkling that it was something 'rude'.

Apart from my debut as a sheep in St Joey's nativity play I made my first stage appearance in drag, at St Anselm's. The senior boys of the main college were putting on a Christmas show and the powers that be thought it would be a good idea if the Redcourt boys joined in the fun with one of their own. The vehicle chosen to display our varied talents was *Hiawatha*, based on Henry Wadsworth Longfellow's long-winded poem. It was a strange choice for an all-male cast as there were scenes that involved giving birth, but the Brothers obviously thought: Ah, *Hiawatha* – perfect for boys, lots of Red Indians and stuff.

I was picked to play Hiawatha's grandmother, old Nokomis. The parents were expected to provide the costumes for their offspring's part in this epic production and my mother spent weeks bent over a decrepit Singer sewing machine, cursing as she tried to run up a Red Indian outfit. It wasn't bad, either, by the time she'd finished: a pair of brown cotton trousers trimmed with yellow looped fringing and a matching waistcoat. To go over the trousers she'd made, as a nod towards Nokomis's sex, a sort of tabard on to which she'd sewn a selection of beads and buttons that she'd found at the bottom of the sewing tin. To complete the look she'd made a wig using grey wool threaded into a hairnet. I was beside myself.

We rehearsed every other day, prompted to learn our lines by the constant threat of the strap. The day before *Hiawatha* was due to open, it was decided that we'd better have a full dress rehearsal for the benefit of the teachers and senior boys of the main college.

*

The curtains slowly parted to reveal a group of Red Indians gathered nervously around a pile of sticks and scrunched-up newspaper to show that they were huddling around a camp-fire, chanting in a slow laborious monotone outside a ramshackle tepee. The full moon hung low and wobbly in the sky.

> 'Downward through the evening twilight
> In the days that are forgotten
> In the unremembered ages,
> From the full moon fell Nokomis,
> Fell the beautiful Nokomis . . .'

At this point I ran on to the stage from the wings in the style of Isadora Duncan, arms raised high above my head, hands flapping, mouth and eyes wide open to denote fear since, according to the text, old Nokomis 'fell affrighted' from this full moon of hers.

Some of the seniors started to snigger. There was even a wolf-whistle from the back, throwing the Indian chorus completely off their stride and causing the Brothers to unsettle the cast even further by loudly shushing and threatening the perpetrators. During this temporary hiatus in the proceedings, I thought I'd try a bit of improv, as they like to call it in comedy clubs. I felt I couldn't just stand there, I'd better do something, at least until the Indians got their act together.

I ran downstage throwing my hands to the sides of my face and giving them the old eyes and mouth 'fear routine' again. Nokomis was scared and confused – she'd just fallen to earth from the moon, for God's sake – and via movement and mime this was my interpretation of the poor woman's plight.

'I know, Edvard Munch's "The Scream",' one of the seniors shouted, to much hilarity. Arseholes, I thought to myself,

160

ignoring them and instead taking off round the stage like a mad thing, clutching my head and letting out a harrowing wail as I ran. It was exhilarating.

'Where am I?' I implored dramatically, now completely as one with the character of Nokomis. I knew this woman. I was this woman. 'What is this place?' I asked, arms outstretched.

'The doctor will see you now,' some wag from the sixth form called out.

'Good, cos I'm going to have a baby,' I snarled at the heckler, inciting a round of applause from the house. My first put-down; not a cracker, I'll admit, but OK by nine-year-old standards.

'In the moonlight and the starlight, Fair Nokomis bore a daughter,' the drama teacher hissed from the wings, desperate to snap the paralysed Indians out of their stupor and restore order. His hysterical voice carried to the back of the hall.

Mild hysteria broke out when, after retiring to the tepee, I gave birth to a bouncing baby daughter – literally, as the Tiny Tears doll that was playing the daughter was dropped by the nervous midwife assisting at the birth and, landing on her rubber head, bounced beautifully off the stage and fell at Brother Ennis's feet.

Then the makeshift tepee, a death trap constructed from two bedsheets and half a dozen garden canes, collapsed along with what little composure the audience had left. I lay in the wreckage unable to move, since the looped yellow fringing on my trousers was caught among the canes.

The Tiny Tears doll grew up to be a big strapping girl who in turn gave birth in the remains of the tepee to Hiawatha him-self, assisted by me. I had no choice in the matter since I was still entangled in the ruins. Powerless to free myself, I lay there and pretended to go to sleep. After all, I reckoned old Nokomis had had a bit of a day of it, what with falling from the moon, giving birth with no husband to support her and then seeing her daughter make the same silly mistake by dropping one herself. She was probably ready to call it a day.

The newly born Hiawatha danced around me in a chamois leather loincloth chanting his verse. The seniors were howling, the Brothers shook their heads and coughed. From my prone position I weighed up the situation. The show was a turkey. The audience were laughing so hard that it seemed the only way to salvage what was left was to play it for laughs. My cue came:

> 'Safely bound with reindeer sinews,
> Stilled his fretful wail by saying—'

I sat up abruptly, as if woken from a deep sleep, and after a hammy display of yawning and stretching absent-mindedly scratched my head, deliberately dislodging my wig so that it hung drunkenly over one eye as I delivered my line in the style of a deadpan Scouse housewife. '"Hush, the Naked Bear will hear you",' I drawled. An embryonic Lily Savage had briefly emerged.

It brought the roof in. Even the Brothers couldn't help smiling. I liked the buzz I was getting from making people laugh, and basked in the praise that was showered on me by the senior boys after the show.

'Where's that boy in the grey hat?' a big glamorous-looking senior asked, piling into the backstage changing area. 'He was really funny.' It wasn't a hat, it was a wig, I almost said but didn't, not wanting to spoil the moment.

Hiawatha never made it to opening night. Brother Ennis thought it best that we didn't go on in front of the parents and governors. He said we were under-rehearsed and the show was more than a little chaotic, a kinder way of saying that we stank. I was devastated, but with the resilience of youth quickly put the matter behind me.

'Next time those Brothers want you to wear a Red Indian

squaw's outfit,' my mother said, 'tell them to make it their bloody selves.'

The morning that my eleven-plus results fell through the letter box of Number 23 just happened to be the day of my sister's wedding. I'd failed, and even worse was being told that my next school would be the dreaded St Hugh's, a secondary modern on Park Road South that we at St Anselm's looked upon as the roughest place on earth and avoided even walking past on our way home.

My mother, who had been convinced that I'd passed, collapsed on to the sofa in floods of disappointed tears, knocking her carefully placed wedding hat to one side as she threw her hands up to her head. 'How could you?' she cried accusingly. 'How could you fail?' She went on to declare that she'd never be able to hold her head up in the street again. St Anselm's had kudos; St Hugh's, none.

For me, the world came to a crashing halt that morning. For a St Anselm's boy to be demoted to St Hugh's was tantamount to suicide in my book. I felt like Cain, cast out into the land of Nod. My brother and cousins had been educated there and told hair-raising accounts of bullying and brutality that made *Flashman* read like *Mary Poppins*. They were probably grossly exaggerated flights of fancy, those stories, but they were enough to strike terror into my eleven-year-old heart.

'If I have to go to the Yozzers,' I wailed, 'I'll kill meself.'

My sister appeared from upstairs, her hair wrapped in a chiffon scarf to protect the Doris Day bouffant she was sporting, set and combed out that morning by Pat of Birkenhead Market. 'D'ya mind not ruining my wedding day,' she pleaded tearfully. 'Dad, tell him, I'm getting married in a couple of hours and look at the state of me mother.' My father, as ever the mediator, calmed my sister down, tried to pacify my mother and consoled me with the promise that first thing

163

Monday morning he would personally go down to the Education Board and get me transferred to another school.

The bride's mother's tears of despair had turned to hot ones of anger. 'I bet you all those Cheshire boys have passed, and let's face it, they're a lot thicker than you,' she ranted, referring to her suspicion that the boys from Cheshire got preferential treatment. Throughout my last year it seemed as though all the boys who lived there were periodically swept away to a class-room and in private sat an exam in preparation for the eleven-plus. This happened quite frequently, and the boys who sat these tests never discussed them with the rest of us. My mother was very suspicious about this and got it into her head that they were being groomed to go on to greater things.

Four boys below me in class position who happened to live in Cheshire had passed the eleven-plus. Two of these boys seemed as dense as a Victorian pea-souper and the others couldn't pass water without supervision. My mother was furi-ous. How could these boys pass the exam when her darling son (who, apart from being a little slow at maths, was smart as a whip) had failed? All the evidence she needed was there.

I hear that these days St Anselm's, Redcourt, is up there with the best and is run on entirely different lines from the hellhouse of my day, the Christian Brothers' reign of terror long over. I hope so, for the kids' sake.

CHAPTER TEN

MY DAD WAS AS GOOD AS HIS WORD AND DID INDEED HAVE a word with the chaps down at the Education Department. Instead of starting the autumn term at St Hugh's, I was to go to Blessed Edmund Campion, in Claughton Village. I felt as if I'd had a last-minute reprieve from the electric chair. My mother didn't care if I was starting at St Trinian's. Her dreams of a college education for me had been dashed and in her pessimistic state of mind it was all downhill from here.

My dad was also bitterly disappointed that I'd not got into St Anselm's main college, but he took a more philosophical view of the matter, accepting that maybe it hadn't been such a good idea to take me out of a school where I'd been performing well and put me in one where I failed to thrive. It was my dad who escorted me on my first day at 'Blessed Eddy's'. My ma still had the hump, and apart from getting another Provident cheque out to buy me a school uniform in the regulation green and black showed little enthusiasm for my new start. The horror of standing in the middle of a packed playground with my dad in tow wearing his best Gannex mac, surrounded by scowling lads who were each and every one of them in a pair of long trousers and sniggering at my short ones, makes me squirm with embarrassment to this day.

*

Most of the pupils at Blessed Edmund Campion came from the North End of Birkenhead. The North End was a tough, predominantly working-class area, at its epicentre a huge circular block of flats known as Ilchester Square, standing at the junction of Laird Street and Corporation Road like a great fortress. Ilchester Square was notorious. It was a powder keg that could explode at a moment's notice; its reputation for violence was legendary, and it was definitely a no-go area for non-residents. Even the police were wary about going near Ilchester on their own and usually turned up in a pack of half a dozen when a visit was required. They hadn't forgotten Bonfire Night, when a fire engine had been turned over by an angry mob baying for blood as the crew attempted to extinguish the enormous blaze roaring dangerously in the middle of the square.

The pub round the side of the block was appropriately named the Blood Tub, and every Saturday night rivers of the stuff poured from battered noses and broken teeth as yet another barney kicked off. Ilchester Square and the mean streets that lay in its shadow was Birkenhead's very own version of Hell's Kitchen. Prostitutes hung around on Corporation Road hoping for a lucky strike with a sailor or a docker who would appreciate a 'ten-bob gobble', the proceeds of which would be spent in the Crown and Cushion on Market Street. I saw a couple falling out of the door steaming drunk one Saturday afternoon, assisted by a poker-thin queen with plucked eyebrows and long fingernails. The women looked like the pair of noisy, motheaten old parrots that sat hunched on perches behind the door of Wirral Pets as they staggered, squawking at each other, down Market Street in killer white stiletto heels that even I could recognize as unsuitable footwear for women of their age and inebriated condition.

My mother shook her head and made a tutting noise as she watched the pair of ageing brasses ricochet from lamp post to wall. 'Keep away from strong drink and women like that,' she said disapprovingly, grabbing my arm and marching me in the direction of the number 60 bus stop. To paraphrase Tallulah Bankhead, she never said a thing about drugs and men.

Corpo Road working girls were nothing like the whores of legend, no golden-hearted tarts ready to ruffle a child's hair with a friendly word before slipping him a couple of pennies for sweets. On the contrary, these women would tell us to 'eff off' if we so much as glanced at them. We used to run past them on the other side of the road and call out 'PROZZIE!' at the top of our lungs, whereupon the 'prozzie' on the opposite pavement would let rip with a stream of invective that would've had the congregation of St Werburgh's dropping dead with shock but made us scream with laughter.

At first I was ridiculed at Blessed Eddy's for wearing short trousers, and laughed at and bullied for sounding 'posh'. Hard to believe now, I know, but back then St Anselm's had weeded out most of my Scouse twang and left me with near-perfect vowels. I was also polite, obedient, compliant and passive – not great selling points in a class full of hyperviolent thugs – and if I was to survive and be accepted I had to undergo a few major changes. I began to wonder if getting a transfer from St Hugh's was a good idea after all. It certainly couldn't have been any worse than Blessed Eddy's, where most of the boys were aggressive and confrontational. Fights broke out daily in the playground; the queue for the bus after school was a bloodbath; and bullies lurked round every corner to steal your dinner money or beat you up. Small fry compared to the guns and knives of today's sink schools, I know, but terrifying at the time.

I hated Blessed Edmund Campion, hated everything about it, and became quiet and withdrawn, retreating to my bedroom after school where I would lie on the bed in the dark, picking at the wallpaper and 'worrying'.

Eventually I ceased to worry and began to make friends. There was a boy in the class who made my life and a few of the other kids' lives hell. He had foetal alcohol syndrome written all over his unlovely face and was a relentless bully. I scored major Brownie points on the day when I eventually snapped and retaliated. He'd stuck a compass in the back of my leg, and I turned on him and punched him so hard in the face that he lost his balance and fell down the stairs. I was given two strokes of the cane for that, but it was worth it.

Then there was the time I scored the winning goal, which gave me, albeit only until my classmates realized that it was a never to be repeated, once in fifty million stroke of luck, the status of footballing god, up there with Bobby Charlton. God knows how it happened. I'd been hanging around the edge of the frozen pitch as usual, trying to look like an eager and enthusiastic team player who had a clever tactical reason for standing so far away from where the action was, when suddenly the 'action' started to come towards me at terrifying speed. Before I knew it I'd lashed out haphazardly with my foot and kicked the ball straight into the goal, thus winning the game. A big handsome lad in the year above me, with curly hair and beefy thighs, whom I'd always been shy of rushed towards me, flung his arms round me and kissed me on the neck. An emotion which had up till then lain dormant and unexplored came to life at his touch. 'I fuckin' love ya,' he shouted, and kissing me hard on the mouth squeezed the cheek of my arse at the same time. My legs turned to jelly and I went limp in his arms like a silent movie heroine – which was unfortunate really as just as I was getting into this malarkey he dropped me and ran on, cheering and waving his arms above his head, leaving me flat on my back on the frozen mud wearing a glazed expression while a flock of Disney bluebirds twittered gaily in a circle around my head.

The gods looked down upon me kindly that day, for even

after he'd cottoned on that my dazzling goal was a pure fluke we became friends. He was taller than me; puberty had come early to him and he looked a lot older than twelve. The word that springs to mind as I try to describe him is 'thrilling', and indeed he was. He was tough, yet not a bully. He was also confident and smart and he taught me how to ride a bike. I'd never met anyone like him before – the boys of St Anselm's were piss-elegant mummy's boys, but he was a different breed altogether, with a touch of the feral about him, raw and exciting. We'd sit in the park after school and have long necking sessions on a secluded bench. 'Pull the hood of your duffel coat up,' he said, 'so if anyone passes they'll think you're a girl.'

There was nothing 'homo' in these lip-locking sessions, we'd reassure ourselves. Homos were old and hung around the men's lavs at Woodside Ferry. This was a different kettle of fish entirely – this was in the name of research. We were plainly and simply practising our kissing technique in preparation for the great day when we actually got to do it with a girl. And so each afternoon we'd sit locked in a passionate embrace, the youngest lovers in Mersey Park, enthusiastically experimenting with our chosen after-school activity, perfecting our skills until reluctantly we went our separate ways home for tea. We never got beyond kissing – in our innocence neither of us really considered it – and we carried on necking in the park until we gradually grew out of it, finding other after-school games to play, pretending that our liaison had never happened. But neither of us was ever quite the same again, and we became awkward and embarrassed in each other's company.

After that I gave up on men. Disillusioned and on the scrap heap at twelve. Never mind, there was always the telly for consolation. Like every other kid, I lived for television. John Steed had yet another new Avenger Girl at his side in the form of Tara King. At first I resented her for daring to try to fill the goddess Emma Peel's leather boots, but slowly and surely she grew on me until I found myself smitten by this auburn-haired beauty. I stuck pictures of her all over my bedroom wall, wrote her name in large letters with black felt-tip pen on my haversack, proclaiming to the world my love for this creature, her of the cold green feline eyes, voluptuous figure and quirky nature. This Amazon who could throw men over her shoulder without compromising her femininity, who drove a scarlet Lotus Europa Mark II and lived in an enormous flat in Primrose Hill that was decorated in shades of mustard, pink and green and filled with fascinating artefacts such as a penny-farthing bike hanging over her fireplace. There could be no other. There wasn't anyone to compare with the Canadian actress called Linda Thorson who played Tara King. I was hooked, and so began the start of a long love affair.

I'd fantasize on the bus on my way to school about working for the secret service and living in London, somewhere smart, probably around Regent's Park or Piccadilly Circus, I thought, in a flat not dissimilar on the inside to Tara's. I'd drive a Lotus down Portland Place, Tara at my side, and after a night at the theatre we'd drink champagne in a glamorous West End restaurant before ending up in a very smart nightclub that had an up-tempo jazz combo playing something on bongos in the corner and a girl in a French maid's outfit selling cigarettes from a tray hanging round her neck like an usherette's. This was one of the many scenarios I'd cook up in my mind as I sat on the back of the bus from Borough Road to Claughton Village, staring out of the window, absently sucking on a pear drop, on my way to school. Be careful what you wish for. My ma was saying that to me long before it became fashionable and, witch that she was, proved to be right.

I've since sat with Linda Thorson many times in the Wolseley Restaurant on Piccadilly, drinking the odd drop or two of champagne before going on to a club – no bongos in the corner or chic cigarette girl, unfortunately, just a DJ and a drag queen collecting glasses. I haven't driven in a Lotus with her down Portland Place, but we've sat in the back of a black cab on the way to the theatre. I didn't end up living in Regent's Park or Piccadilly, nor am I a secret agent (give me time), but I've got a penny-farthing bike hanging on the wall in my London flat. However, all this comes much, much later.

One of my other passions was Batman, me and every other kid in the world who had access to a TV set. There wasn't a kid to be seen on the streets of Birkenhead of a Saturday and Sunday evening. We were all glued to the telly watching Batman. It was nothing like the dark and moody Batman of today: this was the campy Adam West sixties serial that had every kid in the UK addicted.

A boy in school jumped out of his bedroom window, wearing his duffel coat, fastened with one button round his neck as a substitute cloak worthy of the caped crusader, a balaclava and a pair of wellies, and broke both legs when he hit the kitchen roof. Our gang didn't go quite that far but we'd play Batman enthusiastically in the playground every break time, taking it in turns to be the various villains. I was never Batman or Robin. They held no attraction for me; I thought they were ridiculous. They were so self-righteous and boring that they made me want to turn to crime. I much preferred to be either the Joker, Penguin or Catwoman – far more interesting. The game usually ended in a glorious punch-up accompanied by a soundtrack of *Wham*s, *Kapp-ow*s and *Kerrunch*es.

I was fitting in nicely at Blessed Eddy's. I was still paranoid about my school work, believing that I was stupid and unable to learn, a legacy from the Christian Brothers. I gave it my all that first year at school. I revised for the exams every night in bed; on a Saturday morning I'd be found in the reference library hoping that I looked learned and intelligent, a student perhaps, as I sat at one of the highly polished tables, surrounded by books, tapping my teeth with a pencil and listening to the silence. I came top of the class that term. Having been used to hovering near the bottom at St Anselm's, I couldn't believe it. I thought they'd made a mistake. At lunchtime I ran to the phone box in Claughton Village and rang home.

'Barkenhid six height dabble tu,' my mother answered in her telephone voice.

'Guess what?' I shouted excitedly down the phone.

'You better hadn't be in trouble, my lad. What are you doing on a phone in the middle of the day? I hope you watched yourself crossing that road. They come down that hill at ninety miles an hour, bloody lunatics they are. A woman I talk to on the half-ten bus said her sister went six foot in the air and turned a somersault when she got hit by a bloody lunatic on a motorbike on that sharp corner by the pet shop . . .'

The pips started to go. I rooted in my pocket for a coin and put it in as she carried on regardless.

'She was in the General for ten months on traction, poor thing. Got one leg longer than the other now, according to the sister; has to wear a built-up shoe . . . was that the pips? Where are you getting the money from to be making phone calls?'

'I came first in class,' I shouted, seizing my chance when there was a slight pause in her diatribe. 'First!'

'Oh. Well done,' she said flatly.

'Did you hear me? I said I came first in class.'

'Well, let's be honest,' she said after a moment, 'it wouldn't be hard to come first in a class full of idiots, would it? Half of them can't even write their own name. Thick as two short planks . . .' Her voice tailed off and she sighed dramatically. 'I suppose it's better than coming last,' she said, 'but it's a shame that you couldn't manage to come first at St Anselm's. You'd be at college now instead of that sh— oh, well.'

Talk about a slap in the face. A kingsize, razor-pointed hat-pin to deflate the balloon of exultation and bring me crashing back down to earth. My dad was more enthusiastic. 'Well done you,' he said as he read out some of the more glowing remarks. 'Listen to this, Molly,' he shouted to my mother who was laying the table for tea in the next room. "English. If he keeps this up I hold out great hope for a successful CSE result." And this . . . "Art – excellent. Religion – a studious pupil. French – shows great promise." '

'Maths,' my mother chipped in from the middle room, ' "Needs to work much harder. Does not apply himself." He'll never get anywhere in life without maths. Never mind art, religion or French. What good's that to you unless you're going to become a French monk who likes drawing bloody cartoons.'

I couldn't win. There was always something for her to find fault with. Meanwhile, I was changing, physically and mentally. I would soon be thirteen. My nancy-boy posh voice had lowered quite a few octaves and my vowels had become pure Ilchester Square, causing my ma to create blue murder every time I opened my mouth.

'All that money wasted on bloody elocution lessons,' she'd say, referring to Lulu's classes from the glory days when she'd had a St Anselm's boy as a son instead of the North End wacker she was currently emptying a bag of frozen crinkle-cut chips into the chip pan for. 'Just because everyone else in that school is common as muck doesn't mean that you have to act and speak the same,' she'd add angrily, shaking the basket of chips furiously in the bubbling oil, as if it was every last common-as-muck North-Ender in the school that she was frying.

That summer I went to Ireland with my dad to stay at the farm for a couple of weeks. My mother preferred to stay at home as she claimed that it was a good opportunity for her to scrub the house from top to bottom with my dad and particularly me out of her way.

There had been changes at the farm. The house at last boasted a bathroom and toilet, and an extension with two further bedrooms had been built on at the back. My cousin Mickey had three children now, so I shared a sofa bed with my dad in the parlour, not a comfortable experience. Not only was the sofa bed as old as time, but it provided nightly accommodation not just for me and my dad but also for a nest of mice somewhere in among the ancient springs and horsehair.

As well as working on the farm, Mickey was a nurse at Castlerea psychiatric hospital, and when it was time to cut the turf or mow the fields patients who were considered harmless would be released to help, in return for a good wage and plenty of food. When I got up the first morning my dad was already up and out. To get to the new bathroom I had to cross the kitchen, where the temporary labourers from Castlerea asylum sat in a line at the long wooden table eating their breakfast. Every eye followed me as I hurriedly crossed the floor in jeans and a shirt of my dad's. They sat in silence, chewing their bacon, until eventually one of them spoke. 'Jesus, isn't she a little young for him?' he said, nodding towards my dad, who had just entered the room. They thought I was a girl. I stared at myself in the bathroom mirror. I had thick wavy auburn hair and long eyelashes, and was slim and pretty. I was horrified at the realization that I had been mistaken for a girl. I'd sprouted a couple of pubic hairs but that wasn't enough. I wanted to shave. My face was as smooth as a baby's: I had the complexion of a milkmaid.

Oh, dear God, let me sprout hairs on my face and all over my chest, and while you're at it the pubic area could do with being a little more hirsute. It's far too sparse at the moment. Let thick brown hair (not ginger, please God not ginger) sprout all over my body. Amen.

When we got home my mother had decorated my bedroom. One wall was a putrid shade of mustard, another bright red. The door was turquoise gloss, the skirting boards and ceiling bright yellow. She'd hand-dyed the carpet a vivid red and had made curtains and a bedspread from the most lurid floral print that Birkenhead Market had to offer. I was speechless. It was a nightmare. What had possessed her to do this? Was she going crazy? Losing the plot?

'You're always banging on about that one from *The Avengers* and how marvellous her flat is, so I've decorated your bedroom like it. What d'ya think?' She stood back, admiring her handiwork. 'I think it's hideous myself, but I thought you deserved a treat for coming top of the class, so there it is.'

I'll say one thing for my mother: she certainly kept you on your toes. She was as unpredictable as the weather and contrary as a rich woman's cat. I was touched by her attempt to recreate Tara King's apartment in a room as tiny as my bedroom and gradually got over the shock of the psychedelic colours. Eventually I grew to like it. It stayed like that until she died.

CHAPTER ELEVEN

'NOT YET, HANG ON . . . NEARLY . . . QUICK! COME ON, NO, get back, get back I said . . . Now! Come on! Quick, don't dawdle. Jesus tonight, hurry up, there's a bloody big van coming.' My mother was paranoid about crossing roads. She'd grab the arm of whoever she was with in a vicelike grip and hurl herself and her prey across the road at the speed of light, but not before a prolonged and tense period perched on the edge of the kerb, her worried eyes scanning the length of the road, until she eventually decreed that the coast was clear for the moment and the road just about safe enough to cross.

'For Christ's sake, Mam,' I snapped, trying to shake her hand free from my elbow as we attempted to negotiate Old Chester Road. 'Mind me jacket, you're creasing it.'

'I'll put a crease in your lip in a minute,' she said, pulling me up outside Mrs Cunningham's chip shop. 'Taking the Lord's name in vain in the street. You want to get yourself down to confession, you heathen.'

Mrs Cunningham's sister appeared in the window with a tray of fish cakes and gave us a cheery wave. My mother quickly turned from hellfire and brimstone to gracious lady and beamed back at her through the glass. The window had net curtains that were pulled shut when the shop was closed. On the glass in lead lettering was blazoned 'Cunningham's Fish and Chips. Quality First – Civility Always'. Mrs Cunny's fish and chips were the best in Birkenhead . . . no, the world. People came from miles around to sample her peppery fish cakes, savour her chicken snacks and salivate at the sight and smell of a mountain of freshly cooked chips, deep-fried in dripping, surrounding a piece of fresh cod smothered in a crisp golden batter that melted in your mouth after you'd taken the first glorious, crunchy bite. There was usually a long queue so you had to get there early. Mrs Cunny was one of my favourite people. She had a sly, shy smile and she would chuckle privately to herself as she wrapped the fish and chips up in the newspaper and listened to the chatter of the customers waiting in the queue. 'The usual, love?' she asked my mother, leaning slightly across the counter, all smiles in a clean white blouse. 'And how are you, trouble?' she said to me. 'Still on the altar?' My mother gave a nervous laugh and, with the air of a woman who had suffered, declared that I had given up serving at mass as I was thinking of joining the marine cadets. 'And why not?' said Mrs Cunny, laughing and throwing me another sly wink. 'It'll put hairs on his chest.' Exactly what I was looking for, plus some on the face. Thank you, Mrs Cunny, O wise woman of Old Chester Road.

Mrs Cunny was extremely wise. She didn't trade in idle gossip and was, as the sign said on the window, always civil to her customers. She expected and got the same in return. She'd run the chip shop with her husband during the war and after his death took it over herself with a little help from her two sisters. Sometimes the mask would slip and she'd snap at the elder sister who was, to use the parlance of the day, a bit slow. This sister would drag an enamel bucket into the shop from the kitchen at the back and proceed to chip the potatoes in a contraption at the end of the counter. She put the spud in, pulled the lever and hey presto! The spud became chips and joined the others in the white enamel bucket underneath. If you weren't careful you could catch a finger in this machine and chip it along with the spud. The slow sister would chat to the customers from behind the counter as she chipped away, so Mrs Cunny always had one eye on her to see that she didn't lose a couple of fingers. There were plenty of near misses. No wonder Mrs Cunny was jumpy when her sister became animated and lost concentration. 'For God's sake, Jeanie, leave that alone and have a look at those peas.'

Mrs Cunny rose every morning at four thirty to go to the fish market. She always did the job herself, picking out the freshest fish with a professional's eye. She was a supreme mistress of her craft. I've tasted plenty of perfectly good fish and chips since but nothing holds a candle to the magic Mrs Cunny could weave over a piece of cod and a King Edward.

Much to my parents' disappointment, my run on the altar of St Joseph's Church had been a short one.

My old pal from St Joseph's School, Franny Mooney, suddenly turned up in class one day. His peripatetic parents had settled in the North End and Franny had been transferred to Blessed Eddy's. He hadn't changed much, still small and slight with bright ginger hair, an irresistible target for bullies. Franny was resilient, though; he knew how to bob and weave with the blows. Ever resourceful, he had a lucrative sideline as an altar boy.

According to Franny, funerals were the biggest money-spinners. A family bereft was inclined to tip the urchin with the mournful face who stood so beautifully at the graveside of the recently departed more than handsomely. 'And if you can make yaself cry, then they'll have a whip-round for you, make a bleedin' fortune,' Franny added gleefully, rubbing his hands and praying that a plague would strike Birkenhead and wipe out half the Catholic population, providing him with lots of profitable employment.

When funerals and weddings were thin on the ground Franny bragged that he would help himself to a couple of quid from the collection plate. I couldn't do that. I was cursed with a conscience and would've been terrified of reprisals from the Almighty. Not so Franny. The flames of hell obviously held no fear for him. Money for sweets was his top priority and so each Sunday he cheerfully relieved the collection plate of a pound or so, treating it as a legitimate payment for services rendered.

Apart from cleaning up in the way of tips, the other incentive luring me towards joining the altar boys was the shoes they wore. They were made of shiny black patent leather and peeked out from underneath the boys' scarlet tunics as they moved in a slow and dignified manner about the altar. I thought those shoes were the last word in elegance and couldn't wait to get myself kitted out in full altar-boy drag, complete with a pair of the shiniest patent leather shoes ever seen in the diocese, and strut my stuff on a Sunday morning.

I duly delivered myself to the priest's house, attached to the side of the church, for Father Doyle's inspection.

'Serving holy mass is a sacred act,' that good man said. 'You must take time to learn what is expected of you and then perform those duties with humility, devotion and profound reverence.' Providing I got the shoes I'd be happy to lie prostrate on the altar steps wearing a hair vest. I bowed my head respectfully, trying to look like a perfect candidate for the post. After all, he took Franny on, didn't he?

I was handed over to the senior altar server for instruction. He was a religious zealot in his late forties whose one ambition in life had been to become a priest. This had eluded him for one reason or another, and the realization that it was now too late to fulfil his dream had left him more than a little bitter. He didn't want any new kids on his block and made his feelings loud and clear. 'You do nothing,' he hissed. 'You understand? You stay kneeling at the side of the altar throughout the mass and do fuck all. D'ya hear me, you little bollocks?' I was shocked to hear a man of God using such language. No one in our family, apart from Aunty Chris and then only when she was pushed to the limit, said fuck. Plenty of fecks, but no fucks.

The Almighty was obviously shocked as well, because the senior server was struck down as he was coming out of the Beehive pub one Saturday afternoon and broke his arm. That's how I got to swing the thurible, that fascinating, ornate receptacle, straight out of the Arabian nights, that was used to burn the incense. The SS was in plaster and could hardly move his arm. He also had a black eye and a cut on his balding head, but being a member of that group of eternal martyrs he couldn't stay at home quietly and recover but preferred to carry on and let people see how unselfishly he ignored his suffering for the love of his God. I hated him. 'I wish he was dead,' I'd moan to my mother.

'Beware,' she would answer in her prophet-of-doom voice. 'Curses like chickens come home to roost.'

In spite of the SS I liked being on the altar. I enjoyed the ceremony and the elaborate and mystifying preparations that took place before communion, when the thin white wafers magically underwent something called transubstantiation and became the actual body of Christ, while the red wine that we surreptitiously took swigs of in the vestry was transformed into his blood. But most of all I loved those patent leather shoes, polished lovingly with milk before each appearance. My mother couldn't understand why my black school shoes wouldn't do for the job but after a lot of pressure and plead-ing from me she finally gave in and courtesy of the Provident Cheque Company bought me a pair. They came with a warn-ing. 'If I find after shelling out thirty bob for a pair of bloody shoes that you suddenly decide to pack it up like you did the Cubs, then you are in big trouble, mate.'

I'd joined the Cubs when I was nine but didn't manage to

last the month. I hadn't wanted to be a Cub in the first place, but my mother wanted me to and so off I went. I was bored tying knots and competing for badges that involved lighting a fire with two sticks. What was the point when women down the years had lost half their jawbones from phosphorus poisoning working as match girls at Bryant and May's, just to provide us with a far more convenient way to start a forest fire if we so chose? The Scout movement was also a wee bit jolly for me, all that dib-dib-dobbing and calling grown men Bagheera or Akela. It had a sinister whiff to it, and as far as I was concerned I couldn't wait to hand in my woggle and get the hell out of it before some bright spark suggested camping in North Wales.

All went well for a while. I'd been on the altar for nearly six weeks. I'd dutifully turned up for the Sunday masses, was a picture of holiness and had even been entrusted with the task of holding the small silver tray under the punters' mouths as the priest gave them their communion. Rotten teeth, no teeth, foul breath, brown tongues, cold sores, nose hair with globules of snot attached, you saw it all at that altar rail, and when I wasn't suppressing the urge to retch I was usually trying not to laugh at the expressions of exaggerated piety on the faces of some of the congregation.

Even my mother was beginning to believe that this was something I just might stick at. She became so confident of my continued success that she took to mentioning it whenever she found herself in Eileen Henshaw's.

'I'll take six rashers of back, please,' she'd say politely, pointing at the bacon. 'But not that top slice, it looks a bit . . . tired.'

'Aren't we all?' Eileen shrugged, peeling the bacon off the tray and on to the scales.

'Not our Paul.' My mother seized her chance. 'He was serving at six o'clock mass this morning, bright as a button. Father Doyle is so impressed with him that he's considering him for the priesthood.' A blatant lie and she knew it, for in reality, deep down in the back of Father Doyle's mind, there was already a little niggling idea that his judgement might have been slightly impaired the day he took me on.

'A priest!' Eileen couldn't have been more shocked if my mother had said I was joining the Jackson Five. 'I wouldn't fancy my son growing up to be a priest, creepy bloody things.'

'I shouldn't think there'll be much danger of that, Eileen – he'll grow up to be just like his father, an atheist who boils hams. Oh and by the way, I'd chuck them King Eddies out if I were you, they've got more eyes than a spider.'

Yes, all went well until the night a film called *Gypsy* was shown on TV. It's a musical starring Natalie Wood and Rosalind Russell and portrays a highly fictionalized account of the life of Gypsy Rose Lee, the world's foremost striptease artist, and how she rose from an ugly duckling to be the Queen of Burlesque. I'd never seen anything like the characters in the burlesque house scenes: the bugle-blowing stripper with a voice like gravel and the faded blonde and her bump-and-grind 'butterfly ballet'; the boozy pit band playing its raucous, brassy and dirty music while above their heads on the illuminated runway of joy the elegant Gypsy shed her clothing. My first whiff of burlesque was a heady one and made me seriously giddy – I couldn't get the music out of my mind and had taken to standing on the upstairs landing practising my bumping and grinding. I'd been shown a glimpse of a world that I secretly longed to be part of: backstage dressing rooms, touring, performing, fame and noto- riety; an intoxicating and seductive mix. There was the added bonus that you didn't need to have any talent to succeed in showbiz. All you really needed was a gimmick.

The next morning found me serving at ten o'clock mass to a packed house. I was no longer standing in the vestry waiting to form part of a solemn procession behind Franny Mooney, the

SS and Father Doyle. No, in my mind's eye I was backstage at Minsky's Burlesque, about to make a spectacular entrance, when I would step out on to the runway and shed my cassock bathed in the light of a surprise pink spot. The organist played 'Oh come loud anthems let us sing' but all I could hear was the wah-wah mute of the cornet and the rhythmic throb of the tom-tom.

Father Doyle and his troop filed diligently on to the altar. I held back for a few moments, delaying my entrance, and then sashayed out, smiling up to the gallery. My dad, who was sitting in the third pew from the front, shifted uneasily in his seat. I took my position on the altar step and slowly knelt down, making sure that I executed a perfect stripper's dip as I descended.

The SS glared at me from the other side of the altar. I flashed him an angelic smile; didn't he realize that he was witnessing the debut of Birkenhead's very own Queen of Burlesque? I managed to resist the lure of the brass section blaring in my ear and retain a dignified composure for as long as I knelt on the steps. It wasn't until it was time to swing my thurible that I really lost it. I rose slowly to walk down the three steps to collect the censer, pausing slightly at the top before bending my knee and raising my cassock ever so slightly to reveal a well-turned ankle and a patent leather shoe. The crowd fell to their knees as I slowly made my descent, swaying slightly in time to the music in my ears. Picking up the thurible, I started to swing it from side to side, slowly at first, the smoke from the smouldering incense curling sensuously around my legs. Then, as the drummer in my head picked up the beat, I swung it faster, twisting my hips with the merest hint of a grind. The crowd were going wild! The band really cooking with gas! Listen to those horns! That drummer! I slowly turned and made my way back up the stairs. At the top, I gently let the censer chain slip from my hand, lowering my right shoulder and looking over it to give the audience an enigmatic smile to show that my performance had come to its tumultuous climax! The applause was deafening. They were tearing the place apart! The band struck up the reprise, the horns blaring. My God, I'm a Star!

Father Doyle, chalice in hand, coughed as he passed me on the altar steps, interrupting my reverie. 'When you're ready,' he said under his breath, peering at me over his glasses in a very strange way. 'Communion.'

Afterwards in the vestry the SS let rip. 'What the bloody hell do you think you're up to? Mincing around the altar like a dirty great nancy boy. I've been watching you lately. Your mind's everywhere but on your duties. If you don't want to serve the Lord then fuck off.'

Philistine, I thought to myself. He'll see one day.

My days at St Joseph's were numbered. The straw that finally broke the camel's back came when Franny and I had an uncontrollable and prolonged fit of the giggles during a funeral service. Father Doyle was furious, as were the bereaved's nearest and dearest, who didn't leave a tip. We were told to quit the service of the Church and to contemplate our wicked sins, and only to return when we were truly repentant and thought that we might, just might, be able to show a bit of decorum at a graveside instead of behaving like a pair of hysterical hyenas. We never went back. The patent leather shoes were relegated to the cupboard under the stairs, to cries of 'Never again will I waste another shilling on your little fads' from my mother.

School became boring. Apart from the hated maths, I found the lessons easy. No point going in, I thought to myself one morning while I was waiting for the bus, I fancy a day out in the country. So I jumped the bus to Heswall and spent a pleasant day exploring the country lanes. This was better than sitting in a miserable classroom. It was also exhilarating – I was doing something forbidden. Kids who sagged classes could be expelled or caned in front of the entire school at assembly. There was the added risk of getting caught by the school board or someone who knew your parents. It was all very exciting. The world was my oyster; I could go anywhere I wanted to (dinner money permitting), and I did. I explored all over the Wirral, taking the bus to my destination of choice and then walking home. I must have walked miles. It might have been interesting, but it was also exhausting.

Notes from my parents explaining my absenteeism were easy to forge. They were always the same, written in a fairly decent facsimile of my ma's handwriting:

Dear sir,
 I'm sorry Paul was not at school yesterday but he was bilious again.
 Yours faithfully,
 M. O'Grady (Mrs).

I did have intermittent trouble with my stomach so I didn't feel bad about this lie. Soon I was hardly ever at school. I was roaming the streets of Birkenhead instead, as bored now as I ever was in class. Sitting for the umpteenth time in a bus shelter in Heswall on a rainy February morning, cold, hungry and bored out of my mind, I came to the conclusion that it was time to call my career as a truant a day and get myself back to school. If nothing else there were kids my own age to talk to, and it was warm.

'Oh, Mr O'Grady, nice of you to join us,' Mr Broad the PE teacher shouted across the class as he called out the register. 'It's been so long since we last saw you. My, how you've grown. Why, I hardly recognized you. Class, in case you've forgotten, that strange boy at the back is Paul O'Grady.' Huge burst of merriment around the room.

186

Sarcastic bastard, I thought, my face burning with embarrassment. If I had been genuinely ill he'd no right to take the piss, and if he thought he was so bloody smart then how come he never twigged that I'd been sagging? Berk.

'I'm going into hospital next week,' Franny piped up next to me. 'I'm having me tonsils out,' he went on proudly. 'Aunty Kath's bought me a pair of pyjamas and me mam's got me a sponge bag to put me bits in, and I get to eat loads of ice cream.'

I wanted a sponge bag to put me bits in. I wanted to go into hospital. I wa— Suddenly, as in every good Daffy Duck cartoon when the duck hatches a plan or thinks of a brilliant idea, a light bulb came on over my head. That was it! I'd invent an illness and be taken off to St Cath's Hospital and be spoilt rotten. I could get myself into the bed next to Franny's.

There was another reason why I could do with a spell in hospital just then, and that was because my dad had received a letter from the Board of Education enquiring why his son had been absent from school for the best part of the term. The proverbial shit was hitting the fan. My dad had to go down to the education office and explain himself. 'I'll see you tonight,' he had said ominously as he left for work that morning, 'and you better have some answers.' I had to move quickly.

Franny had duly been carted off to St Cath's Hospital, complete with new sponge bag, to have his tonsils removed, and so sensing that there was no time like the present I went into school and dramatically fainted in assembly. I was carried outside and taken into the school secretary's office, just as I'd planned. All sick kids ended up in Miss Savage's office. She was a kindly soul, and because of her name I felt that I had a connection with her. Miss Savage ran off to get me some water and I seized my chance. I quickly took the register for my class from her desk and shoved it down the back of the radiator. There, that was the evidence, the only proof that I hadn't attended class, disposed of. The notion that there might be corresponding records down at the Board of Education hadn't crossed my mind. My degree in low cunning was actually just a low-grade CSE.

'Where's the pain?' a teacher asked.

'Here,' I responded wanly, and pointed to my stomach. Actually my guts were bad that day so there wasn't much acting required when the teacher prodded my side with his finger. 'Does that hurt?'

'OW.' To tell the truth it did, but then that area was usually tender.

An ambulance was called and I was rushed to hospital, causing a minor sensation around the school. However, instead of being delivered to St Cath's and Franny I was taken to Birkenhead General. My plan was starting to come apart at the seams. 'It's the wrong hospital,' I kept telling the ambulance driver.

My mother was telephoned at her work. She was currently putting tops on washing-up bottles at Lever's in Port Sunlight and was not amused at being called to the hospital.

'If this is one of your games,' she said, dropping her handbag angrily on to the counterpane and taking her headscarf off, 'I'll swing for you.' She eyed me suspiciously as I sat in the bed propped up on pillows reading a comic, the picture of glowing health. 'You were fine when you left the house this morning, so what is it exactly that is supposed to be up with you? You don't fool me. I can read you like a tuppenny novel.' The thing was, she could. 'So go on, what in hell is supposed to be up with you?' Jesus, she'd have given them a run for their money in the Spanish Inquisition. I was spared further grilling by the arrival of a doctor.

'Hello,' he said cheerfully. 'Are you the boy's mother?'

'Unfortunately,' she answered, through clenched teeth.

'I'm just going to examine him,' he said, popping on

a rubber glove, and with that he stuck his hand up my bum.

I shot up the bed like a scalded cat and screamed the ward down. The attempted suicide in the screened-off bed next to me roused momentarily from his sleeping-pill-induced coma and groaned.

'Tsk, tsk,' my mother said, 'such a fuss.'

'Count yourself lucky,' the doctor said, retrieving his hand. 'He's about to have his stomach pumped, next door.' He took my mother outside the ward for a private chat, and when they returned a few minutes later her face was grim. The doctor sat on the bed. 'Now, young man,' he said, folding his hands in his lap, 'I've examined you and you have an inflamed appendix, so we're going to pop you up to theatre and whip it out, OK?'

No it's not bloody OK, I wanted to scream. You've made a big mistake. There's nothing wrong with me. I only wanted to come in for a few days' observation and be with Franny and have ice cream and a sponge bag, and now I'm going to be cut open.

'There's no need to worry,' he said, getting up to leave and patting my head. 'It's just a little operation.'

My mother couldn't quite accept that I actually was ill. She still had a nagging doubt in the back of her mind that the pieces didn't quite fit, and that somewhere in this saga was something vital that she'd missed. She took her coat off and pulled a chair up next to the bed. 'Well, if you were putting it on, love,' she said kindly, as if reading my mind, 'it's backfired. But there's no use crying over spilt milk as it turns out you really have got appendicitis after all, and it's better out than in. That explains those stomach pains in the Isle of Man. I must go and ring our Annie.'

Turned out that the appendix was just about to burst. I ended up in hospital for over a month as I caught a serious infection in the wound which meant it wouldn't heal and had to be packed with gauze each day. I lay in bed listening to the radio on the headset and became addicted to *Waggoners' Walk* and was introduced by Pete Murray to Barbra Streisand singing 'Don't Rain On My Parade' – another eye-opening revelation. In all I missed nearly a whole year's schooling, what with playing truant and the appendix fiasco.

CHAPTER TWELVE

IT WAS 1969, THE YEAR THAT THE GIRLS' SCHOOL NEXT DOOR, Holy Cross, joined forces with the boys and became Corpus Christi High. Puberty was really kicking in. I was a raging mass of confused hormones. One minute I was drooling over the girl who worked in the hairdresser's on Church Road, the next I was eyeing up the window cleaner.

A craze went round among the boys in class for joining the forces. Most joined the army cadets, Franny joined the ATC and was instantly nicknamed Douglas Bader, and I went the way of my hero Popeye and joined the marines. Surprisingly I took to it instantly and stayed for over a year, but in any case I wouldn't have dared quit. I'd wheedled a new pair of regulation marine's boots, only this time out of my dad. 'If you give up these marines after ten minutes like you did the Cubs, or get kicked out like you did when you were on the altar . . . the shame of that . . . then you'll be getting buried in those boots, my lad,' my mother threatened darkly. She hadn't forgotten the patent leather shoes.

We didn't do much in the marines at first, just endless drilling up and down the hall of the headquarters in Park Road East. We learned how to clean our uniforms and how to get the toecaps of our boots shining like glass by rubbing Cherry Blossom boot polish on with the back of a heated dessert spoon in a slow, circular motion, followed by a vigorous rub with a rag until, quite literally, you could see your face in them. We marched to the Anglican cathedral in Liverpool for Remembrance Sunday. You kicked the back of your heel if you got out of time to put you back in step. Things livened up for me when we were introduced to weaponry. They taught us how to strip down, clean and reassemble a rifle, then taught us how to use it. Heaven. I was a crack shot on the rifle range and prayed for a war so I could show off my new-found talents.

Walking home one night from the cadets I was jumped by three older lads. They beat me black and blue and stamped on my cap, flattening it. I owe the bend in my nose to those bastards. Our captain was sympathetic but practical. 'We must see that this never happens again, cadet,' he said and packed me off to the Boys' Amateur Boxing Club. I hung around out-side the club for ages before plucking up the courage to go in. I could hear lots of grunts and sounds of sweaty activity coming from inside and it didn't seem encouraging – not my cup of tea at all.

I was put through my paces by a big middle-aged man in a tracksuit with a nose that looked like a large toad squatting on his face. I think his name was Eddy. He watched my pathetic attempt at skipping with mild amusement, and if he was desperate to throw his head back and laugh like a drain at my feeble jabs on the punch bag he disguised it well. Over the weeks he gently coaxed and encouraged me, slowly building up my confidence until I felt that I just might be ready to have a go in the ring. It was a friendly fight, but I got hammered. 'Good,' said Eddy, applying a cold flannel to my cut lip. 'This will sharpen your wits for the next time, put a bit of fire in your blood, give you that edge. You won't let this happen again if you can help it, will you?'

No, I thought, I bloody well won't.

From then on I fought to win. 'Punch through them,' Eddy

would say. 'Aim for what's behind them, it'll give more power to your elbow.' I swallowed an imaginary can of spinach and laid into my opponents with the power of Popeye at my back. Once I'd thrown a couple of successful punches the floodgates opened and I smelt blood. I wanted more.

Occasionally a man would come into the gym and size us up for small local bouts. Dark-haired and expensive-looking, with a whiff of the gangster about him, he never picked me for any of the competitions as I had no technique and only basic skills in the ring. However, four years later, after the Boxing Dinner and Dance at the Kingsland Restaurant, where I had a part-time job as a waiter, he discovered that I had other skills when he gave me a lift home. Not that I ever made it home – I ended up at his 'pad'. Turned out he wasn't a gangster after all. He owned a boutique.

My gentle dad wasn't too keen on the idea of me bashing ten bells of shite out of someone every Tuesday night. He thought it was making me aggressive. He was right – it was. I didn't have a boxer's discipline; at the slightest sign of confrontation I'd punch first and ask questions later. In the end I gave up the boxing, but I stayed in the marine cadets. I really did love it. We went on night exercises to remote parts of North Wales and played war games and survival skills. It was pure *Avengers*, crawling through the undergrowth with a rifle strapped to my back, creeping up on the enemy and immobilizing him. In fact when I eventually did leave the captain visited my parents, much to my mother's surprise (and amusement), and asked them if they could persuade me to stay, as he thought that I might have a career in the marines. But it was too late. I'd moved on to other things, discovered other pleasures.

My brother Brendan was a part-time marine, but he wasn't the reason I'd joined the cadets. It was no big-brother hero-worship; I had no wish to emulate him. I hardly knew him, really. He was thirteen when I was born and deeply resented this late addition to the family, so he more or less ignored me. He was mad on motorbikes; I once fell off the back of his Vincent coming up Sydney Road. I was six at the time and didn't get a mark on me, just bounced when I hit the road and went sailing up on to the grass verge. My mother, on hearing the news, left her station at the gas stove and chased my brother down the Grove waving the frying pan she'd been cooking with round her head and leaving a trail of fish fingers in her wake, to the delight of a couple of moggies. He had a teddy boy's quiff and when he wasn't on his motorbike racing on the Wall of Death in New Brighton he could be found diving with the sub-aqua club off the coast of Anglesey, filling the bath, when he came home, with scallops.

He married a divorcee and left home when I was about eight. She was older than him and had a child, a little boy named Keith. There were a few raised eyebrows when my brother brought his new bride and her son home, but the family soon settled down and welcomed them into the fold. Everyone loved Keith. He was blond and cute, a few years younger than me, and would have looked the archetypal all-American boy if he had not been so frail. The aunties doted on him; Aunty Chris even took him to New Brighton for the day. I'd been usurped! My nose had been pushed firmly out of joint and I glowed an icy emerald green, eaten up with hatred and jealousy and hell-bent on finding a suitable and hideously painful way to get rid of my rival.

I did consider pushing him off the ferry into the murky waters of the Mersey and in fact I came quite close once, but luckily changed my mind at the last minute. On holiday one summer in the Isle of Man I toyed with the idea of holding a pillow over his face and suffocating him. Keith had a wart on his leg, a great crater of a thing, and I had to share a bed with him. He'd pick this wart until it bled as he lay there, turning my stomach and forcing me to give him a couple of good kicks to get him to stop. 'Nan,' he'd scream, 'he's kicked me wart and made it bleed.' For which I'd get a belt across the head. Oh, I could've murdered him all right, quite easily.

The young ladies of Holy Cross came in all shapes and sizes, from the glamorous Monica Summerfield, who looked like Jessica Rabbit in a school uniform, to the Mansfield twins, known to one and all, either individually or as a pair, as 'Twinny'. The Twinny Mansfields were terrifying, small and skinny with pale skin and pink eyes, ginger rat's tails framing their mean little faces. They had vicious tempers and foul mouths and would attack with the ferocity of a particularly evil pair of Jack Russells if they suspected that you were laughing, or even looking, at them.

''Ey yew, worra yew fookin' lookin' at? D'ya wan' us to wool the 'ead off yer?' You averted your eyes when passing the Twinny Mansfields as you would on encountering a pair of gorgons, in case they got it into their psychopathic heads that you were 'takin' the piss'.

Once we'd got over our initial bashfulness at being in the same room with these strange creatures and stopped sniggering and shoving each other every time one of them walked past our desks, we began, slowly, to start seeing them as individuals. The goddess Monica was unattainable. She went around surrounded by a gang of less attractive handmaidens, cold and aloof, a tiger's mane of fiery red hair cascading around her shoulders, and ignored us all. Some of the other girls were more amenable. Susan Ashton let me take her to the pictures. She had legs that went up to her armpits and full luscious lips. Her only drawback was the Deirdre specs she wore. The lenses were the size of greenhouse windows and as thick as the bottom of a milk bottle. We sat through *Mackenna's Gold* at the Plaza. She had a heavy cold and when the poor girl wasn't blowing her nose she was busy fighting me off. In the end she gave in and let me have a snotty snog and a quick grope under her jumper. I wouldn't have known what to do if it had gone any further. I had a vague and inaccurate idea about the theory but had not yet tackled the practical.

Fourteen and still a virgin: it was something that worried me day and night. All we ever talked about was sex. We were obsessed. Some of the boys would whip their tackle out and have a surreptitious wank at the back of the biology class. I'd draw obscene pictures of naked women, anatomically incorrect, I'm sure, but close enough for my classmates' needs.

My mother bought me a book called *The Gift of Life* from the Union of Catholic Mothers. I didn't have a clue what it was about. It was full of ridiculous euphemisms such as 'the man plants his seed in the woman's garden and slowly life starts to grow' – it sounded like a gardening manual. It took Aunty Chris, in her own inimitable style, to explain the rudiments of reproduction to me.

'What in God's name is this rubbish?' she said, flinging *The Gift of Life* on to the couch.

'It's a Catholic book on S E X edu-ca-tion,' my mother said in her deaf person's voice, blushing beet red from the ankles up.

'Why?' enquired Aunty Chris, applying a bit of lipstick. 'Do Catholics do it differently from everyone else, then?'

'Shh,' hissed my mother, hastily shoving *The Gift of Life* under a cushion and nodding furiously towards me before hurrying out of the room.

'Oh, for God's sake,' said Aunty Chris wearily, putting her lipstick back into her bag and sitting down to light up a fag. She'd met Vera Lalley earlier in the day at Charing Cross and she'd been persuaded to go to the pub for a couple of drinks. The unaccustomed alcohol – she'd given up the booze years ago – must have loosened her tongue, as what followed was completely out of character.

'Listen,' she said, pursing her lips and leaning towards me, 'it's all very simple, but if I tell you you've got to promise me that you won't do it until after you're married. OK?'

I nodded eagerly, desperate to know even if it was from Aunty Chris's lips. Better coming from her than either my mum or my dad. I'd have died the death of a thousand shames if they'd so much as mentioned it.

'Well,' she said, beckoning me closer and lowering her voice until it was barely audible, 'what happens is this.' She inhaled deeply on her fag and stared at the ceiling, thinking of a suitable way to put it. 'Well, the man gets his thingy out and puts it in the lady's doo-dah.' She was drawing strange shapes in the air with her hands. 'Then a baby starts to grow and nine months later the lady gives birth to that baby, d'you see?' No, I didn't see, as I tried to match this exposition with the patterns she'd drawn. She sat back in the chair, took a long drag on her fag and nodded, satisfied with her explanation.

'How does the baby get out of the lady's belly, then?' I asked after a moment.

'Well, it comes out of her . . . you know. Don't be so bloody thick. I've just told you, her doo-dah,' she said, flicking her ash casually into the palm of her hand.

'What's a doo-dah, then?'

'The thing a lady sits on, her . . . doo-dah.' Aunty Chris crossed her legs and brushed ash off her skirt. She was beginning to lose her nerve, not liking the way her impromptu sex education lesson was going. 'Get up and get us an ashtray, will you,' she said irritably, 'and never mind doo-dahs.'

'So is the lady's doo-dah her bum, then?' I was relentless in my quest for knowledge. This doo-dah held the key to so many puzzles, and besides, I was enjoying watching Aunty Chris squirm.

'No, it's not her bum,' said Aunty Chris hurriedly. 'I think it's going to rain, Molly,' she called, looking out of the window at the cloudless sky, desperate to change the subject. 'You haven't left any washing out in the yard, have you?'

'Well, if it's not her bum then what is it?'

'Oh, I've had enough of this,' shouted Aunty Chris, getting unsteadily to her feet and scattering fag ash everywhere. 'It's not her bum, it's her Anne Fran.'

'Her *what*?'

'Her Anne Fran ... her Minny ... her FANNY for God's sake!'

'I hope Dot next door isn't listening to this conversation,' said my mother, coming back into the room like an express train and quickly closing the window. 'I've never heard the like, and for your information,' she added, lowering her voice, 'it's not a fanny, it's a va-gi-na.'

Aunty Chris choked on her ciggy and went into a loud and long coughing fit, laughing and gasping for air at the same time.

'You want to give those up, they'll kill you,' my mother said sniffily. 'And hadn't you better get ready?' she went on, not looking me in the eye. 'You'll be late for your paper round.'

As I walked to Prescott's shop to pick up the night's bag of *Liverpool Echo*s to flog round the hospital I mulled over in my mind the mystery of the elusive fanny. Suddenly, as if a bolt of lightning had hit me, I saw clearly for the first time the answer to my questions. The penny had dropped with a loud bang. I understood exactly what the doo-dah was all about. St Paul on the road to Damascus hadn't had a clearer vision.

I ran the rest of the way, delighted that I'd solved the mystery and looking forward to telling Franny all about it the next day at school.

The girls hadn't been impressed with our military uniforms. They thought they were old-fashioned, or 'antwacky' as they say on Merseyside, and slightly naff. They wanted to be seen with smart young men dressed in the latest 'mod gear', not nerds in uniform.

Time to change the image. The Gear Box Boutique on

Borough Road was the place every aspiring man about town shopped in, providing he had the money – mod gear didn't come cheap. As well as my paper round with Prescott's, I managed to get myself another round with a rival newsagent. It meant getting up an hour earlier but who needs sleep when you're driven by the urge to own a gingham Ben Sherman shirt? I got a Saturday job in a fruit and veg shop on Church Road and ran messages for neighbours. Everybody ran then. My mother ran down to church, Aunty Anne ran round to the betting office, my dad ran to the pub. My sister's nylons ran and were repaired with nail varnish, dogs ran around the streets, water ran down walls, my cousin Tricia's hair dye ran, noses ran, people ran for buses, and kids ran to the shops on messages. With a little help from my parents and money I'd got as birthday presents I managed to earn enough cash to buy the full ensemble of clothing and footwear necessary if you were going to be with it.

Up till then my 'best outfit' had been picked for me by my mother and paid for with the ubiquitous Provvy cheque. It was an oatmeal corduroy jacket, cream slacks, beige cord shoes and a fitted orange shirt. I looked like the gay character from a Rita Tushingham film. Not any more. I was going to be stepping out at St Werburgh's disco the epitome of cool.

Admiring myself in the mirror of my mother's dressing table (if the mirror was tilted to a certain angle and you stood on the bed, you got a good view of everything from the neck to the knee) I thought I was the proverbial dog's bollocks. The long-desired gingham Ben Sherman shirt, black barathea blazer with brass buttons, two-tone parallel trousers with turn-ups ending at the ankle and – the pièce de résistance – a pair of beautiful oxblood Como brogues. To complement this outfit I had a new haircut: my thick wavy hair cropped short, with a razor parting down the side, known as the Suede Head.

'Suede Head?' my mother screeched when she saw it. 'You look like you've been shorn for nits.'

I swaggered out of the house leaving a breath-strangling trail of my dad's Old Spice aftershave in my wake to meet my mates at Central Station. We knew of a few pubs that would turn a blind eye to a lad's age as long as he was fairly passable as an eighteen-year-old. Even in our barathea blazers we looked about ten, but nevertheless we sailed into the public bar of the Central Hotel, hands in pockets, shoulders hunched and heads down, emulating the older lads we'd seen going into the ale-house. Sauntering up to the bar, we would nonchalantly ask for four pints of brown over bitter. I hated this concoction and would much rather have had cider, but brown over bitter was considered a real man's drink and consequently I'd sit sipping it, poison or not. It was usually me who was elected to ask the barman for the round of drinks as I had the deepest voice. I'd lower it even more for these occasions, until I sounded like a Scouse Bill Sikes.

'How old are yeh?' the barman would ask, deeply suspicious. 'What's your date of birth?'

'June the fourteenth 1950,' came the well-rehearsed reply, putting five years on my age.

'Don't shit a shitter,' he'd laugh, pulling the bitter into the glass all the same. 'The lot of yeh haven't got enough hair round your bollocks to make a wig for an 'ard-boiled egg.'

I don't remember any of us getting drunk at that age. I'd been drunk in Ireland when I was nine. There, children are allowed in the country pubs. You'd go into the post office, which was also the general shop, and there'd be a little bar at the back with some owld feller enjoying a mid-morning pint of Guinness with his pipe. I was no stranger to a pub called Creggs, which was owned by friends of the family. They were nice, easy-going people who didn't mind me going behind the bar to 'help out', which in reality meant I helped the deliciously creamy Guinness out of the drip trays, ending up stretched on the bar top, blind drunk. Nobody seemed to mind. My dad and the cousins carried on drinking, but my mother sent my dad to Coventry for weeks afterwards and my career as a drinker was nipped in the bud. Shame, as I liked getting slightly tipsy on the odd glass of cider that I was occasionally allowed when out with my dad. But it was nothing stronger than a bottle of Cydrax after that, non-alcoholic but close enough in taste to the real thing.

Five years later, I'd have killed for a Cydrax to take away the awful taste of brown over bitter mixed with a Sovereign cigarette. I wasn't a committed smoker then – that addiction wasn't to take a hold until a few years later – but I'd have one when I was showing off, 'out with the lads', as we thought ourselves.

Even though we pretended that we already had, we couldn't wait to grow up; to shave on a daily basis, to have a wild expanse of pubic hair surrounding a penis the size of a Wall's Pork Banger, to have sex – proper, all the way, full penetrative sex, naked and in bed; to drink and smoke and stay out late. And then came the great day when we queued outside St Werburgh's disco, breathing in and exhaling hard to remove any trace of fags and booze on our breath, in case Father Lennon should smell it on our way in. I was mad for the Upsetters' 'Return Of Django', although the repetitive little dance that went with the music was as boring as it was tiring to do. I executed it with a girl named Anne Downey, who carried it out with military precision, head down and hands clenched. I heard later she'd joined the army. I bet she was a credit to the service. St Werburgh's disco sold orange squash and tea and a parish priest walked around to make sure that nobody got into trouble. The whole affair was hardly Sodom and Gomorrah, yet it was here that I first became intimately acquainted with the female anatomy.

There was a girl in our school – let's call her Jean – who was only a year older than me yet could've passed for a woman in her twenties. She was a hard-as-nails North-Ender with 'experience' written all over her, and was what my mother called 'a dirty bitch'. When not playing truant, which she was most of the time, she could be found working behind the bar of a pub in Laird Street. I was in awe of her. No, I was terrified of her – she was the toughest girl on the planet. She was also startling to look at: extremely tall, with yellow hair and a huge bust, and frighteningly confident. You didn't dare argue with her: she'd have killed you with a head-butt. God knows what she was doing in St Werburgh's disco. She seemed far too worldly for the likes of us.

'Didn't recognize ya all got up like a pox doctor's clerk in your new togs,' she said, standing over me. 'You don't look too bad for a gobshite.'

Her maxi-coat was unbuttoned and I could see that she was wearing a skin-tight jumper and the tiniest of miniskirts. She turned towards her mates and grinned slyly, then turned back to me and ran her hand across my thigh. 'Nice kecks,' she growled. 'Let's have a better look at them, then?' And with that she led me to the back of the hall, pinned me against the wall and began to eat the face off me.

There was nothing remotely erotic about being kissed by Jean; it was akin to being rubbed vigorously in the face with half a two-day-old honeydew melon. However, once the lady had made up her mind to have you, then the only sensible reaction was a passive submission.

'Give us yer 'and,' she grunted impatiently, grabbing my wrist and guiding two fingers inside her knickers. I was rigid with shock. Completely paralysed. I had hold of what felt like a warm, wet vole.

Jean groaned and proceeded to give my groin a brisk rub as if she was cleaning brass. I levitated with fright. 'Nice, eh?' she said, backing off and eyeing me up and down in the way the praying mantis sizes up her mate just before she devours him whole. 'Smell your fingers.' It wasn't a seductive request, it was an order. I reluctantly wafted them under my nose. All I got was a slight whiff of the pickled onion crisps I'd been eating prior to my run-in with Jean. I smiled sheepishly at her. 'Now you know what a real woman smells like.' Her voice was mocking as she pulled what there was of her skirt down and went back to her cronies. The tension left me and I gave a sigh of relief as I watched her, head hunched into her broad back and hefty shoulders, swagger across the dance floor like a prizefighter.

Suddenly, I saw myself as a real stud. Jean had singled me out. That's right, me. The mighty power of the haircut and the Ben Sherman shirt had obviously turned Jean's head. She'd never known that I existed up till now, but all the same it was me – yes, me! – who had been chosen by Big Jean, the girl who only went out with grown men and could swear, drink and fight like a navvy. The very same Big Jean who had let me slip her the finger right in the middle of St Werburgh's disco.

My mates weren't impressed. 'She's takin' the piss out of yer. She'd go with anyone, her,' they said pityingly. 'I wouldn't touch her with two shitty sticks' . . . 'She's the school bike' . . . 'She'd let Captain Hook finger her' . . . 'You'd better go and wash yer 'and before you catch something.'

'You're just jealous,' I said, annoyed at their blasé reaction to my encounter with King Kong. 'She said she's fancied me for ages.' I looked over to where she was standing and smiled, giving her a little wave. She was preoccupied with pouring Bacardi from a bottle in her handbag into a plastic beaker of squash, and, glaring at me, mouthed the word 'Wanker'. Feeling stupid, I went to the Gents and washed my hands, secretly agreeing with my mates that Jean indeed wasn't worth touching with two shitty sticks.

That summer I was allowed to go to Ireland on my own. I flew Aer Lingus from Speke Airport to Dublin, my first time on a plane, feeling like McGill from *Man in a Suitcase*. I had some time to kill before I caught the train to Castlerea, and although my parents had told me not to I went for a mooch around Dublin. I got something to eat in Bewleys Café on Grafton Street, where my dad and I always headed when we got off the boat. Bewleys was dark and smoky, with a turf fire burning in the grate – that glorious smell which, for me anyway, is the fragrance of Ireland. All Bewleys ever seemed to serve were all-day breakfasts, and very delicious they were, swilled down with a mug of liquid tar calling itself tea.

In Easons bookshop I bought a copy of J. D. Salinger's *Catcher in the Rye* to read on the train. I also picked up *The Eleventh Pan Book of Horror Stories*, selected by Herbert Van Thal, just in case the *Catcher* didn't work out, but in the four hours it took to get to Castlerea I finished the book. I empathized with Holden Caulfield, the anti-hero of the story, a skinny, cynical adolescent, who didn't seem able to communicate with either adults or others of his own age. I saw the world through Holden's jaded eyes for the first time. He was right: it was full of phoneys, and there was too much pressure to conform to parental and other irritating adults' ideas. Well, no more. I began to cultivate a suitably louche attitude to go with my new frame of mind and greeted the cousins with a laid-back 'Jesus H Christ, it's good to see ya.'

I didn't dare give the Holden welcome to my aunty Bridget and if my cousins wondered why I was talking through the side of my mouth they didn't comment. Nice people. It's thanks to all those holidays spent on the farm in Ireland that I developed a love for the countryside. I can hear my aunty Bridget's voice in mine when I call the chickens – you make a noise that sounds like *Zook-zook-zook*. Chicken fanciers will understand, the rest of you will just have to believe me.

*

The year 'That Same Old Feeling' by Pickitywitch was released was the year I became Paul O'Grady, Cat Burglar. It was an indefensible crime, and I make no attempt to absolve myself. Why did I do it? That's easy. Boredom, plus an unquenchable thirst for excitement. I can't even defend myself by saying that I was easily led. Not that I wasn't – it's just that in this instance I was the instigator. I was very immature, and in a world of my own, floating somewhere between Planet Batman and Planet Avenger. I went to church regularly every week, did my homework, was a member of the Legion of Mary, turned out every day to flog the patients of St Cath's their papers and fags, still went to the marine cadets, and was available to babysit most Saturdays for my sister.

On the dark side of my moon it was a different story. The evil twin was enjoying himself; the balance of order had tilted in chaos's favour. He could be found running down the street throwing milk bottles at random, hanging around outside chippies in the North End, swigging cider and smoking loosies (unscrupulous newsagents were more than happy to sell loose Park Drive fags to kids), prowling the streets for girls (preferably ones who would go down the back alley with him for a necking session and hopefully a grope) . . . and climbing through bathroom windows to rob houses.

The evil twin was unscrupulous, his bad behaviour knowing no bounds. Smarter than his pals, he used his clever ways to encourage them to become willing accomplices in his mini crime wave.

Our first 'job' was a house in Oxton. It wasn't planned; we were just walking past and it seemed like a good idea to break in. Franny was having none of it and went home, leaving the four of us to slip in through the open kitchen window. We didn't even have to smash it, which I have to say disappointed me – I'd been looking forward to that. Instead, the owners had very obligingly left the house wide open to us. We didn't actually steal anything; instead we browsed around examining every room as if we were house-hunters instead of burglars.

'Look, they've got their own private bathroom in their bedroom.'

'Jesus, look at this. They've got a shower!'

'There's a phone by the bed!'

I swear we took to burglary just so we could have a good nose around the homes of the 'posh'. If *Location, Location, Location* had been on the telly at the time none of it would've happened.

We went further afield, to Heswall, for our next heist and found a suitable des res down a country lane. It was a beautiful house, full of antique furniture and oil paintings. Again, as in the previous house, there were no coin-filled electricity, gas or television meters to rifle, and as we were only interested in cash we chose not to take anything except an oil painting of a ship and an old pirate's pistol which we planned to sell.

We had no idea how to go about this and after a lot of debate in my bedroom with the booty hidden in the loft above, we decided it would be best to flog them to a shop in Rock Ferry that seemed to deal in old paintings and such. Turned out that the pistol was an eighteenth-century flintlock, one of a pair, and the oil was a valuable and recognizable artwork. The manager of the shop, recognizing the worth of our plunder and suspicious as to how a gang of scruffy kids had come by it, called the police and we were nicked. My dad threw up with shock. He actually vomited in the kitchen sink when the police came to the house to tell him that they were holding me at the station.

He came to collect me and we walked home in silence. He didn't look at me, stopping only once to allow me to catch up when I'd paused to tie my shoelace. He just looked through me while I hurriedly tied a knot.

My mother was making the tea. 'Where've you two been?'

she asked suspiciously, coming in from the kitchen, her eyes darting from me to my dad. 'What's going on?'

'He's been arrested and charged with housebreaking,' my dad said bluntly, sitting down and running his hands through his hair. 'I've just been to pick him up from Well Lane police station.'

My mother sat down slowly on the arm of the sofa, her trembling hands clasped in her lap. 'He's done what?'

My dad shook his head. 'You heard me right, Molly,' he said slowly. 'He's been having a rare old time, breaking into people's houses. I'd just like to know why,' he added sadly, staring at me as if he didn't recognize me.

My mother began to rock herself, ever so slightly, back and forth. 'Mother of you, sweet Jesus,' she moaned, 'what on earth are we going to do?'

'If it's any consolation, Mam,' I began, 'we didn't really nick much—'

'Oh, that was very charitable of you,' she said bitterly. 'Those Brothers at St Anselm's had your cards marked all right. What did Brother Kearney say? "Born to trouble as the sparks fly upwards" – never a truer word spoken.'

'Now, Molly, don't take on,' my dad sighed. He looked tired and old, as if all the life had been knocked out of him, which for the moment it had.

'How could you?' my mother shrieked, suddenly lunging towards me. 'You thieving, robbing, lying little whore.' She pronounced it 'who-er'. 'I'll bloody well swing for you.' She grabbed me by the hair and laid into me with the flat of her hand. I wriggled out of her grip and ran upstairs.

She carried on all night, slamming doors and muttering curses. I stayed in my room, out of her way, mortified with shame.

'You know you'll go to prison for this,' she roared up the stairs. 'And it'll serve you right.'

Aunty Anne and Aunty Chris came round to calm her down.

207

The three of them hunched round the fire would've given Macbeth's witches a run for their money. Sitting on the stairs, I could hear them in the front room. My dad had retired to the Black Horse to drown his sorrows and try to make some sense of his son's behaviour.

'I know now that I must have taken the wrong baby home from St Cath's,' my mother lamented, dunking her biscuit in her tea. 'He has to be a changeling. He's evil incarnate, that one. I don't know where he gets it from.'

From my seat on the stairs I knew, without being able to see her – not from the gift of X-ray vision, but from years of experience – that she was pointing her finger in the direction of Rose Long's house. 'Imagine *her* when she gets a load of this little lot. Oh, she'll have a field day. It'll be round the neighbourhood quicker than a bloody tornado . . . and imagine if the *Birkenhead News* gets wind of it – or the *Echo*? Mother of God, the shame and disgrace.'

She'd got it into her head that the world's press would be beating a path to Holly Grove to get a glimpse of and hopefully an exclusive with the leader of the 'Birkenhead Four'.

As it happened, when I did appear before the beak some months later I had the fear of God put into me and was given a sixty-pound fine, a lot of money at the time. My dad paid it religiously at the rate of a pound a week, and I paid him back when I started work. Or at least, half of it – he didn't have the heart to take any more off me after the first few payments. He told me to keep it, adding, 'You'll only have it off me again anyway when you're skint and on the cadge.' I didn't deserve him.

CHAPTER THIRTEEN

I WENT STRAIGHT, IN THE CRIMINAL SENSE, AFTER THAT. OH, I was the model penitent. I'd soon be sitting my O levels and CSEs and leaving school. I had no idea what I wanted to do with my life and no one to point me in the right direction. The careers officer was as much use, to quote Aunty Chris, as men's tits. According to him, there were two options. You could apply to Cammell Laird's for an apprenticeship in various trades, everything from ship's fitter to electrician. My mother was all for this. You could go anywhere in the world once you had a trade under your belt. 'There's always employment for a skilled artisan. Jesus was a carpenter,' she'd say cheerfully, ignoring the wonky coffee table with the tilt to the left that I'd spent two years making in woodwork. The other option was an apprenticeship with my dad's employers, Shell Oil. My dad arranged an interview for me as an electrician. It was fortunate that I got on the wrong train at Rock Ferry that morning and went to Chester instead of Ellesmere Port; if I hadn't, Shell Oil probably wouldn't be there today. I was totally uninterested in anything as mundane as electric wiring, and would probably have blown it up. I had no desire to be an electrician or a boiler-maker. I'd decided that my career lay in journalism. In my mind's eye I saw myself as a hard-boiled hack, lurking in the shadows dressed in a Sam Spade-style mac and trilby, tab-end stuck to my bottom lip, covering another dangerous assignment for a big London paper.

'A journalist?' My ma's eyebrows hit her hairline. 'You mean on a newspaper? A reporter? Good God, what next? You know nobody likes a reporter, don't you?' she said. 'They're the lowest of the low, in the same league as coppers and big dogs – you can't bloody trust 'em.'

Nevertheless, I wrote to the editor of the *Echo*, impressing on him how much the readers of his paper would benefit from my ace cub reporter skills, and to prove that I was serious about that week's chosen profession I signed up for a course at Sight and Sound, a Liverpool typing agency that taught the inept and cack-handed how to type and interpret the mysteries of shorthand. I didn't get through the introductory course, which seemed to me to be a form of brainwashing.

Unfortunately, the editor of the *Echo* turned me down, but pointed me in the direction of the *St Helens Star* who were looking for an enthusiastic youngster willing to sign his life over to that paper. Surprisingly, the editor of the *Star* did offer me a job, but my dad put the kibosh on that. He equated St Helens with the Outer Hebrides and declared that it was too far to travel and no place for an immature lad like me to live and work.

'And besides,' my mother added dryly, 'you need a careful eye keeping on you in case you feel inclined to put on your striped jersey, grab your swag bag and start looting the poor sods of St Helens.'

It was always the way. My dad was protective of me, my mother suspicious.

I contemplated art school. I enjoyed drawing and was fairly good at it, forever scribbling and doodling on every surface I came across. ('D'ya know he's drawn a woman's face on the lav door, Paddy?') One of my many fancies at the time was to become a children's illustrator, or even – the ultimate dream –

to be a Disney artist. But how does one get from Birkenhead to California? Via the Laird School of Art? I took my artwork off for an audience with the principal. He said it was promising and that I had a degree of talent. There was one painting that he really enthused over, raved in fact, and that was a dazzling abstract in violent shades of red. 'This is wonderful,' he said, standing back to admire it. 'Forget all the other little boring daubs and doodles and concentrate on producing more remarkable work like this.'

I was annoyed. The 'remarkable work' wasn't actually mine – I'd borrowed it from the portfolio of an artistic genius who had left school the previous year to become a welder and slid it in among my 'daubs and doodles'.

'Why don't you attend a few classes,' the principal said, 'see how we get along?'

We didn't. The still life class was made up of what we of the Suede Head persuasion called 'trogs'. A trog was basically a hippy – afghan coat, tie-dye T-shirts, bell round the neck, the whole patchouli-smelling kit and kaboodle and the exact opposite of everything the Suede Heads stood for. The twain were never to meet. Trogs were mainly middle-class *Monty Python* fanatics, quoting their favourite sketches ad nauseam to each other. I thought they were a bunch of prize twats and wanted to kill them all – I couldn't wait to get out of there. Besides, they were all brilliant artists, making my pathetic attempts resemble the kind of stuff that appeared on the gallery wall in *Vision On*. In traditional style, I stuck it for less than a week.

I loved *Vision On*. Tony Hart, the presenter, had that indefinable quality called IT. Inspired by the way he'd made art look so easy and uncomplicated, at the age of eight I dashed off a painting of Polperro Harbour, copied from a print bought in Boots that hung behind my dad's chair, and sent it in. To make doubly sure that my work ended up as one of those chosen to hang on the holy of holies, the Gallery Wall, I wrote a pitiful little letter explaining that I was deaf and dumb. At the time *Vision On* was aimed primarily at children with hearing difficulties and I thought my note might tip the balance in my favour. My picture was chosen, my name was flashed up on screen and I nearly wet myself on the front-room carpet as I saw my painting proudly displayed on that Sistine Chapel of children's entertainment, the Gallery Wall. I told my mother.

'I thought that you had to be deaf to get your picture accepted?'

'No, anyone can send a picture in.'

'Did you tell them you were deaf? Well, did you?'

'Yeah.'

'Oh, you wicked little boy, get down to confession and tell Father Lennon what you've done.'

When I did confess I could hear the priest sniggering behind the grill. 'Shocking,' he said, coughing. 'Say ten Hail Marys.'

For once, though, my parents were relieved that I hadn't stuck at something. They didn't want an artist in the family; it was an unreliable profession. They wanted me in a good steady job, such as a trade, with two weeks' paid holiday, sick benefits, sports and social clubs, a good chance for career advancement and a nice little pension waiting at the end of it. Safe for life. The thought secretly horrified me, but I was keen to start work in a proper job and looked forward to becoming a wage-earner.

I toyed with the idea of being a chemist's assistant and wrote off to various companies who were advertising in the back of the paper for just that. I fancied messing around with chemicals, making potions and maybe even discovering a cure for a terminal disease, eventually going on to win the Nobel Prize for Medicine.

One company said that they would take me on depending on my O level results. Maths and at least one science subject were essential for the job. I knew there and then that I didn't stand a hope in hell of getting it. I hadn't even bothered to sit maths O level; I had a go at CSE arithmetic, something that Cheetah the Chimp would be able to get through with very little effort, but the answers to even the simplest of questions evaded me and I was marked ungraded. I ended up with four O levels, in English lit and lang, art and biology, and a handful of CSEs.

'Not bad, lad,' Aunty Chris said from the top of a ladder, 'but I take it you won't be going to Oxford.' She was hanging wallpaper in the front room and had a length of woodchip pasted and draped professionally over one arm, ready to go.

'A restricting garment, six letters,' Aunty Anne said absently, her head buried in a crossword book as she ambled into the room. The floor and furniture had old sheets draped across them, and the windows were covered, in the absence of the net curtains, in a thick pink coating of Windolene, as a safeguard against any passing 'nosey bastards' who might dare to glance in and catch Aunty Chris in her rollers.

'Look where you're going,' Aunty Chris roared from the top of the ladder. 'Don't kick that bucket of paste over, you dozy mare.'

Aunty Anne briefly looked up from her book to make sure that there weren't hazards in her path and, ignoring her sister, repeated the question.

'Two down, restricting garment, six letters.'

'Straitjacket,' Aunty Chris said, concentrating as she lined up the paper, letting the first loop of the roll stick to the wall. Brushing it down, she deftly repeated the process until she'd reached the skirting board, finishing it off with a series of hard sweeps with her brush. 'Look at that,' she said proudly, standing back to inspect her handiwork. 'Not a bubble in sight.'

'Too many letters, straitjacket.' Aunty Anne gave the freshly papered wall a cursory glance, absorbed in the pressing problem of her crossword.

'Corset then.'

'No, cos that would mean three across is wrong.'

'Well, I don't know,' Aunty Chris snapped irritably. 'Get out of my bloody way, can't you see I'm busy? I'll end up in a straitjacket myself trying to paperhang with you two under my feet.' She pulled a tab-end out of her overall pocket and lit it. 'Why don't you get yourself down to the Labour Exchange, Paul,' she said, coughing. 'They're looking for people for the Ministry of Defence. That's who James Bond worked for, isn't it, Annie?'

'MI5, same thing,' Aunty Anne replied, sucking on her pen, still pondering the solution to the elusive restrictive garment. 'And what were you doing in the Labour Exchange?'

'Oh, I just threw my head around the door to see if they had anything on the books I might fancy in the way of a change. Good job for our Paul, that, though – Ministry of Defence. Now sling your hook and let me get on,' she said, rolling out another length of paper on the rickety pasting table.

So it was actually possible to get into this mythological ministry after all? The same ministry that 007 and, more importantly, Steed and Tara worked for? That was it then. I was going to be a secret agent.

'Basque!' Aunty Anne suddenly screamed out. 'Restricting garment – a basque!' She was delighted with herself as she scribbled the answer into the book.

'She amazes me at times, she really does,' Aunty Chris sighed, slapping a mixture of Polycell and fag ash on the back of the paper. 'The things she comes out with. You want to take her down with you to the Ministry of Defence, she'd be another Odette with her command of French.'

I was interviewed in the Liver Building by an immaculate civil servant who could have stepped out of an Ealing comedy. I was in Avenger land, I told myself, and indeed I could've been – there was something surreal about the situation, sitting in a musty old office at the top of the Liver Building convincing a Richard Wattis clone that I was just what the ministry needed, and being brought a cup of tea and a digestive by a lady I could've sworn was Pat Coombes.

Knock me down with a feather and call me Gladys – he took me on, offering me a job as a clerical assistant, eight pounds a week plus luncheon vouchers and one day off a week for day release at Birkenhead Technical College, starting at the end of September. That gave me nearly six weeks off and in the interim I was offered the chance to elevate myself from senior paper boy at Prescott's to working behind that most hallowed of all hallows – the counter.

The shop had a steady stream of customers all day, but come hospital visiting time the place was mobbed, so that Mary, the full-time assistant, had to vacate the room at the back where she spent most of her time, drinking tea and dragging on a Regal, and reluctantly slop out in her Dr Scholls to serve the baying horde with boiled sweets, Lucozade, comics and fags to take to their loved ones in St Cath's just across the road. If you can imagine Maureen Lipman with a black beehive and fly-away specs, in a striped overall with a cardigan draped in a casual manner over her bony shoulders, chewing nonchalantly on a wad of gum and staring myopically into your face, then you have Mary.

She'd tell outrageous tales about the customers: 'You know that woman who comes in with the blind one hanging off her arm?' she'd say confidentially, stacking Milky Ways on the counter. 'Well, the blind one is really a prostitute . . . you have to hand it to her.' She'd cackle at her joke and roll her chewing gum round in her mouth, delighted with herself.

Or 'You know the old feller who comes in, gets a quarter of barley sugar for his wife? You wouldn't credit it in a hundred years but he's a secret millionaire, owns half of Oxton, worth a fortune but a terrible miser. Well, he fancies me rotten, and the other day' – at this point she'd lower her voice – 'he shoved something down the front of my blouse and said, "Have a little drink on me, Mary." I hoped it was a couple of quid, well you would, but when I shoved me hand down me bra and pulled it out, it was a tea bag.' Hairy old gags, I know, but new to me at the time and very funny. I enjoyed my summer in Prescott's, drinking tea and laughing at Mary's non-stop cabaret, and was sorry when the call to arms came from the civil service.

'There's been a mistake,' I was saying on the phone to the recruiting officer, 'I've been put in the wrong department. I applied to join the Ministry of Defence, or failing that the diplomatic service, but the letter I've got here says that I'm to report for duty at the DHSS, Canning Place.'

He explained that you were placed where you were needed, and right now there were very few openings with the MOD or the diplomatic service in Liverpool. However, there were several within the DHSS, so tough titty. In other words, take it or leave it.

My mother was in her element. She didn't care if it was the DHSS or the SS as long as it sounded official.

'Civil service,' she shouted over the counter to Eileen Henshaw, in a voice that could be heard on the Isle of Man. 'I'm taking him over to Liverpool now on the ferry to sign the Official Secrets Act – he can't start work until he signs it. Government secrets, you know – you can't go blabbing about what you've seen. It wouldn't do for you, Eileen, would it?' I was shrivelling up beside her with the speed of a salt-covered slug, desperate to get out. She gently opened the shop door to leave, still smiling radiantly. I wondered if she'd had a turn. 'Let's be honest, I don't know why we bother buying papers when you can stand at that counter for five minutes and learn everyone's business.'

'The local shop is the hub of the community,' Eileen rallied, quoting something she'd read in the *Grocer*. 'I can't help it if customers discuss certain—'

'Gossip I think you'll find it's called, idle gossip. Thank you . . . bye-bye,' Ma called out merrily, letting us out of the shop, pausing on the pavement and smiling up into the late summer sun. 'I love getting one over on her.' She chuckled malevolently under her breath. 'C'mon, son, we can't be late for the Official Secrets Act. If we get a move on we'll just catch that 60.'

The Official Secrets Act turned out to be a disappointingly ordinary form, on which I dutifully wrote my name (in triplicate, of course) in my best handwriting using the Good Pen that my mother had brought along especially for the occasion. In the lift on the way down, she turned into Rose Kennedy.

'You can never reveal government secrets to anyone now, under pain of death,' she said dramatically, and I believed her, not that I imagined there would be much call for the personal details of other claimants on the part of any Soviet agents who happened to find themselves signing on at Steers House.

I didn't have any idea where Canning Place was, but my mother did. She knew Liverpool like the back of her hand and would probably have made a good cabbie if she'd ever bothered to learn to drive. But driving wasn't for the likes of us. Nope, we travelled by public transport or on foot, something my mother loved to do and frequently did. She adored a good mooch or a bus ride on an unknown route that led to previously unexplored territory.

Canning Place was part of the fast-diminishing Old Liverpool, a row of boarded-up Georgian houses and a pub called the Custom House that was straight out of *Treasure Island*. Even in its present state of disrepair and neglect Canning Place was impressive. It had charm, a piece of the city's heritage and character that had survived the bombing in the war but was no match for the inner city redevelopment of the late sixties and was now awaiting demolition.

The modernity of Steers House, a concrete and glass cube, was bleak in comparison with the faded gentility of Canning Place. In the middle of the block was Dolphin Square, a rain-swept, miserable arena that had a solitary sweet kiosk standing incongruously in the middle, as if it had just landed from Kansas, and a soulless pub that was predictably called the Dolphin. The square was as bleak as anything East Germany had to offer, the icy winds off the Mersey permanently howling around the grey concrete pillars as if trying to find an escape route. I looked at it with mixed feelings. My stomach was turning and I had that tingling in the groin that for some reason is called butterflies, when it actually feels like mini-volts of electricity. No doubt the word was coined long before Mr Edison was a spark in his daddy's eye.

'Come Monday morning you'll be up there,' my mother announced proudly, looking admiringly at Steers House. 'Ooh, it's lovely and modern. Aren't you looking forward to it? You should be, it's your first day of a new life.' She'd been reading too many Angélique books, but her optimism was infectious and we were in a fine mood as to Blackler's 'we repaired for some liquid refreshment and a teacake', as Noël Coward might have said had he been living on Merseyside and about to start work for the Social Security.

Blackler's Store on Charlotte Street was a Liverpool institution. It was the home of the Christmas grotto which featured every year the famous 'Dancing Waters', bursts of illuminated, coloured water that would appear to dance to music. Blackler's sold everything and anything at bargain prices, from a mousetrap to half a yard of turquoise feather trim, and for the weary shopper there was a café on the first floor in which you could drink tea and eat cheese on toast while observing the punters below. 'She could do with losing a bit of weight . . . that's a nice coat, bet that cost a pretty penny . . . wouldn't you think she'd wipe that kid's nose, poor

Dragged up in my
Maureen's swimming
me, aged three, at
re, North Wales.

m (left to right): Dad,
eith and Mum on the
f Man in the 1960s.

Clockwise, from top left: Maureen, John, Tricia and me at Talacre; Ireland – Maureen, Dymphna and me, aged seven; Mam in her Kim Novak glasses, me, Aunty Anne and young Nora Fenton on another pilgrimage, this time to Pantasa, North Wales; my ma and the Union of Catholic Mothers – marching, marching, always marching!; me, aged eight, with my dad in the Isle of Man; Keith, Mum and me; in love with a calf, aged four.

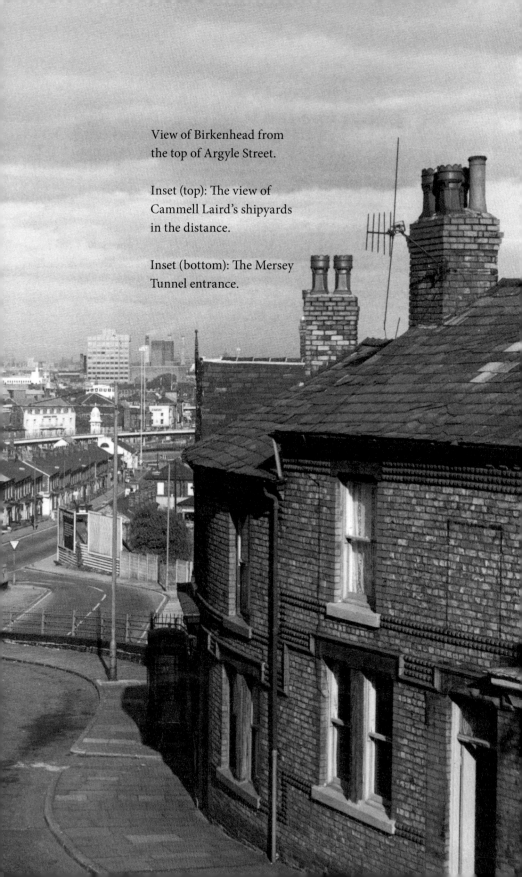

View of Birkenhead from
the top of Argyle Street.

Inset (top): The view of
Cammell Laird's shipyards
in the distance.

Inset (bottom): The Mersey
Tunnel entrance.

Top: Sheila's wedding in 1966.

Middle: Me, Mum, nephews Paul and Michael, and Sheila – Treader Bay, Anglesey

Bottom: (left) Sheila, m Mum, Anne, Maureen and nephew Michael; (middle) me aged twelv with nephew Paul; (right) sunbathing.

Top: Dad, Mum, Sheila and her husband Peter, Uncle Mick and Aunt Addie in the front room at Holly Grove.

Middle: The Addams family wedding – Chrissie, Harold, Annie, Ada Hannigan, Mum, Lily Fawcett.

Bottom: Dad and Ada at my cousin John's wedding.

Clockwise from top left: Aged seventeen, dishing up beans in Diane's kitchen; it seems that all photos were taken in the garden at Holly Grove – look at the hair!; the White Rose of Athens? No, it's Diane in the skirt that got her banned from using the lifts in George Henry Lee's; me with nephew Michael.

little bugger . . .' My mother provided a running commentary as the hordes passed by.

The work at the Department of Supplementary Benefits, Steers House, was mind-numbingly boring. Each claimant was interviewed by a clerical officer who wrote the claimant's name on a slip of paper which was given to one of the Searchers – not the group, but me and a few other miscreants, the lowest of the low, the clerical assistants – who then had to run around the building searching for the claimant's casepaper which was never in its proper place, filed away in the enormous bank of filing cabinets that sat in the middle of the room, conveniently located so we could lean on a few open drawers and talk to each other over the top until our hysterical supervisor screamed at us to stop talking and get some work done.

The CAs really were the drones of the hive, flitting from table to desk in search of errant casepapers: Slow Dave, with his blond feather-cut hair and dandruff, lurid kipper ties, and permanent residue of white spit flecked in each corner of his mouth; Christine from Wigan, who loved the song 'Johnny Reggae' and went about her search for casepapers singing it over and over again until the supervisor's nerves finally cracked and he threatened to kill her; and Flo, who was the eldest of the bunch and looked and sounded like one of Marge Simpson's sisters.

Flo was one of the old guard who had been transferred from Renshaw Street to Steers House. Renshaw Street wasn't pretty or of any architectural merit; it was a dump, literally falling down around its residents' ears, yet they loved it. An archaic, derelict hovel, ill equipped to deal with the increasing number of claimants looking for Supplementary Benefit, it was eventually closed down before it fell down and the staff and clients were transferred to the concrete and glass Steers House. They hated it, lamenting the loss of their rat-infested, inadequately plumbed toilets and the cosy family atmosphere that had apparently existed in the cramped and overcrowded office. Flo had the knack of always managing to look busy; she was a very crafty delegator and clever at getting others to do the running around for her without their realizing it.

'It was never like this at Renshaw Street,' Flo would say, tapping her lip thoughtfully as she studied a claimant's slip. 'We knew where everything was there, see, not like this place, but I've seen this casepaper somewhere . . . now let me think.' She'd close her eyes and concentrate as if she were a medium trying to locate the name of someone's dead relative. 'I've got it,' she'd eventually declare, pulling out a packet of Park Drive and lighting up. 'It's on Jim Shelley's desk in Fraud. Run up and get it, will you, while I have this fag.' Of course the paper was never there; it was another of Flo's ploys to offload an irretrievably lost casepaper.

Occasionally a claimant, tired and frustrated after waiting all afternoon to be interviewed, would snap and provide us with a bit of very welcome diversion. They'd abuse a member of staff or throw a chair over the partition. The supervisor, who was supposed to deal with situations like this, would always overreact and call the police, when a few calming words and the promise of a Giro would've done the trick. He was good at bullying us, but not so brave when it came to dealing with the public.

We were always grateful for the odd bomb scare to break the monotony of the daily routine. These phone calls were invariably made by disgruntled punters who'd been turned down for benefit, yet the police always insisted on evacuating the office, much to the boss's disgust, allowing us half an hour's freedom while they searched the building for any stray explosive devices. 'Better to be safe than sorry,' we'd say to him as we strolled back into the building after we'd been given the all-clear. Apoplectic, he would retire to the executive lav and have a good cry.

*

I was sitting in Cousin's café eating my favourite lunch of salmonsaladbarmcake, cup of tomato soup and a pasty, washed down with a glass of Coke – a feast that cost all of three luncheon vouchers – when John, the schoolmate from the necking sessions in the park days, came back into my life. He'd joined the merchant navy after leaving school and I hadn't seen him since. Predictably, I'd considered, along with just about every other profession, joining the merchant navy as a steward, but jobs at sea were as rare as hen's teeth by the seventies. At one time it was easy; someone who was already a merchant sailor took you down to Liverpool pierhead dock office and signed you up. You got a pass book with the name of the vessel you would be sailing on and the date and off you went. One of the Fawcett cousins offered to take me down to sign up, but my dad put a stop to that.

'There is no way that he's going to sea,' he said, dismissing the idea as a non-starter. 'He's too daft. It's not a life for the likes of him.' I never got the chance to find out.

'Budge up then, Ogger,' John said, calling me by my nick-name from our schooldays and moving me along the seat with his hip as he sat down next to me with his tray. 'Long time no see. What'cha bin up to?'

He'd filled out and grown taller since I'd last seen him and his recently acquired tan showed off his blue eyes and white teeth in their full seductive glory. He flashed me a smile, and somewhere in the room an almighty explosion went off. I heard bells and whistles. The orchestra in the back of my mind who were on permanent stand-by suddenly struck up the theme from *Gone with the Wind*. Dizzy with lust, I could feel my face slowly flushing a deep scarlet as I struggled with an overpowering urge to drag him on the floor, right there in the middle of Cousin's, among the barm cakes and office workers.

I managed to hide my sudden rush of excitement at seeing

221

him again and conduct myself in a suitable fashion. We talked about jobs, girlfriends and sex, mainly sex, and if John was to be believed he'd had every woman from Rotterdam to the South China Seas since joining the merchant navy: not bad going considering we'd left school less than eight months ago. We chatted about school, conveniently pretending that the snogging sessions never happened, and parted after agreeing to meet up for a drink later in the week. How was I going to wait till Friday? I floated down the street like a lovesick schoolgirl. I wanted him worse than bad and by hook or by crook I was bloody well going to have him.

We went to New Brighton for a drink, and ended up in a disco called the Golden Guinea. The pangs of jealousy I felt when John chatted up a girl gnawed at me with the ferocity of a rodent ulcer, but I kept up the 'get stuck in there, John' jovial hetero banter befitting a best buddy. Talk about *Brokeback Mountain*.

As usual, I ended up with the mate, whom I didn't fancy in the least and who I knew in my boots felt exactly the same about me, but we showed willing and after a couple of drinks and a slow dance we went through the motions of a half-hearted snog and a cursory grope at the bus stop.

Before long John and I were spending all our spare time together, listening to records in my bedroom, going to the wrestling matches every Friday night at the Liverpool Stadium and attempting to pick up girls (reluctantly on my part) at every opportunity. I'd buried my passion for John, as it was clear that there was no point ruining a perfectly good friendship by hankering all the while for a sexual one. The plotting and manoeuvring to get him into the right situation was becoming tiring, so I gave up hunting him down and enjoyed what we had.

Then one night we were at a party in Liverpool, and the father of the girl whose do it was asked John and me if we'd like to stay over, seeing as we lived on the Wirral, and adding the magic words 'that's if you don't mind sharing a bed'. Thank you, fairy godmother. We were both a bit pissed and the room was cold so we wasted no time, getting undressed down to our underpants and into the narrow single bed as fast as we could. There was no slowly, slowly catchee monkee approach, no tentative meeting of legs to test the water, no casual hand falling where it shouldn't. We fell on each other like wolves who hadn't eaten for a month, John obviously as keen as me to see what all the fuss was about.

In the morning we didn't mention the intense night we'd just spent. Instead we went about the business of washing and dressing as if nothing had happened. It was only when we were on the train home that John turned to me and asked if I thought that the night's activities made us homos.

Homos were few and far between and hung about lavs wearing dirty macs and women's suspenders, so no, we couldn't be what you called proper homos. 'I think,' I said after a while, 'we're sort of blood brothers.' He thought for a second and then nodded, not entirely convinced by my risible explanation but letting it go for the time being. We sat in silence as the train came out of the tunnel and into Hamilton Square station. 'Here's my stop,' he said, getting up. It was now or never.

'Are you sorry we did it, then?' He didn't answer me, just got off the train. I knew there and then the meaning of 'I wanted the ground to open up and swallow me'. Before I had a chance to get the boxing gloves out and beat myself up he banged on the window and gave me a sly smile, then ran off up the stairs and vanished into the crowd. It was my very own *Brief Encounter* moment: colours bled into sepia, an unseen orchestra swelled to Rachmaninov's second piano concerto and the train, belching great plumes of steam, slowly pulled out of the gas-lit station, our respective hearts breaking, never to see each other again.

As it happened, we didn't. He joined a ship a few days later and wrote to me from Greece, concluding, *I fancy you more than I've ever fancied a girl but I don't want to be a homo, so I think it's best if we pack it in. All the best, your mate, John.*

Can't say I was heartbroken. I'd like to say that I stood on the dock clutching his letter with tears coursing down my cheeks as I watched his boat sailing into the distance, but I didn't. You see, I'd moved on. I'd discovered the Theatre Darlings!

I'd read somewhere that the theatre was absolutely teeming with homosexuals and so, inspired by this piece of inform- ation, I joined the local amateur dramatic club in the hope of meeting a few of these theatrical homos. The Carlton Players, based on Grange Road West in a converted church known as the Little Theatre, had been going since the thirties and was very much a closed shop, their productions nearly always featuring the same cast. It was hard for a newcomer to get a toe on the bottom rung of the ladder, let alone be allowed to appear on the tiny stage of the Little Theatre.

'You have to work your way up, laddie,' I was told by Mr Harold Rowson, the company's producer and main man – the Binkie Beaumont of Grange Road West. His elderly wife, who had once been a stalwart of the company but who now, due to lack of mobility, rarely graced the boards, was treated like Dame Edith Evans whenever she made one of her surprise visits.

'Ah, our neophyte player. I've heard all about you,' she said in a full, rich voice. 'Why have you come to us? What drew you to the theatre?' I could hardly tell her that it was in the hope of getting a shag so I mumbled something about wanting to be an actor.

'Work hard, learn your craft and one day,' she said, her

face crinkling up into a benevolent smile, 'you may be fortunate enough to become a member of that distinguished profession.'

I didn't know if I was meant to genuflect or not, but before I could make up my mind she hobbled off. 'Who is he again, Betty?' she said regally to the woman who was holding her up.

'Whoever he is, dear, we could certainly do with another pair of hands backstage.'

Backstage? Backstage? I haven't come here to lug scenery. I'm going to be an Actor. Did you hear me? An Actor, you daft old . . .

'Are you a new member of the company?' A feller who'd have looked more at home behind the counter of a branch of the Halifax Building Society than in the green room of a the-aterrr interrupted my train of thought. 'Welcome to the lunatic asylum,' he said, weighing me up. 'Have you decided on your audition piece?'

Audition piece? What audition piece? No one mentioned a bloody audition piece to me. I'm not auditioning to get in here, it's not the RSC, it's am dram . . .

'No, I don't need one cos I'm just going to help out backstage or something, I think, so, erm, I'm not an actor or anything . . .' I could hear my ma's gay little nervous laugh ringing in my ears, only this time it was me who was making it. I was also blushing to my roots. Piss off, Halifax, you're getting on my nerves.

'Well, nice to have met you,' Halifax said cheerfully, rushing back to his cronies to break the news that I was 'only crew' and therefore not worth bothering with, 'unless he's lighting, darling'.

The 'Actors' of the company jealously guarded their positions within the pride and were deeply suspicious of any newcomers who might tread on their toes or steal their limelight. They prided themselves on their professionalism and

225

were more 'pro' than the pros, obsessed with always appearing as 'the utter professional'. This lot would've gone on wired up to a life support machine if it meant not missing a 'performance', and prided themselves on being 'off the book' by the first day of rehearsal. There was less rivalry, gossip and petty jealousy at the court of Elizabeth I than there was in the rehearsal room of the Little Theatre. They watched each other like hawks and were always on the lookout for one of their number to step out of line, which gave the others the opportunity to say in the pub afterwards, arms folded across chest, superior expression on smug gob – and providing the offender was out of earshot, of course – 'Well really, I do call that behaviour highly unprofessional.'

Two of the leading lights of the Carlton Players were Reg Triplett and Betty Begley. Reg was considered a versatile actor who could play everything from low comedy to high tragedy. He looked upon the Little Theatre as Olivier did the Old Vic, and like most of the others he lived and breathed theatre. He wore a car coat and carried his scripts in a leather-bound folder with his name embossed on the front. Betty Begley had the distinction of having been a professional actress, appearing in her time in a Norman Wisdom film – or so Halifax told me. She'd retired from a life in front of the camera to bring up her two children, Sally and Kim, who, like their mother, were active members of the Carlton Players.

Betty was a very attractive woman. She fancied herself as a Margaret Lockwood or Honor Blackman type. She strode around the rehearsal room in a fur coat and leather boots, script in one hand, pencil in the other, proclaiming, 'Dahling, do you rrreally think Eleanor of Aquitaine would say it like that? She is after all one of the world's most powerful women. I'd rather try a different approach if you don't mind, something with a bit of wallop in it.'

The Carlton Players' production of *The Lion in Winter*

caused quite a stir among the patrons of the Little Theatre. When Betty, as Eleanor, dressed in a cloak and cowl that had previously been worn by the Wicked Queen in a Christmas panto, lifted a necklace up to her bosom just before the end of Act One and announced in her ripe, throaty voice, 'I shall hang this from my nipples,' an audible gasp of horror went round the audience. A few of the outraged even threatened to withdraw their membership.

Richard the Lionheart's homosexuality caused a few more raised eyebrows and tut-tuts among the more conservative of the blue rinses, even though the subject had been dealt with 'in a most discreet and delicate fashion'. I was helping with props in the wings and had hoped that the Carlton Players were going to break down barriers by allowing a modicum of heavy petting and a little light sodomy in that scene, but it wasn't to be – maybe Birkenhead audiences weren't quite ready for that just yet.

At Christmas the company put on a show for members and friends of the theatre, a frightening bunch of people who thought that just because they'd made a financial contribution to the place they now had the God-given right to swan about as if they owned it. The play, complete with musical interludes and comic monologues, was set in Victorian Birkenhead and involved a convoluted tale of three washerwomen from the North End taking a trip to Oxton to visit the daughter of one of the women who was in service in a big house there. Harold Rowson himself played the master of the house and his wife, Dame Norma, came out of retirement to execute the role of the grand matriarch. The setting was a Victorian drawing room where a refined musical soiree to celebrate Christmas was in full swing, Betty's daughter Sally, a real beauty, played the youngest daughter of the house. I thought she looked enchanting in her Alice in Wonderland costume and developed an instant crush on her. Her brother Kim, who had a fondness for long suede waistcoats and wearing his jeans tucked into his knee-high boots and seemed like he had a very high opinion of himself, played the young army captain. Betty was the Glamorous Music Hall Artiste whom the eldest son, a bit of a roué swell and general cad about town played by Reg, had brought home in an 'ansom from the Argyle music hall, for a bit of supper. The role gave Betty carte blanche to get her ample cleavage out and give her all as cockney tart. She warbled a rendition of 'I'll Be Your Sweetheart' at the piano with the male members of the family gathered around her, lustily joining in the chorus while the womenfolk looked on unamused.

I had been given the part of youngest son, which involved little more than sitting stage right in a chair throughout the entire performance, miming having fun. I didn't care; it was showbiz. I longed to do more, but for the time being was grateful to sit half hidden by the curtain and display a range of emotions from ecstatic joy to sorrowful recollection each night. My face was inch-thick in numbers 5 and 9 of the sticks of Leichner greasepaint that I'd bought from Owen Owen's and kept in a cigar box like a real pro. You blended these colours into your face until you'd achieved the healthy glow of a severe angina attack. After finishing it off with a light dusting of powder, a speck of carmine and a dab of clown white on the end of a hairpin for the corner of each eye, and a dash across the eyebrows with a black pencil, you were ready to hit the green.

There was a party on the last night and everyone got very drunk and luvvy.

'A huge hit. It'll run for years,' Reg shouted over to Betty, toasting her with his glass of mulled wine. It did in fact run for years for Betty and Reg; they took their final bows on the Little Theatre stage twenty-two years later in 1993, in a production of *The Right Honourable Gentleman.*

Feeling brave after a couple of drinks, I told Sally Begley that I thought she was a great actress and that she should be on a professional stage. She threw her arms round me and kissed me. 'Thank you, sweet boy,' she whispered theatrically. *Carpe diem*. It was snowing outside and I asked her if she'd like to see it. She said that she would. The planets were aligning in my favour at last.

It really must be Christmas, I thought, standing there in the softly falling snow with my tongue down the lovely Sally's throat. I made a silent promise to God that I'd get up and go to early mass in the morning.

I floated down Grange Road West. It was deserted, covered in a blanket of virgin snow. The stars were bright and the air was still and silent. The combination of mulled wine and cider, the gently falling snow, the Christmas lights hanging overhead and the potent spell woven by the combination of the stage and Sally Begley's kiss was a powerful enchantment that bewitched me, and transformed this normally unremarkable street into something truly magical. I didn't want the moment to end.

CHAPTER FOURTEEN

PREDICTABLY, MY LOVE AFFAIR WITH THE THEATRE, OR AT LEAST the Carlton Players, was short-lived. It wasn't that the Players weren't welcoming; they were, once we'd got to know each other, but I still felt like an intruder from another planet. I didn't know what to do with myself; I was not part of the enviable group who were rehearsing for the forthcoming production, nor was I often needed or welcome backstage, apart from one occasion when I stood in the wings and opened the curtains for a local dance school who'd hired the theatre for the night to stage their 'Dance Extravaganza'. This was a very long, complicated production that went on for about fifteen hours, or at least it felt like that. My concentration would occasionally lapse, as it did during 'Clair de Lune' when I brought the tabs in a fraction too early, resulting in a tirade from a nine-year-old étoile who wiped the floor with me, calling me, among other things, predictably 'unprofessional'.

I hung around the green room pretending to be absorbed in the contents of the noticeboard or tidying up the magazines and emptying the ashtrays. Out of sheer boredom and frustration I volunteered for front-of-house duties, a bad decision as this was another closed shop ruled over by two antique harpies who after a while condescended to let me show the patrons to their seats, a thankless task as the faithful piled

231

out of their minibuses, stampeded into the theatre and sat where they liked. It was first come first served, and with ten tons of crimplene bearing down on me I thought it was prudent to get out of their way and let them get on with it.

Once the curtain had come down on the infamous production of *The Lion in Winter* I got my coat and went home. There was no point hanging about here any more so best take my square peg out of their round hole and find another diversion.

I'd been transferred from Steers House back over the water to Birkenhead. It was not a move I was happy about, even though I was bored stiff at Steers House. I couldn't see Horden House being an improvement. After all, it was the same tasks, just in a different workplace. I'd miss getting the ferry over to Liverpool; it made the start to the day an event. It would have been easier and a lot quicker for me to take the underground, but there was something special about going to work on a boat, taking your morning promenade on the top deck, enjoying the bracing estuary air and the view across the Mersey to an approaching Liverpool, and following it with a corned beef sandwich and a cup of tea made with condensed milk in the little café below deck. The underground was mundane in comparison and I always went to work on the *Mountwood* or the *Woodchurch*, enjoying it every time.

No more ferry boats. It was up and at 'em after the usual prisoner-of-war-camp wake-up drill.

'Paul, it's eight o'clock. Get up or your head'll go flat.'

'I'm up.'

'It's ten past eight. Are you getting up or what?'

'I'm up.'

'This tea's going stone cold down here, and your toast's rock hard.'

'I'm up,' this time accompanied by throwing a leg out of the bed and banging haphazardly on the bedroom floor with the foot.

'Are you having a fit?' Mother's voice sounds too close to be coming from downstairs; I open one eye and see that she is standing menacingly over the bed, grimly observing the leg action. 'UP!' Curtains flung back and window opened wide accompanied by usual monologue. 'You needn't think that you're lying stinking in your pit all day, my lad. You can get yourself out of that bed, down them stairs and out of this house for work double bloody quick.'

Camp Commandant retreats downstairs. Breathe sigh of relief and crawl under the bedclothes to evade arctic blast coming from open window. Enemy returns with secret weapon; plugging it in she leaves it running on the landing, right outside my bedroom door, until I am forced, screaming, unable to bear the noise any longer, out of my warm bed and across a freezing bedroom to switch it off. This was below the belt. Worse, it was an extreme and inhuman form of abuse that would've been frowned upon by Amnesty if they'd been aware of the torture by Electrolux vacuum cleaner that was occurring in Holly Grove.

I'd also got a part-time bar job in the Royal Air Force Association club in leafy Oxton. During the week I served in the little bar downstairs with Audrey, who was the quint-essential barmaid of a certain age found on Bamford postcards. At weekends the ballroom upstairs opened and the members danced with their wives to a Palm Court trio who played the same limited repertoire week in week out; there was always 'Ramona' played in the tempo of a rumba, 'The Street Where You Live' as a perky foxtrot and 'Martyr' to the beat of a strict tango. On Saturdays when the joint was jumping the band threw caution to the wind and went with something a little more contemporary. The room rocked as a sea of geriatric ravers gyrated to the strains of 'Rock Around The Clock' and 'Let's Twist Again'. These days I'd see the irony and enjoy it,

probably join in, but in 1972 I found it as painfully and embar-
rassingly naff as the shapeless maroon nylon jacket and
matching bow tie that I had to wear behind the bar. I can't say
I liked many of my customers. The majority of the male
patrons of the club were fusty old snobs who congregated at
the bar with their large Scotches and cigars and condemned
everyone from 'the Blacks' to the damn government for the
abolition of hanging.

'I'm glad it's been abolished,' Audrey piped up in her 'wickle
girl voice' from her permanent position wedged on a stool at
the end of the bar, 'because now I can shoot my ex-husband
and get away with it.' Much merriment and fussing of Audrey
from the gentlemen of the bar.

'Get this young lady a drink.' Audrey had the men eating out
of the palm of her Thumbelina-sized hand.

She'd worked for some years in a golf club before divorcing
her husband and coming to the RAFA. She carried a torch for
the days when she'd stood behind her elegant bar with fifteen
different kinds of malt whisky and held court to a bunch of
well-heeled, Pringle-sweater-wearing, randy middle-aged
admirers instead of the boring old men that she had to put up
with in this unsophisticated, fuddy-duddy fossil hole, waiting
on a league of gentlemen who surreptitiously leered at her
when their wives were about but tried to paw her when
they'd left them safely at home. She was tiny and doll-like with
a mass of viciously teased up and backcombed hair in four
dubious shades of red framing her ageing baby-doll face,
giving her the look of a Busby Berkeley chorus girl dressed as
a poppy.

She belonged to the Aunty Chris School of Maquillage and
adhered to the golden rule that you never appeared in public
without your make-up. Audrey's technicolour paint job
made Aunty Chris's face look well scrubbed. She kept
vanishing to the Ladies every five minutes to touch up, pausing

on the way to do a bit of subtle touching up of a different nature with some of her regulars.

I walked into the snooker room to collect glasses one quiet night, and found her pushed up against the snooker table by a member of the committee, trousers round his ankles and his saggy old buttocks flapping as he gyrated his hips like two tired old pillowcases drying in a breeze. Her skirt had ridden up to reveal an expanse of wobbly white thigh hanging obscenely over the top of her black nylons, strangely reminiscent of a pint of Guinness with an overflowing head.

'Don't say anything, will you?' Audrey pleaded afterwards. 'It was just a bit of company, two unhappy people snatching a quick bit of affection.' Don't worry, I assured her, I wouldn't be discussing this with anyone ... except maybe Denise, Barbara and Robin, who made up the rest of the bar staff. I'd been momentarily struck dumb by the sight of two old people having sex over a billiard table. Ugh. It was not a memory that I was keen to hang on to.

'There's been no man in my life since I divorced that bastard,' she whined, wobbling unsteadily for a moment on her four-inch heels; she'd been at the brandy again, 'and I'm the kind of woman who needs to be looked after by a man, if you get my drift,' she added with a wink.

Audrey went in for a lot of pouting. Her lips fascinated me. They were coated à la Kathy Kirby with a gallon of red gloss, which shimmered perilously on the surface when she spoke so that she hardly dared move them in case the reservoir of gloss broke away into a rogue estuary and took off down the side of her mouth. It made her look like a ventriloquist's doll. She stank the place out with her liberal use of a heady and whory perfume and sounded like a temple dancer in full flight whenever she moved her arms and jangled her numerous charm bracelets and bangles.

Mrs Mack the bar steward and some of the members, mostly

the wives, looked down on Audrey with her big bust and flirtatious manner and resented the way their husbands bought her large brandies and held on to her hand for longer than necessary when receiving their change. They thought she was 'fast', and not quite the kind of barmaid one might expect to greet one when ordering a port and lemon at the RAFA club.

Meanwhile back at the Social all was not well. I was in trouble again, and summonsed to appear at the head office in Bootle to face a disciplinary hearing. The charge was all the usual offences: not amenable to discipline, spends far too much time talking, does not concentrate, is frequently late or absent, shows no aptitude for advancement . . . in short, why was I still in the employ of the civil service and wasting everyone's, including my own, time? Good question.

At this so-called disciplinary hearing I was taken into a room and verbally abused by two senior officers. It was as if I were being interrogated by the police for a bank heist: these two highly un-civil servants did everything but hit me.

'I ask you again, for the umpteenth time, give me one good reason why I shouldn't dismiss you, O'Grady,' said one of my inquisitors, who obviously saw the bully Flashman from *Tom Brown's Schooldays* as his role model in life.

I sat calmly contemplating these two officious jokers, and then I suddenly became aware of my own voice saying that I could honestly think of no good reason why they shouldn't sack me, but to save them the trouble of all the form-filling in triplicate that a dismissal would obviously require, why didn't I just give 'em a week's notice and we'll call it quits, eh, boys?

The slapping sound I could hear was the noise shit makes as it hits the fan, but I didn't care. I felt exhilarated by my sudden stand against authority, but how the hell was I going to explain to my parents that the good steady job and the pension that went with it had just bitten the dust?

I sat on the top deck of the bus watching Stanley Road go by. My decision to quit couldn't have come at a worse time. Nerves were very fragile. My nephew had been rushed to hospital near to death with gastroenteritis, my sister had miscarried and Aunty Anne had lost her husband Harold after a long fight with cancer. All these disasters had happened within three weeks, and now to chuck the cat among the pigeons I'd gone and walked out of my job.

I'd have to find another one quickly. Maybe I'd try a shipping office or a pub . . . and then a thought hit me. Why not get a job in London? I'd dreamed about living in London for years. It was Avengerland, a mythical place where everybody lived in a smart pad in either Westminster or Primrose Hill and drove around deserted West End streets in a Lotus Europa on their way to chic soirees and discotheques. What was I dithering for? Here was a chance to actually make it happen, to say goodbye to Birkenhead and make a go of it in the Promised Land. What could I do? A bar job maybe, in a hotel or pub, living in – that would kill two birds with one stone. My mind was racing. There was an employment agency at the bottom of Wood Street that specialized in catering work, called Lifeline. It was written on the whitewashed wall in big black letters, with 'Proprietor, T. Brailey' in a smaller hand underneath. I tore up the two flights of stairs, anxious to see if the mysterious T. Brailey could indeed throw me a lifeline.

John Christie's back bedroom was never as grim as the waiting room of that agency. The walls and ceiling had been painted in a depressing bottle green and brown, and traces of ancient lino clung to the bare, uneven floor, absorbed into the very grain of the wood by time and wear, refusing to leave even though the rest of it had crumbled and gone west years ago. A small gas fire with most of its elements burnt out popped in the grate, creating a claustrophobic atmosphere in the airless little room.

I wanted to turn on my heel and get the hell out of it but was halted in my tracks by the arrival of a pale, ethereal creature enquiring if I were looking for flats or employment. One half of the office was devoted to finding suitable accommodation for their clients and was run by herself, she explained, while the other half, the employment agency, was the domain of her sister Thelma who would be with me shortly, that is if she was correct in her assumption that I was seeking employment within the hotel and catering industry. She spoke like a character from *Cranford*, one of the vaguer, more wistful ones, and had a whiff of mothballs and lace gloves about her. Her sister Thelma, the T. Brailey of the sign outside, exploded out of the inner office. To describe Thelma Brailey is to describe Renee Houston as the arts mistress in *The Belles of St Trinian's* crossed with Jennifer Paterson of *Two Fat Ladies* fame.

Thelma was a powerhouse. Small and stocky, she wore her hair up in a bun that she anchored together with two pencils wedged in the top. She had a tendency towards sloppy Joe sweaters, once popular with beatniks, black leggings and biker's boots.

'Yes, what can we do for you?' she demanded, scrutinizing me through a pair of enormous specs that magnified her watery eyes to startling proportions. 'Have you had any experience in the catering field?'

I told her about the RAFA club, which went down very well, and assured her that I could get a reference from them.

'And are you in the employ of anyone at the moment?'

She was very impressed when I told her that I was a civil servant.

'You're not a common or garden barman,' she said, rifling through a mountain of papers on her desk. 'You're management material, and I know of an excellent hotel in Virginia

Water which is looking for a smart lad with ambition like yourself to fill the currently vacant position of trainee manager. Does that appeal?'

I couldn't believe it. It was that easy. Within minutes I had the prospect of a fabulous job.

'Is Virginia Water in London?' I asked her.

'Just round the corner from Piccadilly Circus,' she said without missing a beat, picking up the phone. 'Just fill in that form while I give the manager, a very charming man, a call.'

Thelma was wasting her talents in this dismal little office. She'd have made an excellent white slaver, crating up unsuspecting would-be chambermaids and shipping them off to the opium dens and brothels of Shanghai.

'Yes, he's here with me at the moment,' she was saying down the receiver, rubbing her forefinger on her forehead as she spoke. 'He's very smart, very bright, a civil servant who also has years of experience in the catering field and can run a bar single-handed if required. Impeccable references, just what the Wheatsheaf is looking for . . . I'll put him on the phone.'

I was interviewed down the line by the manager who was, as Thelma had said, a 'charming man'. I was to learn all aspects of running a hotel, would work both in the bar and in the restaurant, and if I were to consider taking this position would not only get all my food provided free, but would receive an excellent salary and the promise of a never-ending stream of generous tips. Also included in this once-in-a-lifetime offer was my own room within the hotel, overlooking the lake in Windsor Great Park. I was instantly sold on the idea and agreed without considering the consequences to start work in a week's time at this glorious Wheatsheaf Hotel. 'Welcome to the Wheatsheaf,' I envisioned myself saying as I greeted guests from behind my plush Crossroads Motel-style reception desk or mixing a pre-dinner martini behind a chic cocktail bar to the accompaniment of a Laurie Johnson bossa nova piped through the ultra-modern muzak system. I just had to get round my parents.

'I've quit the civil service and I'm going to work in a hotel just round the corner from Piccadilly Circus.' No, honesty was not always the best policy, especially where my mother was concerned. I gave it a bit of thought on the ferry going home and decided the best option was to lie. I'd tell them I'd been offered a temporary transfer to an office in London with digs in the civil service hostel. Far easier and gentler to feed them this line. The truth was only going to cause a third world war.

'London? You mean London down south London? That London?' My mother's reaction was as I expected.

'Well there's only one London, Mum.'

'You wouldn't know with you, it could be a London anywhere.'

My dad took a bit of persuading. I painted a rosy picture of helping with the Christmas rush on Giros in a nice little office in Euston, protected from the evils of the big city by the omnipotent civil service who looked after their young employees like a parent, even going to the trouble of caring for them in the monastic confines of the mythical civil service hostel.

'Where is this place you'll be staying?' he asked suspiciously. 'What's it called?'

'The Wheatsheaf Hotel. It's in a place called Virginia Water.'

My mother pounced. 'That's in Surrey, not London.' Unable to comprehend the speed at which the civil service required my transfer to London, she was looking for holes in my flimsy plot.

'It's only round the corner,' I answered airily. 'Takes about ten minutes to get to the West End.' I knew this to be a fact, for in *The Avengers* wouldn't they be in a city street one minute and then turn a corner and be in a country lane the next?

'This tale is as far-fetched as a bucket of shite from China,' my mother said, poking me in the chest with her finger. 'And if I find out that you're up to no good, or if you dare to bring trouble to this door again, then I'll swing for you.'

In the end it didn't take her long to rumble the whole story. Thelma Brailey sent me written confirmation of my new job and my mother opened the letter. My parents were waiting for me when I got home from my final day at Horden House. My mates had thrown a leaving do for me in the pub and I was more than a bit pissed, but I sobered up pretty quick when my mother waved Thelma's letter under my nose. My dad was saddened that I'd lied to him and couldn't understand why I'd even want to consider running off to work in a strange hotel.

'Why would you want to wash dishes all day?' he asked. 'Or wait on people? Bloody kowtowing to someone who thinks they're royalty just because they've spent two quid on a meal?' He wasn't angry with me, which made it worse, just confused, unable to comprehend my irrational behaviour. It took some time to persuade him but in the end he reluctantly agreed that I should 'give it a go', adding none too convincingly that it might be the making of me.

My mother had taken to her bed and lay in the dark staring up at the ceiling, clutching a hanky dramatically to her breast.

'I can't believe it,' she sobbed accusingly. 'You've gone from the civil service to domestic service. What in the Mother of God's name has come over you?'

'I'm going to be a trainee manager,' I pleaded, 'and it's not domestic service. Times have changed.'

'Trainee manager my arse,' she spat, propping herself up on one elbow. 'You'll be skivvying behind a bar all the hours God sends. Hotel work is the lowest of the low, always has been, it's the last knockings of service and attracts every loner, misfit and deadbeat that God ever put in shoe leather who can't get a decent job anywhere else.' She slumped back on to the pillows and sobbed into her hanky.

'You did it,' I said. 'You ran away to a hotel in the Isle of Man.' Maybe Aunty Chris was right, maybe what was in the bitch came out in the pup after all. But I didn't dare say so.

'Yes, and I wish that I'd stayed there,' she snapped, sitting bolt upright in bed again and pointing at me accusingly. 'I didn't have a good job in the civil service, unlike some; I didn't have opportunities that I carelessly threw away. I had nothing . . . nothing.' She lay back down on the bed, exhausted by her temper. 'Get on with it,' she moaned, closing the subject. 'I don't care any more.'

I went to my bedroom and packed my holdall with what few clothes I had, including my one good suit for my 'managerial duties'. When I got downstairs my mother was in the kitchen filling a flask.

'I've made some tea and a few sarnies for the coach,' she sniffed, not meeting my eye. 'And I want this flask back.' My dad slid a five-pound note into my hand, 'in case of emergencies', as we said our goodbyes. What with that and what was left of my week's wages and holiday pay, my finances came to the grand sum of a tenner. London, here I come.

There are many lonely places on the planet but none so bleak as the stop for the overnight X61 Crossville Coach for London. Standing there waiting, alone and feeling sorry for myself, watching the last bus pulling out of Woodside terminus as I braced myself against the biting December wind that howled up the hill from the river, I wanted nothing more than to pick up my holdall and go home to my nice warm bed and the security of 23 Holly Grove and pretend that the whole ridiculous turn of affairs hadn't happened – but I couldn't. I'd burned my bridges, and having made the decision to go off to London, or Virginia Water or wherever it was Proprietor T. Brailey was sending me, I had to stick to it.

London was everything I thought it would be. At five thirty

in the morning I woke from a brief and fitful sleep to the delights of the Finchley Road. My God, this was it, this was London. My stomach was doing cartwheels and I silently willed the coach to go faster as I looked out of the window trying to spot a recognizable landmark. Driving past the white Regency houses of Regent's Park towards Park Lane I nearly leaped out of the coach. These houses are only the same ones that were used as locations in *The Avengers*, I wanted to scream excitedly at my fellow passengers. Look at that big white house, that was in 'You'll Catch Your Death'.

There were half a dozen people scattered about the coach. Aunty Chris would've described them as 'lost souls on life's highway, all with a story to tell'. (Aunty Chris was a big fan of *The Untouchables*. She looked upon the late night café at Woodside Ferry as if it were a painting by Hopper and wore her black mac with the collar up and belted tightly at the waist, imagining herself as a world-weary gal who had bin dun wrong, as indeed she had.) She'd have loved the loners on the coach and would've spent the trip imagining reasons for their being there. 'See that one sat at the back? You know why she's going to London, don't you? Why do you think? For an abortion, God help her. Men, they make me sick.'

Outside the Playboy club on Park Lane was a bright red Lotus Europa Mark II, exactly the same as Tara King's. It was an omen. London was going to be exactly as I'd imagined. It wouldn't be long before I had a mews house tucked away behind the Houses of Parliament, I told myself encouragingly, maybe even have a Lotus myself parked outside the Playboy club.

The coach swept past Buckingham Palace on its last lap towards Victoria Coach Station. Someone shouted that the flag was up, which meant the Queen was home and was probably still in bed. I tried to imagine the Queen in bed. Did she sleep with a head full of rollers and a chiffon scarf? What side of the

243

bed did she sleep on? How far did she have to run if she wanted to go to the lav in the middle of the night? Did she have an electric blanket . . . and a Teasmade? My excitement quickly turned to nerves as the coach pulled in and stopped at the station. This was it – I was finally in London.

First things first. I checked the time of the coach to Virginia Water. The journey, I was told, took just over an hour, which meant that the Wheatsheaf was hardly 'just round the corner from Piccadilly Circus' as I'd thought up to now. The penny finally dropped. I'd been stitched up like a kipper by Thelma bloody Brailey. Well, since I was here I might as well give it a go. My initial nervousness had gone and I was feeling fairly optimistic and desperate to explore the city. I had at least eight hours to kill before I needed to be in Virginia Water, which meant the best part of the day could be spent doing just what I wanted. I went down into the gents' lav to give my face a swill and clean my teeth. I could hear my mother's voice as I got a whiff of piss and bleach.

'If you have to use a public lav when you're out be very careful – you get all sorts in there. Always go into a cubicle to do your business, even if you only want to stand up. You don't want some dirty old sod looking at your willy.' Looking at some of the dubious characters hanging around I remembered her wise words and, paying my penny, went into one of the lock-ups.

The graffiti was fascinating, as were the graphic illustrations of crudely drawn men with highly exaggerated and oversized penises doing strange, and what looked like physically impossible, things to each other. Victoria Coach Station's very own *Kama Sutra*. I sat there engrossed. There was a hole in the wall the size of a half-crown, and I froze as I realized that there was an eye peering through it at me. I slapped my hand over the hole and dragging my trousers up ran out of the cubicle. I stood at the sink and splashed my burning face with water. There was the sound of a toilet flushing and a door opening behind me, and I could see in the mirror the owner of the eye casually toddling over to the sink next to me. I took a sly look at him. He was little and fat with a bald patch and a comb-over. He was wearing a black and white top and tight black trousers, and there were traces of white make-up and lipstick on his puffy face. He looked like a swollen Marcel Marceau.

''Ello, love,' he said matter-of-factly, stroking his eyebrow in the mirror. I gave him a curt nod that my mother would've been proud of. He glanced around to see if we were being observed before slowly leaning over and slyly grabbing my crotch. 'Nice carts, dear,' he simpered, giving me a good squeeze. I leaped ten feet in the air and let out a strangled shriek.

'All right, dear, no need to scream the fuckin' cottage down,' Marcel said, swishing past me in a huff. 'You fuckin' feely hommies shouldn't be getting it out if you don't want trade,' he added, swanning up the stairs.

I had no idea what he was talking about. I'd yet to learn Polari, the language of the queens, and for all I knew he could've been speaking Polish with an East End accent. If this was a London homo then I was bitterly disappointed. He looked nothing like the sophisticated models who stood around casually in their underpants, pointing out something of great interest in the distance to a colleague who also happened to be in his vest and underpants while he enjoyed his pipe, on page 342 of my mother's catalogue.

I had a cup of tea in the café to gather my wits before dumping my holdall in left luggage and venturing out for a wander. It was still dark; it was also cold and I was suddenly aware of how tired I was. My eyes itched and burned and my lips were dry and sore, but I brightened up when I stumbled upon Eaton Place. This was where the Bellamy family and their staff lived in *Upstairs, Downstairs*. This was the very street that the defiant Sarah marched down after walking out on a life below stairs to seek a career on the 'alls. London was like a giant film set and Eaton Place particularly unreal in the half-light of the early morning. I knew then why I had come to London. It was beautiful.

I made my way to Victoria Station to find the tube. I had no idea about the mysteries of the London Underground and spent half an hour studying the tube map on the station wall, trying to make sense of the coloured lines as I plotted my course to Piccadilly Circus. I'd read an article in my dad's Sunday paper entitled 'Twenty-four Hours in the Life of Piccadilly Circus' and noticed with interest that 'homosexuals lurked' (*sic*) under the arches of the Fire Insurance Building. The journalist went on to say that this was a well-known 'haunt' of male prostitutes and their homosexual clientele. Maybe I'd be mistaken for a male prostitute and be whisked off my feet to some millionaire playboy's pad to become his plaything.

I'll never forget my first glimpse of Piccadilly Circus, climbing the stairs from the confusing bowels of the underground with the anticipation of a child into Regent Street and a burst of light to find that the sun had risen and it was a bright crisp morning. I found myself outside a shop called Swan and Edgar's (now Tower Records). It was still early and the shop was closed, but even if it had been open I wouldn't have had the nerve to go in. It looked too posh. To my right was the statue of Eros, although I knew from my ma that it was really Eros's twin Anteros and that it was a monument to Lord Shaftesbury; to my left were the neon hoardings and the arches of the Fire Insurance Building.

I stood drinking it all in. I no longer felt tired; I was exhilarated by the mere fact that I was actually standing in the centre of London. Piccadilly bloody Circus. Crossing the road towards the Fire Building I looked to see if I could spot any male prostitutes 'haunting' the arches, not that I had any idea what a male prostitute looked like, but it was disappointingly deserted. I hung around for a bit to see if I could tempt any millionaires who might be driving past on their way home from a smart nightclub in their Bentleys or E-type Jags and 'looking for a bit of company', but there was nothing doing. Business must be slack of a Saturday morning. I felt stupid leaning on the railings and besides, hunger was beginning to get the better of me, so I went in search of breakfast. In Denman Street I found the New Piccadilly Café. It was like stepping back in time to the fifties: Formica tables with chairs covered in bright plastic, glass coffee cups and saucers and a large horseshoe-shaped menu displaying the bill of fare, yet another exciting and eccentric location in London's film set for me to play in. It was unsophisticated, strangely comforting and, most important, cheap. I ordered the full English and a cup of tea.

'You enjoying that, my friend?' the man behind the counter shouted over to me as I shovelled down the food. 'Where you from?' he asked as he brought my tea over to the table. He told me his name was Lorenzo and that his father had opened the café in the early fifties. 'Brasses on every corner and bloody Budapest street rats fighting the Bubble and squeaks in the street,' he told me, speaking yet another language that I didn't understand.

I told him a condensed version of my tale, trying to make the Wheatsheaf Hotel sound like the most marvellous place on earth.

'Ah, hotel life,' Lorenzo said sadly, shaking his head and going back to his counter. 'It's very hard life.' He brightened up enough when I was leaving to wish me good luck and tell me to visit again soon. I assured him I would but had no inkling that this was no idle promise, as I was to be a customer of the New Piccadilly Café for over three decades until it was finally closed down to make way for 'development' in December 2007.

In Great Windmill Street opposite the theatre there was a

247

shop that had a noticeboard in the window. I read the strange assortment of cards pinned up on the board with drawing pins and tried to make sense of them. There was a lady who gave enemas to discerning gentlemen and another who was a nanny and claimed that she was particularly good at dealing with naughty boys and bed-wetters. These I could more or less understand, but the others? *Large Chest for Sale, Soho. Phone Miss Blossom*, or *TV and Wardrobe for Sale, Marble Arch* and *Old Chair Bottoms Re-Caned. Phone Miss Swish*. What did it mean, I asked myself, why were all the single women in the area selling off their furniture?

Here was a woman who had a rubber mackintosh and boots for sale. Were times so hard she was having to sell off her mac and wellies? And another poor soul forced to give tango lessons at a very strict tempo in a Soho garret. Obviously not everyone found gold paving stones in London then.

I puzzled over those cards for years until a friend eventually put me right. I genuinely had no idea that they were euphemisms for something else entirely that had nothing at all to do with the sale or repair of second-hand furniture or clothing.

I wandered round Savile Row, New Bond Street and Oxford Street. London had started to come to life but the big crowds were yet to descend and I was able to study Selfridges' Christmas windows in peace. The theme was Alice in Wonderland. There was a film of the same name being released in the New Year and the producers obviously saw Selfridges' windows as the perfect place for a plug. They really were out-standing, though, dressed with sets and costumes from the forthcoming film. I stood there for a good half-hour, amazed by the detail in the incredible costumes and the ingenuity of the sets. I was used to Blackler's Dancing Waters and papier-mâché puppets – I'd never seen anything of this quality before. This was pure magic.

I was hovering round the door, contemplating whether to go inside or not, when a woman swept past me. It was Honor Blackman. Cathy Gale, the original Avenger girl who had left to become Bond girl Pussy Galore, had just brushed past me in a huge white coat. The doorman greeted her and she replied in that unmistakable voice. I'm surprised I didn't have a seizure. I tore after her through the perfume and make-up department, beginning to feel an empathy with Alice as she chased the White Rabbit, not that I was or am a fan of Alice. Personally I think she was a snotty little prig and I wish I'd sat behind her in school so I could've put chewing gum in her hair.

Standing by each counter, an assortment of women with hair higher than a Maori's hut and startlingly thick make-up posed with bottles of perfume enquiring if 'Madam would like to test?' Honor Blackman swept past them all, declining their offers; she was probably very particular about what sort of scent she used, I thought. She would wear something heady and sensual from Paris that was so expensive that a six-ounce bottle was the same price as a house in Lowther Street. She reeked of elegance anyway and didn't need or want a blast of Blue Jeans, the discerning woman. I studied her as she examined a pot of cream, putting it back quickly with a polite but firm 'No thank you'. God, she was elegant. She had hardly any make-up on, but she made those living shop-window dummies hawking their wares and spraying their noxious scents look like a raddled grab bag of overpainted drag queens. I desperately wanted to go over and speak to her but I didn't have the bottle, and I didn't want her to think that I was a crazed fan, autograph book in hand, stalking her around Selfridges. Instead I watched her, John Steed's right-hand woman, rise majestically up on the escalator and out of sight.

London was a marvellous place, I thought, as I watched her vanish. It really was a Wonderland where anything could and obviously did, happen. I desperately wanted to be part of it.

CHAPTER FIFTEEN

I DIDN'T FEEL AS ENTHUSIASTIC ABOUT VIRGINIA WATER OR THE Wheatsheaf Hotel. When the coach dropped me off on the other side of the busy road, the hotel hardly lived up to the glowing reference that T. Brailey had given it; it was an unimpressive and slightly neglected-looking coachhouse-style pub/restaurant. It also looked disturbingly deserted. The place was in darkness.

Two Scousers, a boy and a girl not much older than me, were hanging around outside. They'd been ringing the bell for half an hour with no success and were starting to panic.

'D'you work here?' the girl asked. 'Cos if you do, get this door open. I'm freezin' me tits off standing here.'

'I think the dump's closed down,' the lad said, blowing on his hands as I tried the bell. 'That mad cow from that Lifeline must be taking the piss.' Two more suckers of T. Brailey's, I thought to myself, giving the door a few good bangs. A light suddenly came on and the door was flung open.

'Where's the fuckin' fire?' said a large podgy man with no shirt, standing hands on hips in the doorway, glaring at us in the overhead light. He looked us up and down, and sneered. 'We don't serve gyppos.'

'We're from Lifeline,' I answered in my best St Anselm's voice, speaking for all of us. 'We're the new staff.'

251

'Oh, are you now? Well isn't that just tickety-boo,' the podgy one said, scratching the nipple of one of his pendulous man boobs. 'God help me,' he sighed theatrically, 'the deadbeats of the north that woman sends me. Well, you'd better come in.' He took us through the entrance hall with its faux wooden beams and hunting prints to a dark flight of stairs marked *Private*. 'I was having my hair blow-dried,' he complained as we followed him up the stairs and into the staff room. 'The hotel doesn't open until five, you should have known that. This really is most, most inconvenient, you know.' He had a big fleshy backside and hips that swayed from side to side, and I hated him on sight. Let's call him Paul Finch. He told us, with a smug expression on his pink shiny face, that he was the deputy manager and under no circumstances were we to refer to him by his Christian name in the public areas. In those sacred places we were to call him Mr Finch and nothing else. 'In fact,' he added grandly, 'until we get to know each other better you are to address me as Mr Finch at all times.' He had the girlish complexion of a eunuch and a pursed snapdragon for a mouth. He obviously fancied himself, sat there on a kitchen chair, his belly spilling over the top of his shiny black trousers, having his blond-streaked hair blow-dried by a creature in a padded blue dressing gown who turned out to be called Carol.

She was from Liverpool and had spent most of her working life as a live-in barmaid. She'd worked everywhere, chasing the seasons from Butlins holiday camps to the Isle of Man and Blackpool, but for the time being she'd given up her peripatetic lifestyle to spend the winter months at the Wheatsheaf. She was an odd-looking woman, prone to wearing short, girly pinafore dresses that were far too young for her. She was what my ma would call 'big-boned' – broad-shouldered with chunky thighs and thick ankles. She had a mournful face and large watery cow eyes set a little too far apart in her head. What with all this and a heavily pronounced overbite, even the most charitable person couldn't have called her pretty. She wore her mousy hair in a tight little beehive with a slide either side of her fringe, making her moon face look even fuller. She spent a lot of time on this hairdo, but only on the bits she could see in the tiny little dressing-table mirror in her cupboard of a room. She was forever asking 'Is me hair all right at the back?' to which I always replied yes even though it looked like a collapsed bird's nest.

Paul summoned a minion to show me to my room. I was to be sharing with a guy named Chris, which I wasn't very happy about as the manager had promised me my own room. Paul roared laughing when I told him this, and then turned on me. 'Who the bloody hell do you think you are?' he said scornfully. 'You're lucky to have a roof over your head at all. You're all the same, you bloody whingeing Scousers. Piss off.' He paused in his tirade to light up a Consulate. 'Don't worry, though,' he went on, throwing his match at the overflowing ashtray and missing, 'you won't be spending a lot of time in your suite. You'll be working hard, I'll see to that. Now pick up that match.'

I lay on one of the single beds in my dismal little room. It had a sloping attic ceiling that I knew would give me concussion every time I sat upright in bed. The carpet was threadbare, its original pattern now undistinguishable under greasy patches and dubious stains. Apart from a few photos of page free stunners torn out of the *Sun* and stuck unevenly with Sellotape on the wall over what I took to be my cellmate's bed, the room was bare and painted a depressing shade of light blue. In one corner stood an old-fashioned wardrobe whose door, if not fastened properly, had an unnerving tendency to swing open in the middle of the night. It reminded me of the landing cupboard in Lowther Street. In the other corner was a sink which had come away from the wall and hung drunkenly to one side. Underneath it, the patch of carpet was damp and heavily stained and there was a slight whiff of pee. Obviously the former occupants of this hovel weren't averse to taking a leak in the sink. I was exhausted. The last time I'd slept properly was Thursday night, and it was now Saturday afternoon. I'd just close my eyes and have forty winks . . .

'Come on, wake up.' A hearty rugger type was shaking me forcibly. 'We've got to go down for dinner. Hurry up – you don't want to be late.' The rugger bugger introduced himself as Chris. There was no shade on the light and even though the bulb couldn't have been more than ten watts it hurt my eyes, which were burning and heavy for want of sleep.

Like me, Chris was a trainee manager, and he'd been at the Wheatsheaf for over a month. He was a real jobsworth and a crashing bore, and he looked upon the management as gods. He kept up a running commentary in his West Country accent as he changed his shirt. 'After you've eaten, Paul – that's Mr Finch to staff when we're downstairs in the bars – wants you to collect litter from the garden.'

'But it's dark.'

'There's a torch by the bins. Then he wants me to show you round before leaving you with Carol in the upstairs bar. She'll show you what to do. Then just before we close he wants you to help out in the kitchen.'

'Doing what? Cooking?'

'Washing glasses and helping with the dishes. The restaurants are always fully booked on a Saturday and the bars are packed. The Wheatsheaf is a very popular hotel, you know, so there's lots to do. Come on, then, shake a leg – and don't forget you have to wear a shirt and tie and black trousers. They'll give you a waistcoat to wear downstairs.'

The red nylon jacket at the RAFA club had been bad enough. I couldn't wait to see Chef and Brewer's badge of servitude. I rolled grumpily off the bed and unpacked my now heavily creased managerial suit and a few shirts from my holdall.

'You'd better iron that,' Chris said, looking disapprovingly at my dishcloth of a shirt. 'Chef and Brewer send inspectors round from time to time and you never know when one might turn up. They just appear unexpected like, and a creased shirt could mean instant dismissal. The iron's in the staff room. You know where that is, don't you?'

He droned on and on like an old woman. I wanted to beat him to death with the wobbly leg of the solitary chair that stood under the curtainless window and then hot-tail it back to Holly Grove.

'I want a bath,' I moaned. 'I've been travelling all night and day.'

'No time for that,' he trilled. 'Just time for a quick wash and brush up.' He sounded like an old-fashioned barber. I mooched off sulkily in search of the iron.

The kitchen staff and waiters were mostly Spanish. They responded to Chris's introduction with a bored nod. Many faces came and went at the Wheatsheaf and as far as they were concerned I was just another bit of flotsam passing through. I sat in silence as I chased my meal of lamb chop and boiled potato around the pool of grease it floated in on my plate. I was usually fussy about food but tonight I didn't care. I was so hungry I'd have eaten anything. Looking around I could see that my spud wasn't the only thing swimming in grease. The kitchen floor and worktops positively ran with it. I smiled at the waiters but they totally ignored me and carried on jabbering among themselves in Spanish. Fuck you, I thought, wolfing down half a spud. Over by the stove a strange creature, like a ghost, with a shock of white hair that matched his apron, stood stirring a huge pan and staring at me.

'Where you from?' he asked in a broad Irish accent, pausing to scratch the papery skin of his cheek.

Here was someone trying to be friendly, I thought. 'Merseyside,' I answered brightly, giving him my best forced smile.

He scowled at me and snarled, 'Fucking Scousers. The place is crawling with them.' The smile died on my lips and I carried on chasing the congealed lamb chop around the slippery plate in silence. I knew now how my dad must have felt when he arrived in Liverpool from Dublin and received a similar welcome.

The Wheatsheaf had two restaurants and an assortment of themed bars. Downstairs in the Cellar Bar the décor was Chef and Brewer's idea of hip: blue neon lighting that made the customers' teeth glow, psychedelic posters on the walls, and loud music. It was where the beautiful young people of Virginia Water gathered. I hated them because I was jealous of them. With their beautiful clothes, shiny hair and suntans they all seemed enormously sophisticated and made me feel ugly, awkward and very, very provincial in comparison. The other bars had sporting motifs. The Jockey Bar had a racing theme, another had a stuffed fox in a glass case, and apart from the trendy Cellar Bar they all had the ubiquitous huntin', shootin' and fishin' prints on the walls. Carol's bar was off the upstairs restaurant. She was extremely territorial and resented the intrusion of a newcomer.

'You can collect all the glasses, empty the ashtrays, wipe the tables down and then stack those mixers on the fridge shelf,' she said with a face of doom, 'and then if it gets really busy you'd better help serve, but under no circumstances are you to make the Irish coffees and you better hadn't mess my till up or waste any stock. Just keep out of my bloody way an' we'll be fine. I know how this bar works, see.' She was an efficient but surly barmaid, her face like a mournful Jersey cow's as she shuffled behind the bar in her Dr Scholls dispensing gin and tonics with a chilly smile. I tried to strike up a conversation with her.

'What part of Liverpool are you from, Carol?'

'Why d'you want to know?' she snapped. 'I left there a long time ago and have no intention of ever going back. As far as I'm concerned I'm a southerner now, so don't mention it again, understand? Now there're some empty glasses on that table over there that won't wash themselves.'

After the pub closed and I'd washed what seemed like every glass and plate in Surrey I was finally allowed to go to bed. I lay there hallucinating from sheer exhaustion, trying to ignore the list of tomorrow's tasks that Chris was reeling off in the dark from his bed opposite mine.

'We get up at eight and then after breakfast you have to empty all the bottle skips. Phew, I don't envy you that. We were really busy tonight so there'll be millions of bottles to sort. Once you've done that you go upstairs and clean Carol's bar. Don't forget to take the coffee machine apart and give it a really good clean, and when you mop the Gents out don't forget the disinfectant blocks for the urinal . . .' He rambled on gleefully until I drifted off, to dream of coach journeys and beer glasses, too exhausted to remember that I was homesick.

The Wheatsheaf had a pecking order to rival the Forbidden City.

Number one was the big boss, the manager, whom we very rarely saw. He preferred to stay in his nice spacious flat with his wife and kids and delegate. Next to God was Paul Finch; he was assisted by his two henchmen, the bar and restaurant managers. The restaurant manager could be affable enough when it suited him, but he was not to be trusted. Neither was the bar manager, a real creep who prowled the bars looking for an empty glass on an unwiped table so that he could tell you what an inept, lazy fool you were and how you would never make it to a managerial position.

I didn't want one. Despite my best efforts I realized that a career in hotel and catering was not for me. Trainee hotel managers were at the bottom of the pecking order. We were the skivvies, exploited and expected to be passively compliant at all times with Paul Finch's whims, and do every dirty job that he demanded under the masquerade of 'training'.

'If you want to become management you have to learn every aspect of the job,' he would preach as he sent me off on yet another hideous task. 'Now go and unblock that toilet in the Ladies. You'd think those uncivilized bitches would learn to put their sanitary towels in the bins provided.'

I was permanently cold. Our garret was freezing. It was too cold of a morning to do anything but splash your face quickly with water from the lopsided sink, jump into some clothes and throw yourself down the back stairs and into the kitchen for a warm around the stove.

Breakfast was cornflakes and toast except for Sundays, when there was bacon and egg – providing the Irish Ghost was in the mood. The Irish Ghost only cooked for the staff. He didn't touch any of that fancy muck, as he called it, that went into the restaurants. He'd worked in hospital kitchens for years before ending up at the Wheatsheaf, which explained his lumpy mashed spuds and boiled-to-death cabbage. He was a terrible cook. His steak and kidney pie had a crust thicker and tougher than a paving stone, and the handful of grey gristle that called itself steak and kidney sat in a puddle of thin, watery gravy. He deeply resented the restaurant chefs' invading what he saw as 'his' kitchen, and there were frequent spats that provided a welcome diversion as I washed plates.

'Call yourself a professional chef?' he'd roar across the kitchen at the man who came in each night from Egham to prepare the prawn cocktails and steak and chips for the Wheatsheaf's discerning diners. The pro word again. 'You've been using one of my knives, haven't you? A real chef wouldn't touch another chef's knives. They're sacred, the tools of his trade. Touch them again and I'll have your bloody hand off.'

Occasionally the man from Egham would rise to the challenge and argue back, and once or twice they even came to blows, but usually, disappointingly for me, he ignored the Irish Ghost, preferring to get on with his job.

Each morning I had to clear out an endless number of skips, full to the brim with empty bottles which had to be put in their appropriate crates. It was a hanging offence if you put a Britvic orange bottle into a Schweppes bitter lemon crate. The skips stank of stale booze and fruit juice. The tomato juice was the worst – the smell of it and the feel of it would make me retch. This was cold, filthy work, and since gloves weren't provided I frequently cut my frozen hands on broken bottles, my lifeblood merging with the pool of stagnant tomato juice in the bottom of the skip.

'Haven't you finished yet?' the hated Finch would shout down to the yard from the staff-room window. 'You've got the Sports Bar to clean and open up yet, and don't forget to give those skips a really good hose down. They were a bit smelly last night,' he would add, waving a piece of toast under his nose as if it were a fan. I wanted to kill him. I wanted to kill every single member of staff in the Wheatsheaf Hotel and go home. Hatred kept me going. I'd lie in bed listening to Chris farting and scratching his psoriasis in the dark and invent enterprising ways to dispose of him. Remembering my ma's botany lessons, I'd drift off on a mephitic cloud dreaming of foxgloves and death cap toadstools. He revolted me. Sometimes I'd hear him crying in the night and would ask him, not out of sympathy but to shut him up, what was the matter.

'I miss my girlfriend,' he'd sob. 'I really love her, really, really love her.'

Stupid big fruit, I'd think to myself, but instead of saying so I'd look at the photograph he carried in his wallet of a particularly ugly troll and make soothing noises of appreciation and tell him how lucky he was to have such a beauty waiting for him back home.

His feet stank and he wore his socks in bed, and as well as the weeping psoriasis he confided in me that he was being treated for syphilis. I was surprised the troll had it in her, but it appeared that he'd caught the dose not from the troll but from a girl in Grimsby he'd met when he was on a course. I'd never come across anyone with a venereal disease before and was suitably shocked and fascinated at the same time. I told my mother when I rang her from the phone box across the road.

'Don't let him touch your towel,' she warned me. 'I remember when I was auxiliary nursing at Clatterbridge the syphilis patients had ulcers eating into their backs. They were so big you could put your fist in them. Better go – *Corrie*'s on in a minute. God knows what Miss Nugent sees in that Ernie Bishop, but still, every pan has a lid.'

Christmas drew nearer. The hollow ache of homesickness in the pit of my stomach refused to go away. I'd been well taught by Mrs Mack at the RAFA club and after a week was entrusted by Finch with the running of one of the smaller bars, the Jockey Bar. 'You still have to do all your other duties as well,' he warned me, mincing off upstairs for a quick slug of vodka in the office. He was a drunk and a mean one at that.

I met him once coming up the stairs after his afternoon off, which was usually spent drinking in a nearby pub. 'D'ya know what you need?' he slurred, wrapping his arm round my waist and pulling me close to him. 'You need a nice cock up your arse.'

I was completely stunned. No one had ever said anything

like that to me before. I laughed, not wanting to rile him but at the same time firmly removing his wandering hand from my backside. 'Don't worry, you'll keep,' he giggled as he watched me stomp down the stairs, my face burning. I went out into the garden for a smoke. Finch had scared me, and I was annoyed to see that my hands were shaking as I lit my cig. Were all homos like Finch and the one in the Gents at Victoria Coach Station? Were they all predatory, effeminate freaks? If so, then I was sticking to girls.

In the Jockey Bar you wore a waistcoat in racing colours. Mine hung on me like a sack on a cadaver. Its previous owner must have been ten stone heavier than me but as it was the only one available I had to wear it. On my first night behind the bar of my new domain, Diana Dors came in with her husband. I recognized her by her bouffant of unnatural white hair. She was starring in a sitcom called *Queenie's Castle* at the time, a popular comedy about a hard-boiled matriarch who lived with her family in a council high-rise. She didn't look that far removed from Queenie in real life, poured into a white miniskirt and sweater which might have looked reasonably OK if she'd been twenty years younger and three stone lighter. She leaned across the bar and beckoned to me with a podgy hand that made me think of a pound of Irish sausages.

'Could I have a glass of water, please?' she groaned. 'And then let me find a chair to collapse in and take the weight off my feet. They're fucking killing me.'

It was easy to see why. She'd forced them into a pair of white knee-length boots so tight that her bunions were clearly visible through the cracked patent leather, and to make matters worse they had elasticated tops that bit cruelly into the flesh of her swollen legs. Her husband, Alan Lake, joined her at the bar. He was your typical medallion man to look at: paisley-patterned shirt undone to the belt buckle of his hipster flares, revealing

261

an expanse of hairy chest criss-crossed with gold chains. He had those mutton-chop sideburns down the side of his face, a single gypsy earring and a diamond ring on every finger. Common, I thought to myself, sniffing disapprovingly, just like my mother.

'Champagne, the best,' he shouted drunkenly at me across the bar, a crazy leer on his face. 'And give us a large Scotch for the wife.' He then proceeded, with the help of a group of hangers-on who seemed to appear from nowhere, to drink the Wheatsheaf dry.

Diana Dors distanced herself from the group. She didn't seem to be enjoying the whisky that she was putting back, and looked tired and unwell. 'How old are you?' she asked wearily, catching me staring at her and pulling herself up to the bar from her armchair. I told her that I was eighteen, although I was really only seventeen.

'Have you seen my film *The Amazing Mr Blundell*?' she asked, turning to look at her husband who was rolling on the floor of the bar with a cushion between his legs pretending to be a jockey. 'I play an old bag with a lunatic husband. Not much change there then, is there?'

I liked Diana Dors. She asked me if I missed Birkenhead and what I was doing for Christmas and if I had a girlfriend, and was the only person who'd shown any interest in me, apart from Finch's unwelcome advances, since I'd arrived. Her husband eventually passed out and was impossible to move. Miss Dors, more from exhaustion than drink, lay on one of the sofas and quietly went to sleep. I couldn't rouse them, so I locked the bar up and left them to it. Finch went ballistic when he found out and there was the usual inquisition in his office until I was eventually allowed, at around 2 a.m., to go to bed. He took a sadistic pleasure in waking me at five, telling me to go down and see if my 'guests' were awake yet.

It was cold in the bar and a grumpy Diana Dors sat hunched on the sofa with her fox-fur coat pulled tightly around her shoulders. 'Who was the bright spark who locked the fuckin' door then?' she shot accusingly at me. 'What do you think you're doing locking me in a bar, you bloody idiot?'

I'd had enough. I was also, like the rest of my kinfolk, dangerous if roused early and unexpectedly from a nice warm bed. Consequently, I told Diana Dors in no uncertain terms what I thought of her and her husband, who lay unconscious, face down on the floor of the bar, throughout my unfaltering rant.

'You're right,' she sighed after a while, slowly standing up and looking at her reflection in the mirror behind the bar, 'but whilst I may be an ignorant fat cow and my husband a dirty flash bastard I'll forgive all for a cup of coffee and the loan of a hairbrush.'

I went to the kitchen and put the coffee machine on and then went up to Carol's room. She wasn't amused at being woken up and even less so when I asked her if she had a hairbrush that Diana Dors could borrow.

'Diana Dors wants what?' she asked, confused and only barely awake.

'A hairbrush.'

'Diana Dors? THE Diana Dors? Wants to borrow my brush? Why?'

'To brush her hair, of course.'

She thought she'd dreamed the incident until she discovered her brush matted with platinum blonde hair and the best part of a can of lacquer missing.

The rodent called homesickness had taken up permanent residence in my guts and was gnawing away at me. The Wheatsheaf was busy with office parties and pre-Christmas dinners and so far I'd only had one afternoon off in the fortnight I'd been there. I'd spent that roaming around Staines in

263

the rain looking for something interesting to do, in the end settling for a Wimpy before catching the train back to Virginia Water. As I walked down the road from the station, with its beautiful houses and fabulous cars parked in the drives, I wondered which one Elton John lived in. Chris had said that he lived round here and that he had a reputation for throwing 'wild gay orgies'. Maybe he's throwing one now, I half hoped as I waded through the piles of leaves on the pavement. And maybe someone will see me and invite me in and before you know it I'll be set up by some millionaire in a Carnaby Street penthouse . . .

There's nothing to do in Virginia Water on a rainy December night, especially when funds are non-existent and you don't know a soul. I should've packed my bag there and then and gone home, but I hadn't been paid and couldn't afford the fare. I was damned if I was going home skint to face my mother's 'I knew you wouldn't last five minutes, I knew you'd be back on the bones of your arse' routine. No, it would be better if I stuck it out for a while.

Back at the Wheatsheaf I weighed up my options: sitting in my garret freezing or going downstairs to the Cellar Bar to blow the last of my money on a half of cider. I chose the latter. Apart from the fact that the Cellar Bar was the only one Finch allowed the staff to drink in when they were off duty, it also happened to be the only bar in the hotel that was in any way lively. The bar staff down here didn't live in. They all lived locally and were young and sexy and thought themselves 'cool'. Standing at the end of the bar in a tank top nursing my half of cider I felt like a dull brown weed in a hothouse of orchids. Then Finch came down and insisted, since I had 'nothing else to do', that I helped out behind the bar. It was getting very busy. Tomorrow was Christmas Eve and people were out celebrating.

I weaved in and out among the happy revellers, collecting the empty glasses and beer bottles, like the spectre at the feast, bleak with homesickness, consoling myself with the odd half of

Woodpecker cider. At the end of the night, as I was helping to clear the bar, confident and chatty after half a dozen ciders, a girl asked if I'd like to go to a party up the road. Maybe this was my chance to sample one of Virginia Water's 'wild gay orgies', although I was less keen on the gay after Finch's advances.

The girl's name was Laura. She was small and pretty and very eager to go to the party. 'We have to take a bottle if we want to get in,' she said. 'Can't you find one somewhere?' Flushed with cider and thrilled with the opportunity that had come my way, I helped myself to an unopened bottle of Campari from behind the bar, knowing that I'd have to replace it with a bottle from the off-licence in the village before the daily stock check in the morning. 'There you go,' I bragged, pulling back my coat and showing my new paramour the booty. 'One entrance fee.'

The party turned out to be dreary. Laura dumped me as soon as we arrived and there was not a sign of anyone wild or gay, let alone a whiff of anything orgiastic, just a few Virginia Water greasers pretending to be Hell's Angels, hunched over a bottle of cider and listening intently to Led Zeppelin. I took a couple of slugs of the Campari, which tasted like cough medicine, and went and sat on the stairs to have a fag.

'Got a light?' a girl said, sitting down next to me, offering her cigarette. I watched her sit back and take a long drag, holding the smoke in her lungs, her face slowly reddening, before she let it go, exhaling a plume of smoke into the air. 'Want some?' she asked, coughing.

'What is it?' I asked in all innocence, staring at her cigarette, which now seemed to be belching out a hell of a lot of strangely fragrant smoke.

'It's grass,' she said, unable to believe that I didn't know.

I had no idea what she was talking about. Was she smoking lawn clippings? Because if so, I wasn't sure it was wise. The place reeked.

'You know, pot,' she said, offering me her joint. 'Take a toke, man. It's from Amsterdam, the best you can get.'

The gates of hell opened up before me. Drugs. I was sitting on the stairs of a strange house with a drug addict, and what was worse she was offering me some of the infernal weed, inviting me to join her in her drug-infested mire. Should I make a run for it or sit here and brave the storm? It was the first time I'd encountered drugs. I really knew nothing about them. Nobody at school had ever taken them and the idea of popping a few pills or smoking a joint had never come up. I wasn't interested and certainly wasn't tempted, declining the spluttering roll-up with a curt 'No thanks.'

Despite my uptight attitude to her joint we got on well. Her name turned out to be Millie and she was back home in Virginia Water from university for the holidays. She had Tara King's green eyes, and after we had knocked back the rest of the poisonous Campari we ended up in one of the bedrooms, where we soon got down to some serious necking and heavy petting. Standing up, she calmly took her dress off and let it fall to the floor; next she removed her bra and stepped out of her knickers. Apart from seeing Diana Rigg get her kit off in *Abelard and Heloise* on stage in Liverpool (tastefully and discreetly lit, of course), I'd never actually seen a female naked in the flesh before – and I'd certainly never seen one at such close quarters.

'Fuck me,' she said, sliding back on to the bed.

I was momentarily shocked to the core by her frankness. What kind of species was she? I'd only ever encountered Birkenhead girls and they kept their knickers on, at least the ones I'd gone down the back entry with had.

'Well, go on,' she said, giving me a dig. 'Aren't you going to get your kit off?'

I hastily tried to undress under the covers, terrified that she should see me naked.

266

'Come here,' she said, throwing the covers back and pro-
ceeding to undo my belt and jeans. I was rigid, not from sexual
arousal but from fright. Had this girl no shame? Within seconds she had my kecks off and was tugging at my underpants.
I hung on for grim death and fought, in the words of the song,
'like a tiger for my honour'.

'What's up with you?' she asked, laughing.

'I haven't got a Durex,' I blurted out, playing for time,
neglecting to add that even if I had I wasn't that sure how long
it would take me to get it on. I was starting to get annoyed with
myself. This was actually it. The moment I'd been waiting years
for – the chance to finally go 'all the way'. I was desperate not
to blow it and show myself up as a ham-fisted virgin.
Nevertheless, eager as I now was to get on with the job in hand
I didn't want our one-night stand to end in fatherhood.

'That's OK,' she said matter-of-factly, 'I'm on the pill.'

Staggering back to the Wheatsheaf, my cherry well and truly
popped, slightly woozy still from the combination of cider and
Campari, I was the happiest seventeen-year-old in the world. It
really was Christmas and I'd just had the best present ever.
Now all I wanted to do was fall into my bed and go to sleep,
contented for the first time since I'd got here.

The bar manager was still up and waiting for me when I got
back. By the expression on his face I knew something was
wrong. There was no sign of Finch. He'd retired to bed feigning exhaustion when in reality he was too pissed to stand and
had left his underling to deal with me.

'Did you steal a full bottle of Campari from the Cellar Bar?'
The man's face was pale and drawn at the best of times, and
tonight he looked like a death's head. I wanted to say I was
hardly going to steal an empty one, but instead I tried to
explain that I'd 'borrowed' one but fully intended to replace it
in the mor—

'Did you or did you not steal a bottle of Campari from the Cellar Bar?' he asked again, cutting me short. He was enjoying this. Aunty Chris was right. Put a gobshite in a position of power and watch it invade Poland.

'Yes,' I said, trying to sober up, 'I suppose I did, but I'm going to replace it, honest.' I was too pissed to really care. Why all this fuss over a lousy bottle of Campari?

'I'm sorry, but theft will not be tolerated and I have no alternative but to telephone the police,' he said, picking up the receiver and taking a perverse delight in watching the blood drain from my face.

Four coppers turned up to arrest me. I was handcuffed and taken to the police station where two of them questioned me for three hours, using the predictable good cop, bad cop routine. It transpired that cuts of meat and turkey had been going missing from the Wheatsheaf's deep freeze as well as alcohol and money from the tills and I was their chief, and for the moment only, suspect. They then removed my belt, shoelaces and watch in case I should attempt suicide and locked me in a cell.

I empathized with Mr Toad. Not much chance here of disguising myself as a washerwoman and escaping, though, I thought as I sat on the floor and looked around the filthy cell, feeling sick and hungover and more than a little worried. A maudlin drunk somewhere in a cell nearby was shouting for his mother. How was I going to explain this to mine? Eventually, after what seemed like hours, they let me go, telling me that I would be receiving a summons to appear in court some time in the new year.

'Happy Christmas, Scouse. Let's not keep in touch, eh?' the 'bad' cop said, handing me back my property and smirking like the cat who got the cream. 'And try and keep your sticky fingers out of the till in future.' I silently cursed him, ignoring my ma's warning that curses like chickens always came home to roost, and instead wallowing in pleasurable visions of the imaginative and painful death I would like to inflict on this obese, swaggering turd. God, being down here was turning me into Attila the Hun.

Having no idea where I was, I followed a road sign for Virginia Water. It turned out to be a longer walk than I'd anticipated and I spent it cursing Thelma Brailey, Chef and Brewer and the police force and all their works. When I eventually found my way back, the Wheatsheaf was closed. The bar manager let me in. The police had rung him to say I was on my way and he'd been waiting up for me. 'Get your things and leave. You have ten minutes,' he said coldly. 'Before Mr Finch sees you.'

I went to my room and packed my clothes. I was completely worn out, both mentally and physically, so I lay on the bed for a moment to gather my wits. Within seconds I was in a deep sleep, only to be woken by a hungover and extremely angry Finch.

'Get up, get up!' he screamed hysterically, shaking me like a doll. 'Get out of my hotel, you little cunt,' and grabbing me by the hair he pulled me off the bed and on to the floor. 'You thieving Scouse bastard!' He was slapping me repeatedly around the head in a blind rage. 'Get out before I kill you!'

I'd hated this man since the day I'd first set eyes on him, and he had it coming. I pushed him off me and landed him a long overdue and highly satisfying punch in the face. He staggered across the room and fell on the sink, detaching it from the wall completely. I was amazed I'd actually done it, and even more stunned to see I'd scored a bullseye.

'Help,' he screamed, rolling himself up into the foetal position and covering his face with his hands. 'Don't hit me, don't hit me!'

Resisting the overwhelming urge to kick him round the room in case he called the police and had me done for assault,

I picked up my holdall and ran down the stairs and out on to the road and kept on running until I thought I was far enough from the hotel to be safe.

Hiding in a bus shelter, crouched down low so that nobody passing in a car could see me, I got my breath back as I weighed my situation up and tried to work out just how I was going to get home to Birkenhead on fifty pence, the total sum of my finances. First thing I had to do was get to London. I thought about hitching a lift but after a half-hearted attempt I realized that I just couldn't do it. Pride got the better of me – I didn't want anyone to know that I didn't have any money and couldn't afford the fare to London. I was no Blanche Dubois, and stupidly refused to let myself rely on the kindness of strangers. Besides, if Finch had called the police I didn't want a charge of GBH added to my fast-increasing criminal record, so best not to draw attention to myself, I reasoned. With no other choice, I walked, making it as far as Richmond, starving, exhausted and close to cracking, some time in the late afternoon. Out of the fifty pence I bought a ticket for Euston, a bag of crisps and a bottle of Tizer. (Try that today.)

Euston Station concourse was packed with people going home for the holidays. Outside the station a Salvation Army band was gathered around a large Christmas tree playing 'Silent Night', and the sense of loneliness and desolation was overwhelming. I sat on the floor of the concourse and tried to work out how to get on a train home with no money. It seemed my only hope was to throw myself on the mercy of the transport police and hope that somehow they would put me on a train.

I told a very sympathetic copper a cock and bull story of how I'd had most of my luggage, including my train ticket and money, stolen from under my nose as I was buying a paper. I didn't have to fake tears: they came readily, I was feeling so dog-tired and desperate. The copper took pity on me, and leading me through a door that bypassed the ticket collector and took us directly to the platform told me to board the train and tell the guard, when he came round to punch the tickets, that I'd lost mine. In all probability he would simply take my name and address and allow me to stay on the train. He did, thank God, and with my newly issued ticket in hand I relaxed for the moment, found an empty seat and fell gratefully into a deep sleep.

'What in God's name are you doing back?' my mother exclaimed, nearly dropping the tray of mince pies she was taking out of the oven as I burst through the back door. 'Don't tell me you've had the sack.'

'I've left,' I lied. 'Couldn't stand it any more. And besides, I wanted to come home for Christmas.'

'You haven't got the police on your tail, have you?' she asked, eyeing me suspiciously. 'You look like you've been up to something, my lad.'

No time, let alone Christmas Eve, was going to be a good time to casually let drop that I'd been sacked and banged up in a police cell, and was awaiting a summons to appear in court for nicking a bottle of Campari, so I kept shtum. I was too tired for a drama so I gave her the less inflammatory version that I'd thought up on the train.

'I knew you wouldn't stick it,' she said, pursing her lips and wiping her hands on her apron. 'I warned you that you'd be treated like a skivvy. Well, I don't know where you're going to sleep. Annie and Chrissie are coming tonight. Wait while I phone our Sheila,' she added, making for the phone in the hall to ring my sister. My dad was out on his rounds, visiting the elderly and housebound, as he'd done for years as one of the Knights of St Columbia. What the hell had he done to deserve me? Maybe my ma was right, perhaps I was a changeling, accidentally swapped at birth by a distracted maternity nurse in St Cath's.

The house was warm and smelt of Christmas. The twelve-inch

artificial tree that had been dug out from the loft as it was every Christmas sat tilting slightly to the right on a little table by the television. The crib that my dad had made out of hardboard and a National Dried Milk tin perched on top of the bookcase, complete with cotton-wool balls on the roof to represent snow and nativity figures bought from Woolies. Christmas cards were strung across the wall and fireplace on lengths of wool, a fire burned in the grate and Val Doonican was on the telly. It was good to be home.

'Our Sheila said that they're looking for porters in St Cath's,' my mother said, coming in from the phone and going straight to the fire. I hadn't been back five minutes and she had a job lined up for me. The word unemployment was not in my ma's vocabulary. 'I'll make you a bite to eat in a minute,' she said. 'You look half dead to me. Jesus, it's perishing in that lobby. The wind howls under that door and straight up the stairs into the lav.' She shuddered as she warmed her hands at the fire. 'Well, you'll just have to sleep down here while Anne and Chris are staying, and you can come to midnight mass with me and Annie.'

I was dropping on my feet but only too happy to agree to sit through midnight mass, I was so glad to be home. I was grateful that she'd taken my version of my exit from the Wheatsheaf so calmly. If only she knew what had really happened . . . but I'd worry about that later. Right now I just wanted to enjoy every moment of Christmas at Holly Grove.

Aunty Chris had retired from the buses and was working as the manageress of Ashe and Nephew, an off-licence in Prenton Hall Road. Her bus had been involved in an accident with a motorcyclist and she'd witnessed his decapitated body hanging from a nearby tree, so she'd hung up her ticket machine and handed in her badge and turned her attention to the retail of alcohol. Strange choice of profession for a woman who no longer drank and claimed to hate the stuff.

As always, Aunty Chris ran a tight ship; anyone who tried to buy booze and didn't look eighteen was given a sharp lecture and ejected from the shop. She was sympathetic and discreet when dealing with her regular alcoholics, and she knew the name and price of every bottle of wine in the shop. She even fought off two robbers who demanded the contents of the till by hitting one of them over the head with a brush, causing them both to turn on their heels and run, Aunty Chris in hot pursuit. She became quite a connoisseur of wine after a while and her 'posh' customers from Pine Walks frequently consulted her.

'This is a lovely little Bordeaux, slightly peppery but nice and light, Mr Mason,' she'd say, presenting the bottle for her client's inspection. 'Goes lovely with cold meats, and very reasonably priced considering its superior nature.' For someone who didn't drink she knew an awful lot about wine.

'How do you know all this?' I asked her. 'How do you know what region the grape comes from and what it tastes like?'

'Easy,' she replied, looking at me as if I were mad. 'It says on the label.'

Christmas Eve was a busy night for Ashe and Nephew. It didn't close until eight thirty and a taxi had been booked to bring Aunty Chris and Aunty Anne over to Holly Grove. It was Aunty Annie's first Christmas since the death of Uncle Al, and she seemed to have shrunk since I'd last seen her. 'Nice to have you home for Christmas, lad,' she said in a tiny voice, giving me a kiss. 'I hope you haven't been up to your old tricks.'

''Eck, 'eck, the return of the prodigal,' Aunty Chris said, coming in the door behind her lugging various shopping bags. 'Nice to see you, but something tells me that you're up to your neck in shite again.'

'Why do you say that?' I asked, turning bright scarlet.

'Because I can read you like a book, love, that's why. Now help me with these friggin' presents, they weigh a ton.' As I've already said, two hundred years earlier and they'd have been burned as witches.

At midnight mass I prayed, with the passion of the good penitent, a childish entreaty that the Almighty had heard many times before. 'I promise I'll never be bad again if you just help me out of this mess one more time . . .'

I saw the new year in at the RAFA club. Mrs Mack had been only too happy to give me my old job back. I was a good barman, surprisingly honest in spite of recent events, and wouldn't dream of fiddling the till or helping myself to drinks, despite having a criminal record and growing by the minute.

'Happy new year,' Mrs Mack cheered, sherry in hand, as the Palm Court trio struck up 'Auld Lang Syne'. 'I hope that 1973 will be an eventful one and full of surprises for you.'

She certainly got her wish.

CHAPTER SIXTEEN

Aᴛᴇ FEW DAYS INTO THE NEW YEAR, THELMA BRAILEY RANG UP. 'I thought you were smart,' she raged down the line. 'I thought that you would go places but I was wrong, the only place you're going is gaol, but before they lock you up you're going to pay me my commission. Ten per cent of your first week's wages, that was the deal.'

'I haven't had any wages, so take a hike and don't ring again,' I said, giving her my best Holden Caulfield and putting the phone down on her.

'Who was that on the phone?' my dad asked, looking up from studying his Pools coupon.

Tired of lying and wanting to start the new year with a clean slate, I told him the truth – a slightly embellished version of it, putting the Wheatsheaf on a par with Blake's 'dark Satanic mills' and portraying myself as an innocent at large, which in retrospect I can see that I was. There was no need to exaggerate when it came to Finch, he spoke for himself. My father went ballistic when I told him about our encounter on the stairs and to my relief and surprise he was outraged by what he saw as their disproportionate reaction to my crime.

'I just might give the manager of that hotel a visit,' he said angrily. 'But first I'm going over to Liverpool to have a word with that woman in that so-called employment agency.'

He didn't have to – she was pulling up outside the house on her moped.

Thelma Brailey was bristling with her own importance and on the verge of spontaneously combusting with fury. My dad was civility itself, inviting her in, politely enquiring why she was so upset.

'Do you realize that you are harbouring a criminal under your roof?' she shouted at my father, determined not to be mollified by his solicitous attitude.

'I'm well aware of that,' he replied, unruffled, 'but you'll be leaving soon.'

'How dare you!' she squawked, jumping up from the sofa as if she'd just sat on my ma's pincushion. 'Are you accusing me of unprofessional behaviour? That's slander!'

My dad in his reasonable way threatened her with everything from having her licence revoked by Liverpool City Council to the Inland Revenue; however, he did pay the old witch the commission I owed her. Despite getting her pound of flesh, Thelma was incandescent with rage and flounced speechless out of the house and down the path, bumping into my mother as she went.

'What's up with her?' she asked, watching Thelma ram her helmet on and mount her bike. 'She's not another Jehovah's Witness, is she? That's twice this week.'

Before my dad could sit her down and explain, there was a knock at the door and my mother ran to answer it. 'If that's her back then I'm going to tell her what she can do with her bloody *Watchtower*,' she said grimly, opening the door not to Thelma but to a young man.

'Mrs O'Grady?' he said, smiling. 'I'm from the Birkenhead Probation Services, here about your son's forthcoming court appearance.'

She took it quite well considering, claiming that she'd known something untoward had happened the moment I walked through the kitchen door on Christmas Eve. She was also slightly appeased by the news that I'd landed a job.

In the early seventies Liverpool was still relatively prosperous, jobs were plentiful and courtesy of the Angela Chapman Employment Agency I went to work for various shipping offices as a bill of lading clerk. There were a lot of ships coming into Liverpool from all over the world, the docks were extremely busy and it was to be a few years before containerization rendered them all but obsolete. I went from one shipping office to another – Nigerian National Shipping Line, Elder Dempster Line, Cunard. I'd leave one job on the Friday and start another on the Monday. I'd been summonsed to appear at Chertsey Magistrates Court and despite my father's protests refused to allow him to come with me, preferring to take the midnight coach again alone. The coach pulled in late and I had to be in court no later than nine. Since I had no idea where Chertsey was I took a black cab from Victoria Coach Station. Luckily I was flush thanks to the regular wage from two jobs, but even so I hadn't banked on spending half of it on a black cab. Not wanting the driver to think that I was a Liverpool scallie up in court for thieving, I told him that I was a reporter from the *Echo* covering a very important case.

To my horror I saw on my charge sheet that stealing a bottle of Campari could mean a custodial sentence. The magistrate spoke of my crime as if it was the theft of an incubator from a premature baby. After threatening me with prison should I ever have the audacity to appear before him again, he fined me fifty pounds and put me on probation for a month. I thanked my guardian angel and left Chertsey vowing that the 'Frank Nitti of Birkenhead', a handle given to me by Aunty Chrissie, would never be up before the beak again, or ever set foot in Virginia Water.

*

277

One evening there was a documentary on BBC2 about the rise of the gay movement.

'Turn that gang of lavatory cowboys over,' my mother roared from her usual spot on the sofa, knitting furiously. 'Have you seen this lot, Paddy?' she asked my dad, who had seen them but preferred to ignore them, clearing his throat disapprovingly and going back to his Spot the Ball in the paper. I was only too glad to get up and turn the telly over. I'd rather have died the slow death than have to sit in the same room when something as sensitive as homosexual liberation, a topic guaranteed to induce toe-curling embarrassment for me, was on the telly.

'Leave it.' My mother stopped me in my tracks. 'Let's see what they're up to.'

Homosexuality had only been decriminalized in 1967. Then in '69, at a Greenwich Village bar called Stonewall, riots had broken out, instigated mainly by drag queens who were sick and tired of repeated police harassment.

'Times are changing, Moll,' my dad sighed, getting up from his armchair. 'I think I'll go for a quick pint.'

I squirmed inwardly as I watched a camp young man in a pink T-shirt, the words 'Gay Lib' emblazoned across his chest, kiss his boyfriend full on the mouth. Had I been alone in the room I'd have relished this chance to learn about gay life, but sat here with my mother it was pure torture. She let out pantomime squeals of exaggerated horror at everything the guy in the pink T-shirt had to say. He spoke articulately about an organization called the Campaign for Homosexual Equality and how there were millions of gay men and women in the world living a lie and it was time to 'come out'.

'Don't let me catch you coming out,' my mother said, returning purposefully to her knitting, tut-tutting like Skippy the Bush Kangaroo. 'Because you'll be knocked right back in again, d'you hear me? There'll be no Gay Libbin' in this house, my lad.'

Scarlet with embarrassment, I asked her what she meant.

'I'm just warning you, that's all,' she said, pursing her lips, 'just in case you fancy taking up with that lot. I wouldn't put anything past you.'

I slunk upstairs to my bedroom and lay on the bed listening to Carly Simon's album *No Secrets* and reading the *New Musical Express*. As fate would have it there was a small personal ad at the back for the CHE with a London phone number. I'd been seeing my old flame Evelyn from school again for a short while, though we were more suited as friends than lovers and both of us knew it. She'd fallen for a male nurse she'd met while training at St Cath's Hospital and was talking about marriage. I was certainly going to miss her but was happy that she'd found her soulmate. When, I wondered, would I ever find mine? Maybe the answer lay with the CHE.

The next day I rang them up and was put in touch with Robin, who ran the Liverpool branch from his flat in Upper Parliament Street. He sounded enthusiastic and invited me to attend the next meeting. 'Oh, before you hang up,' he added cheerfully, 'what's your name?' I didn't want to give my real name in case these people expected me to come out and run through the streets of Liverpool screaming 'I'm gay.' I wasn't ready for such extremes just yet. Best to give an alias, I thought, until I see what they're like.

'Simon,' I answered, Simon being my favourite name at the time. 'Simon King.' No prizes for guessing the inspiration behind the surname.

The day of the meeting I was beside myself with anticipation. Would it be an orgy of unbridled lust and passion, I wondered (I'd read one of my ma's Angélique books), and if so, what would happen if I didn't want to participate? Would I be drugged and gang-raped while unconscious or just thrown out on to the street and mocked for being uptight and inexperienced? I'd cross these bridges when I came to them, I decided. Whatever happened, I was going to meet and experience at first hand what the *Daily Mail* liked to call 'The Twilight World of the Homosexual'.

At the time I was working in the offices of a plastics factory on the Liverpool Dock Road. Having finally exhausted most of the shipping offices in town, I was now dabbling in the mysteries of polythene production. Like every other job I'd had since Christmas, six in all, it bored me to tears and I was restless for some excitement. I hoped the CHE would provide me with it.

I arrived at Robin's flat three quarters of an hour early. He opened the door to me wearing nothing but a short towel, confirming my earlier suspicions about an orgy. Thank God I've had a bath, I thought to myself as I nervously entered this den of iniquity. It transpired that this wasn't Sodom and Gomorrah: Robin had been in the shower when I arrived as he wasn't expecting anyone till eight but he kindly showed me into his untidy front room, left me with a copy of *Gay News* and went to get dressed.

Tonight's meeting was all about Welcoming Newcomers and Robin had recruited a few stalwarts of the CHE to help out. When everyone had finally arrived we were given tea and biscuits, not what I'd expected at a bacchanalian orgy – but then nor was the group. I was discouraged to find that they all seemed perfectly ordinary and unexciting. I was by far the youngest in the room and, looking around, there was certainly no one that I fancied.

Robin chaired the meeting. A tall, gangly, well-spoken student at the university, he seemed nervous and shy as he welcomed this motley bunch of new recruits, telling us proudly that there were now over three thousand members in the UK and that the number was growing daily. It was all so pleasant and genteel, we could've been at a 1930s WI meeting in Tunbridge Wells. The atmosphere was far from predatory or threatening and after our initial shyness wore off we talked freely and openly among ourselves, which made me regret using an alias. These were nice people and I wouldn't mind coming back to attend further meetings.

A guy named Steve, who up till now hadn't had much to say for himself, offered me a lift home. He was older than me, with sly eyes and a small moustache, and he only came up to my shoulder; not really my type, although I was still unsure what my type was. But since the alternative to a lift meant having to stand at a bus stop on Upper Parliament Street, then a notorious red-light district at eleven o'clock at night, I accepted the offer.

'We'll stop off in New Brighton and have a drink at the Chelsea Reach first, shall we?' he said innocently, failing to add 'followed by a session in the back of my van on Egremont Promenade'.

I wasn't agreeable to this suggestion at first but it's amazing how a combination of cider and persistent persuasion can weaken the resistance of a lad who's far too well brought up to say no. Feeling that it was easier just to give in and get on with it, I climbed into the back of the van. If my farewells to John at Hamilton Square station had been my *Brief Encounter* moment, then this was most definitely *A Taste of Honey*.

I got him to drop me off on Church Road. I didn't want him knowing where I lived, and I didn't want to see him again. I'd kept up the Simon King pretence as there was something about him that bothered me. He'd told me that he was an ambulance driver but I didn't believe him, and I was right. It turned out he was really a copper, and a cunning one at that. He found out my real name and where I lived and worked and was waiting for me in his car outside the factory a few nights later. Needless to say I wasn't very happy about this, but saw an opportunity to use the situation to my own advantage.

I made a deal: I'd continue seeing him if in return he promised to take me out on the gay scene and agreed to dispose of all traces of my criminal record. He was a wily bugger but by now I quite liked him, and apart from the van he had a nifty little MG and would take me out to country pubs in it. I still hadn't seen the inside of a real life gay bar and was too scared to go in one on my own. Steve, reluctant to take me to the Bear's Paw or Sadie's, always managed to come up with a fairly plausible excuse as to why we couldn't go. He frequently claimed that, as a copper, it was more than his job was worth to be caught with a seventeen-year-old in a gay club, whereas the real reason he was keeping me away from the bars was because he knew that I was a new face, a young, fresh chicken, ripe for plucking. One of the many chicken hawks, men who hovered hungrily at the bar and around the edge of the dance floor, would be sure to choose prey like me and Steve wasn't taking any chances. He wanted me for himself and guarded me with a jealous eye, coming up with more and more elaborate reasons why we shouldn't go 'on the scene'. I was desperate to go to these mythical places.

The only club, gay or otherwise, that I was getting to see was the RAFA club. I was still working there four evenings a week, growing more and more disenchanted after each dreary shift, resenting the club's hierarchy and committee meetings and all the petty rules and regulations. The crumbling old fuddy-duddies who danced to the resident trio's interpretation of the hits of Vera Lynn and drank sherry and played bowls were driving me insane. Excessive and prolonged exposure to all things boring depressed me at that age and still does. I had bags of energy and an enthusiasm for life that needed constant stimulation, as a plant does water, in order to flourish. I certainly wasn't getting it in the RAFA club or in the plastics factory and couldn't help feeling that somewhere out there a fabulous party was in full swing and I was missing out.

It was my mother who came up with the answer to my craving for change. Together with Aunty Anne she had a cleaning job at the Sandpiper, a nightclub on Conway Street, and she got me an interview with the manager, Lenny Macmillan, for a job as barman. The Sandpiper was done out in a beachcomber theme – fake palm trees, fishing nets, bamboo bar stools and wicker furniture that snagged the girls' tights. Twice a week a resident combo played on the tiny stage at the end of the dance floor. Light years away from the RAFA club's trio, they were really good and sang the hits of Stevie Wonder, Roberta Flack and Donny Hathaway. This was more like it! The Sandpiper was trendy with a capital T, popular with the in-set of the Wirral. The only old people in the place were Lenny and my mum's mate Fanny Roscoe who worked in the cloakroom. Plus the job had the added benefits of being cash in hand and nearer home.

On my first night there Lenny asked me if I'd like to pop over to Liverpool with him in the car as he'd left the keys to the safe in his flat. Lenny wore his shirt unbuttoned to the waist with the collar up and the cuffs turned out and over his suit. He had skin like a crocodile handbag, bleached blond hair and was adorned with the usual array of medallions and gold chains.

'Keep your hand on your ha'penny,' one of the barmaids warned. 'He does this every time we get a new barman. He's a harmless old queen really, just don't let him get you into his flat.'

Here we go again. What was it with these old fruits? And why did they single me out? What am I going to do if he tries his hand? I've only just got this job and I don't want to lose it, and if I don't oblige then he might not only sack me but Aunty Anne and my mother as well. All these questions ran through my mind as we drove through the Mersey Tunnel in Lenny's E-type, with me keeping a careful check on Lenny out of the corner of my eye.

'You've got nice long legs,' Lenny said suddenly, running his hand along my thigh. The nice long legs stiffened and froze. 'Relax,' he said, taking his hand off me and changing gear. He was wearing beige leather driving gloves and half a gallon of Aramis and I couldn't have had sex with him if my life had depended on it. Besides, I was off men for the moment. I'd finally given Steve the Copper, as I'd come to think of him, the elbow and had taken up with a girl called Susan whom I'd met at the Cabin Club, a dimly lit dump where you stuck to the carpet if you didn't keep moving but that had great music and atmosphere. Nope, no more gays for me, least of all the likes of permatanned Lenny bloody Macmillan.

'I've got a girlfriend, Lenny,' I said, trying to sound casual. 'I'm not gay.' And to prove it I lowered my voice.

'What makes you think I am?' Lenny sounded slightly rattled and put his foot down as we left the the tunnel.

He invited me into his flat, an offer which I politely refused, and after he found his supposedly lost keys we drove back to the club in silence.

'Tell me,' he said, as we pulled up outside, 'how old do I look?'

This is always a dangerous question to answer as you invariably offend – or at least I do. I hesitated, then muttered, 'I haven't got a clue, I'm no good at guessing ages.'

'Go on, guess,' Lenny persisted, combing his yellow hair with his fingers.

'Fifty-five?' I hazarded, smiling.

There was an awful silence. The smile slowly faded from my lips as Lenny leaned towards me, distinctly unamused.

'I'm thirty-two.'

Oh, beware the wrath of an evil queen whose vanity has been dented. He didn't speak to me much after that, which suited me fine. I didn't last long though, only a couple of months, after which he sacked me for not dressing trendily enough for the Sandpiper's image. He replaced me with a pretty blond lad in skin-tight flares. Bastard.

Susan had long gone. She'd turned up unexpectedly one
night at the club and caught me being more than friendly with
one of the customers, a girl who lived in Rock Ferry and who
just happened to work in the same building as her. I was back
to being single again and for want of something to do of an
evening I'd started going back to the odd CHE meeting. It was
beginning to bore me as it was all talk, talk, talk and not
enough action for my liking, but to show willing I'd agree
to run off a few leaflets for the first big conference to be
held in Morecambe on the roneo machine at work, when the
secretary, who watched over it like a guard dog, was out at
lunch.

None of the CHE lot were scene queens, and rarely if ever
went to the gay pubs and clubs in town. This left me feeling
very frustrated and wishing I had the bottle to go in on my
own, but I didn't so that was that.

It was time for another change of employment. I applied for
a job in the Liverpool Magistrates Court as a trainee court
clerk. If I was to get the job I'd start in the court collecting
office before moving on to the dizzy heights of the courts
themselves. My mother was delighted when I was successful
and couldn't wait to drop that one next time she was in Eileen
Henshaw's shop.

'That's right, clerk of the court, he's the one who sits
underneath the magistrate and advises him,' she'd say grandly.
'Is that ham fresh?'

And so life went on.

I met Steve coming out of the courts after my interview.

'They finally caught you then?' he shouted after me as I
walked down Dale Street. He was wearing his uniform. It was
the first time I'd ever seen him in it and it was quite a surprise.
He looked as if he was in fancy dress.

'D'ya fancy me dressed like this then?' he asked.

'No,' I replied, 'you look like a music-hall comic.' I didn't find a copper's uniform possessing of any aphrodisiacal qualities whatsoever, quite the opposite in fact. It served only to remind me of the swaggering great shit I'd had the misfortune to encounter back in Virginia Water.

Steve agreed to take me to the clubs if I agreed to go out with him again. I did and a date was set for Friday night. I immediately started planning what I was going to wear and was as nervous and excited as any deb about to attend her coming-out ball.

The great day finally dawned. I rushed home from work and started getting ready as soon as I got in. I was meeting Steve at James Street station at nine o'clock and that gave me less than three hours. Better get a move on . . . I spent a lot of time getting ready to go out when I was a teenager; it's a five-minute swill and brush-up these days.

'Where the bloody hell are you going to, all tarted up like a pox doctor's clerk?' my mother shouted after me as I charged down the stairs and out the front door, leaving a trail of Musk behind me. 'Pooh, and what's that you're wearing, you smell like a tart at a christening.'

'Goodnight, Mam, won't be late.'

Our first port of call was the Lisbon, an old subterranean pub on Victoria Street. You entered through a pair of swing doors and descended to the bar down a set of small but perfectly formed marble stairs. Dolly Levi's arrival at the Harmonia Gardens was re-enacted at least twice a night on these stairs. The ceiling, stained a muddy yellow by a layer of nicotine, was covered in highly elaborate and ornately carved plasterwork. It was a fairly large space with Arts and Crafts-style wooden tables and chairs dotted about that matched the oak panelling, and the walls had intimate little booths with leather seating set into them.

The place was packed to the rafters. Over the noise of the jukebox and the sheer volume of conversation I heard a solitary male voice at the bar shouting out for two large gins and a pale ale, and from somewhere over in the corner a woman laughed hysterically. It was everything that a Victorian gin palace should be. Ornate brass lamps shed their warm, golden glow on the engraved mirrors behind the bar and caught the bevelled edges of the glass so that the light flickered and danced, and the atmosphere was heavy with cigarette smoke and the all-pervading smell of beer. It was loud, bawdy and lairy. I stood by the jukebox trying to look inconspicuous as Steve fought his way to the bar. To be on the safe side I kept looking straight ahead, pretending to be totally preoccupied with Suzi Quatro, who was belting out 'Devil Gate Drive' on the jukebox. Out of the corner of my eye I saw two strange creatures making their way purposefully through the crowd in my direction. Thankfully it wasn't me they were after but the middle-aged man stood next to me.

'Don't I know you from somewhere?' the smaller and scrawnier of the two asked the bemused feller, who obviously didn't have a clue who either of them was. 'I'm sure I do . . . Get us half a lager while I think on,' he added, pushing the older man towards the bar. He was quite an operator, hard as nails, with a tough little face set in a permanent scowl and a mass of coarse badly bleached hair that looked like the stuffing from the back of an exploded horsehair sofa. He was wearing a T-shirt with the word 'Girl' spelt out in multi-coloured lettering on the front.

'This is me mate Francessss,' he said, drawing out the s's through tight, pinched lips, inclining his head ingratiatingly as he dragged his companion forward to be presented.

Frances was smartly dressed in a black sweater and white shirt, the enormous cuffs of which he'd turned out over the sleeve. His black flares were severely pressed, the toecaps of his white platform boots peeked out from underneath and his clothes looked like they had been literally sprayed on. He

287

was poker-thin with a pronounced stutter and moved like a snake.

'I'll have half a laaar. Half a laaar . . . half a—'

'She'll have half a lager, won't you, girl, same as your sssissster Penny,' his friend said, jumping in.

I stood there listening to them, horrified that they were calling each other by women's names and referring to each other as 'she' and 'girl'. There was no way that I was going to be known by a woman's name, I vowed, willing Steve to hurry up with the drinks.

'Got a light on you, girl?' Penny was at my side and waving a Park Drive in my face.

'I'm not a girl,' I said firmly, in spite of the fact that I was terrified of him.

'Fuckin' hell, listen to the gob on this one, Frances. Looks like Julie Andrews, sounds like Lee Marvin,' Penny hissed. 'Don't throw your dolly out the pram, la. Well, have you got a light or not?'

I lit his cigarette for him, cursing Steve for taking so long getting back.

'Thanks,' Penny said, taking a hefty drag of his ciggie before passing it on for Frances to get a light from. 'I'd offer you one but we've only got five between usss. We haven't got a fuckin' bean so we're on the lookout for a mush to get a few bevvies out of. Looksss like I've scored,' he said, nodding towards the 'mush', who was returning from the bar and trying to work out how he'd just been conned into buying two halves of lager for two characters he didn't even know.

'What's a mush?' I asked Steve when he eventually returned, complaining that it took ages to get served when in reality I'd seen him chatting up a bit of rough by the bar.

'Who's been telling you about mushers?' he asked, blowing the head off his pint.

I nodded towards Penny.

'You want to keep away from the likes of that,' he said, looking at Penny as if he'd just crawled out from underneath a lavatory tile, 'and keep away from mushers. They're dirty old men who get conned into buying drinks on the strength of an empty promise – and just in case you've got any ideas, the next round's yours.'

We moved on, first to the Masquerade Club, a tiny little place off Dale Street in Hockernall Alley, an address straight out of Harry Potter, as were the few desperate-looking in-habitants of the club, and then on to the place I most wanted to visit, the Bear's Paw. The majority of Liverpool's gay clubs were hidden down small alleys and the Bear's Paw, in Dorans Lane off North John Street, was no exception. Steve knew the owner of the club, Gordon Shearer (known as Norma to some of the older customers, but never to his face), and his business partner, Dennis.

Steve rang the bell and, after close scrutiny through a small metal grill in the door, a tough young ex-squaddie (rumoured to be – probably out of jealousy – Gordon's rent boy) allowed us in. He ushered us down a flight of stairs to where Dennis, sat behind a small desk, greeted us and took the twenty-pence entrance fee.

'Hello, darling,' he said, offering his cheek for Steve to kiss. He was a fussy little thing, dressed in a neat black suit, a pair of large black horn-rimmed spectacles perched on his nose and the remaining strands of his dark hair Brylcreemed and combed artfully over his balding pate. He could've passed for one of the court ushers or even a magistrate if it wasn't for his camp manner and the startling array of diamond rings and gold sovereigns that adorned his long slender fingers. 'And who's this then?' he asked Steve, offering me his hand in the manner of Queen Victoria. I nervously introduced myself, not knowing if I should shake his hand or kiss it, settling for a gentle squeeze. His hand was warm and clammy.

'Listen to that voice,' he said, throwing his hands up in surprise. 'Sweet little face like that and the voice of a docker.'

I wasn't too happy at being called sweet and made a mental note to toughen up my image, maybe go back to having my hair cropped short instead of the bouffant mop of shoulder-length curls that I was sporting now. The club was split into two: upstairs there was a dance floor and a bar, while downstairs was an unintentional temple to kitsch. Gordon and Dennis firmly believed that the brass jugs and chipped plates that adorned the flock-covered walls, the beaded curtain that hung from the bar and trailed in everyone's drinks, the Swiss murals in the alcoves and the large jolly lady with brassy gold ringlets who nodded her head and smiled indulgently as she ran her fingers over a Hammond organ added a touch of sophistication. The Bear's Paw attracted the 'better type of queen' according to Dennis; the rougher sort were not encouraged and went to Sadie's in Wood Street instead.

I left Steve talking to Gordon at the bar and shot upstairs to investigate the disco. I couldn't believe it – men, grown men, of all shapes and ages, blatantly dancing together, arms entwined around each other's bodies, heads resting on shoulders. There was even a couple openly necking on the dance floor. Oh, this was too much to take in! Men dancing together didn't seem right somehow. I sat down, unable to believe my eyes. My mother would drop dead on the spot if she saw this lot.

There was an unwritten law in the Bear's Paw that I was as yet ignorant of: it stated that if somebody offered to buy you a drink and you accepted, it went without saying that you had just agreed to sleep with them. I accepted four drinks that night, had quite a few dances and had a bit of explaining to do when Steve came up to collect me. A particularly terrifying old queen in a white polo-neck sweater, known among the patrons as 'the Glider' after the strange way he glided around the dance floor, pausing to strike a pose every now and then, accosted me on my way down the stairs. He'd bought me a drink earlier and it was payback time.

' 'Scuse me,' it hissed, 'I thought I was having you tonight.'

'It'll take more than a half of cider to get me to go to bed with you,' I muttered, pushing past him and making a hasty exit.

'What would it take then, rent boy?' he shouted after me. 'Ten shillings?'

'No, a friggin' general anaesthetic.'

I was learning fast.

CHAPTER SEVENTEEN

'LIBERALS TO TAKE OVER LIVERPOOL,' MY DAD SAID, REPEATING what he'd just heard on the radio, with more than a hint of disgust in his voice. 'First Ted Heath and now that Jeremy Thorpe, a right pair of bloody clowns, God help us.'

I ignored him. We weren't getting on very well lately. He annoyed me for no other reason than that he was my father and I was an angry teenager looking for a victim to be angry with.

'Where are you off to?' he said, watching me disapprovingly as I combed my hair in the mirror.

'Me mate's,' I answered irritably. 'We're going to a club in Liverpool so I'll probably stay at his,' adding grudgingly, 'if that's OK.'

'You spend a lot of time staying with "mates",' he said suspiciously, looking at me over his glasses. 'Who are all these "mates"?' He didn't like me staying out and worried – justifiably – that I might be up to no good.

Tonight's mate in question was Diane, a girl I'd met at work in the court collecting office. She was nine years older than me and a bit of a party animal. I kept my gay side from her at first, reluctant to come out to her, though things might have turned out less complicated later on if I'd been honest about my sexuality in the first place. The fact was I was unsure of what my true sexuality was, still experimenting with both sexes, unable to make up my mind which bus to get on. I was sure of one thing: bisexuality made life very awkward at times.

Diane introduced me to Liverpool's club scene. The Babaloo, Ugly's, the Mardi Gras, these were trendy places to be seen in; the one to avoid was the She Club, which had a reputation for being popular with dog-rough man-hungry divorcees. It was said that in the She, along with the Grafton, the women bought the men the drinks. I became very close to Diane and it was inevitable that we ended up sleeping with each other.

I was no stranger to the Bear's Paw by now. The shy young man who was shocked at the sight of two men dancing together had all but vanished, though I was still contemptuous of the young, screamingly camp queens who referred to each other as 'she'. I had learned to give the more malevolent entities and predatory letches a wide berth, and along the way I had managed to make quite a few friends.

My new best pal was Tony. Tony and I hit it off after a prolonged bitching session one night, though we were like chalk and cheese. He enjoyed a bit of verbal sparring and I'd had the best tutors when it came to that. He took me under his wing. He lived in Gayton, an area considered very posh in our house, and was two years older than me in age but wise beyond his years in experience. He was small, dark and handsome, well-spoken, intelligent, charming, didn't smoke and had an excellent job as a Customs officer. My mother adored him. He was everything I wasn't and she encouraged our friendship, hoping that his influence would rub off on me.

What she didn't know was that among his other attributes was an evil tongue, a wicked sense of humour and a voracious appetite for sex. He also had the biggest penis on Merseyside, not that we were lovers – ours was a strictly platonic relationship, sisters out on the prowl together – but he was inordinately proud of his enormous member and quite unabashed when it came to whopping it out, a trick that made him very popular. Tony had no inhibitions and it was him who taught me not to be so uptight and that, if you played your cards right, being gay could mean having a lot of fun.

'Let me be your fairy godmother,' he said in his best Mae West, a film star whose attitude to life and men he greatly admired. 'I'll show you a good time, kid.'

He was as good as his word. His current squeeze had something to do with the New Southport Theatre; Marlene Dietrich was appearing there and Tony asked me if I'd like to go. 'Call it an early birthday present,' he'd said. I'd been interested in Marlene ever since I first saw her on the telly singing 'Black Market' in the Billy Wilder film *A Foreign Affair* (one of her finest if you want my opinion, but let's not get into a queeny discussion over the films of Marlene Dietrich right now and get on with the plot). She fascinated me; she was different from anybody else I'd ever seen. Aunty Chris had a bit of a look of her and there was an air, reminiscent of Marlene, in the way she handled her cigarette, but the real McCoy was something special – unbelievably glamorous and undefeated even though she ended up getting shot or arrested in most of her films. I jumped at the chance to go and see this mythical creature in the flesh, incongruous as the prospect seemed of glimpsing this ethereal goddess of the silver screen in somewhere like Southport. A Parisian whorehouse, a Wild West saloon, yes, but respectable old Southport?

Apart from a few school trips, of which a matinee of *School for Scandal* is the only one that sticks in my mind, a performance of *Abelard and Heloise* memorable only for a naked Diana Rigg and Keith Michell, two pantos, the Little Theatre's production of *The Lion in Winter* and a Gang Show, the only other time I'd been near a theatre was when my mother threw herself on the bonnet of Johnnie Ray's car outside the Empire. I was about six and my mother couldn't afford the ticket, and even if she had, there was no one she knew to go with, so she'd ambled across the water with me in tow, telling my dad she was 'going to look at a nice little church'. She adored Johnnie Ray; her eyes filled with tears whenever she heard him on the radio. 'Poor Johnnie,' she'd say, smiling sadly at the transistor radio, lost in her dreams. 'God love him.'

I don't know if she ended up sprawled across his windscreen by design or by accident. I like to think that she lost her balance as she stepped forward in her eagerness to catch a glimpse of her idol as he drove past. She slid from the bonnet to the road without so much as a momentary glance out of the window from her hero. The car drove off smartish, leaving her, with her stockings laddered and knees bloodied, sat on the road outside the stage door of the Empire and feeling very foolish. 'Don't tell your dad,' she said, bribing me with a box of Poppets from the machine on the platform as we waited for the train to take us back to Birkenhead.

The New Southport Theatre was undergoing a refurbishment and was only half finished. It smelt of newly laid carpet and fresh paint on Marlene's opening night and the brightly lit foyer was teeming with people, mainly men, waiting to worship at the feet of their idol. I was introduced to the Lord Mayor and given a glass of champagne, and thought I'd really arrived. Tony, I noticed, was dressed soberly in a smart grey suit with a shirt and tie. I secretly thought that his dress sense was a bit square and was glad I'd 'put the dog on': scarlet corduroy fitted jacket, pink shirt with batwing collar, brown flares and bright red two-inch platform boots, all of which clashed beautifully with my flame-red, hennaed hair.

Marlene wasn't what I'd expected her to be. She'd grown old since *Foreign Affair*, and although still beautiful, it was a beauty that was artificial. She seemed frail buried underneath that big white coat, her eyes tired and empty as they peered out from under an unnatural-looking wave of blonde hair into the gloom of the auditorium. She seemed very nervous and unsure of what to do as she sang her opening song. She kept shuffling around and staring into the wings, a little old lady, vague and confused and caught in the spotlight of an unfinished theatre. It was shambolic. Her microphone, fixed to a stand that could be raised or lowered, went out of control during a particularly poignant song and shot up comically towards the flies as if in a Morecambe and Wise sketch. I felt sorry for this great old lady, reduced to singing in a seaside theatre that seemed totally unprepared for her. After endless curtain calls and flower-chucking from an army of young men, who, delirious and hyperventilating with adulation and unable to contain themselves, ran down the aisle screaming like mad things to pelt their goddess with bunches of flowers, I was asked if I'd like to meet the great woman. Curious, Tony and I were ushered backstage into the area by the stage door to wait for her.

Marlene was not in the mood for pleasantries with strangers. She was complaining about her dressing room to a woman who was carrying a huge bag. This was her daughter Maria. I'd hoped Marlene would be swathed in furs, exuding wafts of some heady perfume as she glided by, a sultry smile on her lips, before vanishing mysteriously into the night. I hadn't banked on an ordinary-looking pensioner in a blue trouser suit and an odd Baker Boy-style cap holding a carrier bag. She could have passed for one of the well-heeled older ladies who sat in the coffee bar of Beatties of Birkenhead and drank frothy coffee from glass cups. I could hear the tail end of her conversation as she walked towards us. 'It's enough to make me take up smoking again,' she said before turning to me.

'Give me a cigawett,' she demanded.

Since I had only half a crushed packet of ten Cadets in my back pocket and a dog-eared penny book of matches and didn't want to embarrass myself by getting these out in front of her, I told her that I didn't smoke.

'I thought all you Liverpool boys smoked,' she said, slightly mocking. 'How old are you?'

'Eighteen in June,' I answered, feeling, much to my annoyance, that my face was turning a bright red. I couldn't quite comprehend that the nice old lady I was talking to was the very same woman who fought Jimmy Stewart in a bar in *Destry Rides Again*.

'What's a young boy like you doing watching a silly old woman like me?' she cooed playfully. 'Go home to your momma,' she added, pinching my cheeks.

I did just that, but Momma wasn't very impressed.

'Never mind hanging around that old Kraut,' she said, 'you wanna get out and kick a ball.'

One night after a concert at the Philharmonic Hall, Tony had literally bumped into the conductor John Pritchard. When he first mentioned this John Pritchard to me and told me that he was a conductor, I assumed that he meant on the buses. I had no idea who he was and why would I? They had met as they both attempted to get in the same taxi and Tony, ever the gentleman, insisted that John Pritchard take the cab. In return JP invited him back to the Adelphi Hotel for a drink. Tony was no shy, retiring violet and, recognizing a golden opportunity, didn't hesitate to accept.

They became great friends. Tony was fanatical about classical music and they had a lot in common. Tony was also the type who would never embarrass JP in public; he was discreet and smart and could slip in among the Glyndebourne set without inviting comment or gossip. Theirs was never a sexual relationship. JP liked having a bit of eye candy around him but it was very much 'look but I don't want to touch'. Tony was crazy for opera and enjoyed the trips to Glyndebourne and Covent Garden, and now he wanted someone to share the fun with him so he thought it was about time I was introduced to

the great JP. I was dubious at first. I didn't want to find myself
in a compromising situation with an old man (old man! he
was in his early fifties) in return for board and lodging with a
bit of fancy singing thrown in, no matter how plush the venue.
Tony reassured me that there would be nothing like that and
rang JP up there and then to engineer a date.

'JP, do you remember that friend I was telling you about? . . .
That's right, the funny one with the long legs. Well, would it be
OK if I brought him with me to Glyndebourne? He's never
seen an opera.'

And nor did I want to either. Opera was my mother warbling
'One Fine Day' or Mario Lanza and Kathleen Ferrier on
Sunday afternoon radio.

'Here, have a word with him. He'd love to say hello.'

I didn't want to say hello and expressed this by jumping up and
down, flapping my hands and mouthing NO like a demented
mute. Tony ignored me, shoving the receiver into my hand.

'Hello?' My voice annoyingly adopted my mother's half-
crown telephone voice and it came out as 'Hilla'.

'Hello, my dear,' JP said breathily, 'I've been hearing all
about you from Tony. When are you coming down to visit us?'

And so it was arranged that we were to spend the weekend
with him and attend the opera. 'With the Friday night spent
in London on the pull,' Tony said gleefully. He threw away
his fairy godmother hat, replacing it with his Professor
Higgins.

'If you don't mind me being brutally honest, we have a lot of
work to do,' he said, sizing me up. 'For a start, those clothes
have to go.'

'These are brand new,' I protested, holding out the folds
of fabric that made up my emerald green Oxford bags. The
waistband came up to my armpits and they were twenty-two
inches wide at the bottom with a four-inch turn-up. 'They're
the latest fashion, everyone's wearing them.'

'Exactly, that's my point. Who wants to be a member of the common herd?' Tony said grandly. 'You must throw them out or give them to a beggar with no taste, and while you're at it, ditch the shirt and those awful boots.'

I secretly agreed with him when it came to the trousers. They had been an expensive impulse buy and I was determined to get my money's worth out of them, regardless of the fact that they flapped noisily around my skinny legs like a tarpaulin caught on a flagpole at the merest hint of a breeze. But the boots and shirt? This was blasphemy! My red platform boots and candy-striped shirt in varying shades of green were the ultimate in up-to-the-minute fashion. Tony was a square, he dressed like an old man and was trying to get me to do the same. This new look he was recommending sounded very much the same as the old look, the one that I was spending every penny that I earned trying to get away from.

He went on, ignoring my protests. 'For this weekend at least, you are going to be très chic. The look will be public-school boy: grey trousers, casual black sweater – preferably cashmere, crisp white shirt and an old school tie worn loose at the neck. The hair has to go. We'll have to get that Maggie May red cut out.'

I stopped him mid-flow. 'D'ya want me to have elocution lessons as well?' I was laughing in spite of myself at his sheer gall and the outrageousness of this proposed makeover.

'Unfortunately not, I'm afraid,' he continued, really getting into his role of Svengali. 'Elocution lessons would be pointless at this stage, given the limited time available. I can do nothing with the voice. Just try not to swear and remember to keep it down to a respectable level.'

I gave in and made my debut at Glyndebourne looking, as Tony had remarked, 'like a choir boy'. I'd even had my hair cut. I wasn't keen on it as it made me feel like the old Paul O'Grady, but looking around at the Glyndebourne crowd I was grateful that I wasn't wearing the Oxford bags and capped-sleeve T-shirt. I'd have stuck out like a sore thumb and died of mortification. Instead I was feeling quietly confident, knowing that I was soberly dressed head to toe by Carson's of Birkenhead, a transaction made financially viable courtesy of the Provident Cheque Company.

John Pritchard was what Aunty Anne would have called 'a real gentleman'. He was charming and generous and extremely kind to me. There were no embarrassing advances made, no unexpected lunges while strolling round the garden and no fumbling in the drawing room after dinner. He had a soft spot for long legs, and wanted little more in the way of a thrill than to gaze adoringly at my long skinny pins as I lay self-consciously in the garden in a minuscule pair of speedos provided by the house. Tony, totally unabashed by nudity, would parade around naked, his enormous schlong nearly giving JP, and most of the staff, a heart attack.

I was determined not to enjoy the opera. It was the first production in the UK of *The Visit of the Old Lady* by Von Einem and JP was conducting. However, I soon forgot my prejudice and was completely blown away by the magnificence and spectacle of it all as the story unfolded of the single mother banished by her village as a young girl and returning years later to wreak her revenge. I mentally rewrote it imagining Aunty Chris in the part, arriving on the stage not by steam train but on the back of a 42 bus.

In the interval we sat on tartan blankets spread out on the lawn, eating smoked salmon sandwiches and drinking champagne from a Fortnum and Mason hamper by the side of the lake. It really was idyllic and a lifestyle that I could've got used to, but I realized that such pleasures were transient and tried to enjoy the moment for what it was.

JP liked me because I made him laugh and I was happy to play the court jester. He loved to hear about Tony's and my sexual exploits, both real and imaginary, and we were frequent visitors to Carter's Corner Place, his beautiful house in Herstmonceux, Sussex. He had some very interesting parties in the summer of '73. I remember streaking across the lawn with Tony, butt-naked in the middle of a garden party, in front of Lord Snowdon and Dame Joan Sutherland. Embarrassing now when I think about it but exhilarating and liberating back then, and JP loved it. Having a pair of rough-arsed scrubbers charging around naked in among the flower beds and ladies in big hats made him feel daring and deliciously disreputable.

He had a flat in King Street which he generously, if not foolishly, let us use on our visits to London. BR had recently introduced a new weekend deal and for three pounds you got a return ticket from Liverpool to London. We certainly made good use of it and, arriving in London, would go directly to the flat, get changed and head for the Coleherne, a gay pub in Earl's Court, popular with the leather fraternity. We'd stand at the bar smoking Sobranie Cocktail Cigarettes to show that we were sophisticated.

When JP was in town he took us to the theatre. We saw *Gypsy* with Angela Lansbury and an extremely young Bonnie Langford at the Piccadilly. I'd seen the film years earlier on telly, but watching the stage production I saw for the first time the dark side to the story: the tatty dressing rooms and crummy hotels, the whistle-stop tours and one-night stands and the struggle to succeed in a notoriously cruel business – none of which put me off the idea of a life treading the boards. Quite the opposite, it made it sound all the more interesting. The old longing to get into showbiz that had lain dormant stirred in my gut again. What I was actually going to do when I got there God alone knew, but I mentioned my secret ambition to JP over dinner in Mr Chow's in Knightsbridge.

'With legs like those you should be a dancer, my dear,' he said. 'I have a friend with a studio around the corner from the flat, I'll take you over tomorrow. You'll be a marvellous dancer.'

I neglected to tell him that I had two left feet, I was so caught up in his enthusiasm. By the time I left the restaurant I was full of confidence that I was going to be the next Nijinsky. The friend turned out to be Lindsay Kemp, the avant-garde choreographer and dancer. He'd recently choreographed and appeared in David Bowie's show at the Rainbow and it was said that he was responsible for Bowie's metamorphosis into Ziggy Stardust. He ran a class at the Dance Centre in Floral Street, Covent Garden, long before it became a fashionable venue.

I felt stupid. I had no desire to be a dancer, I only went along to please JP and Lindsay Kemp knew it.

'Have you ever had lessons, dear?'

'No.'

'Did you dance as a child?'

'No.'

'Why do you want to be a dancer then?'

'I don't really.'

'Fuck off, dear, and stick to whoring.'

Thus ended my interview with the great Mr Kemp. I had no idea who he was and put him down as a crabby old queen, but seeing the sheer genius of his performance a year later in his unforgettable production *Flowers* I realized just what a fool I must have seemed at that interview.

Tony and I guarded our entry to the finer things in life like Scylla and Charybdis, keeping him well out of range of any pretty young fortune hunters and constantly on the lookout for threats to our position as head catamites. We'd been invited to tea at the Ritz by an old friend of JP's called . . . well, let's call her Lady J.

Milady never went anywhere without her houseboy. None of them ever stayed very long in her service as she wore them out, going through them at the same speed as she went through a bottle of Gordon's Gin. She was a demanding hypochondriac who enjoyed her imaginary ill health. Her latest houseboy, a good-looking blond Dane called Stefan, seemed to be made of sterner stuff. He knew exactly which buttons to push and could play his mistress like a Stradivarius. He flirted with her and flattered her and the silly old goat revelled in his constant attention – as, to our horror, did JP.

We hated this Stefan on sight. He had JP wound round his little finger in minutes and we were more than slightly concerned when we heard him inviting Lady J and, of course, 'this charming boy' to stay at Carter's Corner for the weekend. We were going back up north and wouldn't be around to protect our patch. 'You'll be greatly missed, my dears,' JP said, not quite convincingly enough for our liking, his eyes glazing over with lust as he gazed at Stefan, 'but I'm sure I'll find other distractions.'

'If we don't do something quick to get rid of that ponce we can say goodbye to halcyon days,' Tony muttered as we stood outside the Ritz watching Stefan help Lady J into the car while JP gushed adoringly.

Our chance came a couple of months later. Since the arrival of Stefan, phone calls and invites had been few and far between from JP, who was captivated by him. We'd heard that JP had invited Lady J to the flat in Covent Garden and, unable to attend, she'd sent Stefan in her place.

Tony had been plotting a way to depose this usurper, this brazen cuckoo who had ousted us from the nest, and finally he had a brainwave. It was not common knowledge outside music circles that JP was gay, although he had a partner, Terry, whom he usually referred to as his personal assistant. He was very discreet and expected others to act the same when out with him in public.

We decided to club together to pay for a large ad reading 'Stefan Loves JP' in the personal column at the back of *Gay News*, in the hope that JP would see it and go crazy. Surely, we cackled evilly, such a blatant display of affection to an old closet queen like JP would warrant nothing less than banish-, ment for the hated Stefan. Childish but very effective, the plan worked brilliantly. It got rid of Stefan quicker than Swarfega on grease. Tony was ecstatic and cracked open half a bottle of 'the widow' from his parents' cellar. 'To us!' He raised his glass. 'That'll larn them.'

The last time I saw JP was a few weeks after my eighteenth birthday. He'd asked Tony and me to join him at a small party in Portmeirion, the village in West Wales used as the location for the cult series *The Prisoner*. It was a beautiful Sunday after-noon, and the hot sun beating down on the Italianate village made you believe that you were on the Amalfi coast. We had lunch in the hotel dining room with the architect and creator of the village, Clough Williams Ellis. He'd not long been knighted and JP was making a big fuss of him. He was in his eighties but full of life and great company, giving me a signed copy of his book about the village which I've still got. After lunch I retired with JP to his suite in a Hansel and Gretel cottage in the grounds. He asked me to lie on the bed with him. This is it, I thought, bracing myself, time to pay the piper – but I was wrong. We lay there side by side, holding hands and listening to the birds.

'I'm going to America soon,' JP said, breaking the silence, 'so I don't know if we shall see each other again, for a long while at least.' I was surprised and slightly horrified to see a tear running down the side of his cheek and into his ear. He was in a maudlin mood. 'When, hopefully a long time from now, you hear of my death, think of me fondly.'

Years later, when I read his obituary in *The Times* as I sat waiting for my first day of filming as Roxanne, the copper's nark, in *The Bill*, I did remember him fondly and silently thanked him for making the summer of '73 a memorable one.

*

Tony was part of a rummage crew. Along with other Customs men he searched the cargo ships entering the port of Liverpool for drugs. This gave him ample opportunity to check the crew out, sniff out the ones who were desperate for a bit of male company (and there were many!) and discreetly arrange a liaison with them in a pub on the Dock Road called the Dominion. It was a notorious prostitutes' pub, frequented by sailors and the kind of queen you weren't supposed to have anything to do with. I'd get a phone call when he had a catch.

'Get your arse down the Dominion tonight, we're meeting a few Persian sailors.'

'Who was that on the phone, Paul?'

'Only Tony.'

'Oh yes, what did he want?'

'Wants me to meet him and some of his friends from work for a drink tonight.'

'That's nice.'

If she'd known that the friends were a pack of extremely randy Persian sailors she wouldn't have been so agreeable. The Dominion was a pretty scary place; the word rough didn't come into it. Tony, not in the least bit bothered, elbowed his way past two hard-looking women and ordered the drinks from the faded queen behind the bar. I lit a cigarette and stared self-consciously at my shoes in case I caught anyone's eye. When Tony returned with the drinks I relaxed and looked around. Penny and Frances, the two queens I'd seen in the Lisbon, were sat with a gang of sailors having a rare old time. Penny, drink and fag in hand, inclined his head towards me regally, screwing his face up in a smile that was meant to translate as 'look what I've got'.

'Who the fuck is that?' Tony asked, scanning the group of sailors to see if he recognized any who might have been poached by the arachnoid Penny and Frances.

'Oh, just some queen called Penny.' I was trying to look casual as I slyly examined the rim of my glass to see if it was clean. I was aware that it was a gesture my dad would've made if he was in a strange pub and resented him for it. I didn't want to feel like my dad standing in the Dominion, I wanted to feel the exact opposite of everything he was. I wanted to be bad.

The sailors Tony had arranged to meet turned out to be not at all what I'd expected. Instead of the rowdy bunch of sex-crazed pirates that I'd half hoped they'd be, I shook hands politely with a group of shy but devastatingly handsome young men. They could easily have risen straight from the pages of Jean Genet, ruggedly masculine yet as beautiful as girls. Tony was in his element. 'What would you chaps like to drink then?' he asked the group at large. Their leader, a stunner called Paul who spoke the best English, was having none of it and insisted that they buy the drinks. 'Nope,' said Tony, 'you're our guests and I insist on buying you a drink.' Turning to me as he went to the bar, 'We don't want them to think that we're a pair of Liverpool scrubbers like your friends over there, do we?' he said, winking at me slyly.

The Dominion started to get busy so we moved on, showing them around the town, popping into the Bear's Paw for a couple of drinks, the navy paying by now, keeping a possessive eye on the sailors in case some lairy queen had designs on any of them.

'You want to be careful, you do,' Brian the sardonic barman said as he cleared our table of empty glasses. 'You'll get a bad name hanging around sailors.'

We ended up back on the ship, which was easier said than done as you had to get past the copper on the dock gate first. Luckily, Tony was an old hand at this and knew where the 'whore's entrance' was – a hole in the fence that we could get through without detection. It was exciting climbing up the gangplank and boarding the ship, that smell of oil and seawater as heady a perfume to my nostrils as any rose. Below deck, an orgy was in full swing. There was some sort of sexual activity going on in every cabin. On the way down the corridor I saw Penny stepping gingerly out of a cabin, so drunk he could hardly stand. He stared at me quizzically, trying to figure out where he knew me from. ''Scuse me,' he slurred, pointing at me with his bottle of lager, 'what are you doing on board? This isn't the *Royal* fuckin' *Iris*, you know. And don't let me catch you giving it away,' he shouted after me as I brushed past, 'I'm sick of you lousy free fucks.' We sat in Paul's cabin drinking bottles of Oranjeboom, talking and flirting, and I felt totally at home. The company was good, the booze and fags in plentiful supply, the cabin cosy and compact and a young man with the body of an Olympian god stretched out on the bunk in a vest and shorts was smiling at me. I silently cursed my dad for not letting me go to sea.

A woman with a small baby in one arm appeared at the door of the cabin asking if anyone had a bottle opener. The boys obviously knew her well as they made a great fuss of her and the child, inviting her in and offering her a drink. She was one of the many prostitutes who lived on the ships. They went from ship to ship, living on board with one of the sailors until it was time to sail, then moving on, hopefully finding lodging aboard the next vessel that came into port. She introduced her-self to me and Tony as Dot, adding that she was known in the locality as Dry Dock Dot. Considering that her transient life must have been unbelievably hard and unpredictable, she was a surprisingly optimistic soul.

'It's not a bad life,' she said, dipping the tip of her little finger in the bottle of Oranjeboom and giving it to her baby to suck. 'I get to see the world and I don't even have to go anywhere.'

*

If all the nice girls love a sailor then so do some bad lads. I've always had a soft spot for the navy ever since Popeye and then John, my paramour from school, who left me for a life at sea. There's something romantic about the notion of a sailor, a seafaring nomad with a girl or boy in every port, leaving a trail of broken hearts from Rangoon to Southampton. There was no commitment with a sailor: it was here today, gone to-morrow, with a good time had by all guaranteed, which at the time suited me just fine. I enjoyed playing the wisecracking slut. I was even getting over the embarrassment I suffered when leaving a ship in the morning and having to walk the length of the dock to a chorus of catcalls and wolf whistles from the dockers. Fuck 'em. Instead of running, head down, for the hole in the fence I was sashaying, head and two fingers up, out of the front gate.

Partying on the ships was a complete contrast to working in the dour atmosphere of the Magistrates Court. I'd been elevated from the court collecting office to the courts themselves and I was now a trainee clerk of the court, sat reverently underneath the magistrates, next to the clerk who handed over forms for costs, probationary reports and any other reverently information required by the beaks. I was in Number Three Court and it was here that the cases of prostitutes, drunks and vagrants were tried. It was one of the busiest and smelliest courts to work in and after a three-hour session on a hot day you needed a gas mask. It was entertaining at first, but after a while I realized I was listening to the same old excuses from the same faces who appeared week after week in the dock. I got to talk to some of them while I was having a quick fag in the main hall. One woman was never out of court: a shoplifter and part-time pros-titute and not a very successful one judging by the times she was up before the beak. We'll call her Marlene Corby.

'I was standing at the bus stop with me mate, eating a bag of chips, when this bloke approached and asked me if I wanted business. I was actually thinking of goin' home but I thought fuck it, and said to me mate, "Hold me chips while I give this one a quick seeing-to, and keep your eye peeled for that bus." How was I to know he was a friggin' copper?'

Marlene was the prototype for Lily Savage's criminal side. One morning I was telling her about my mother, who'd been having strange pains in her chest and I was worried about her.

'I'll light a candle for her, lad,' she said piously, patting my hand.

Marlene managed to stay out of the courts for a few weeks until she was nicked one night for soliciting while drunk and disorderly. She was not a pretty sight standing bleary-eyed in the dock the next morning.

'Marlene Corby, you are charged with—'

Marlene interrupted the clerk as she suddenly recognized me. 'Oh, hello, love,' she trilled, giving me a wave. 'How's your mother's chest?'

The magistrates above me spluttered with indignation. One of them leaned forward and tapped me on the head with his pencil. 'How do you know this common prostitute?' he asked.

'Common? Common?' Marlene squealed with self-righteous ire. 'I may be a prostitute but I am certainly not common,' she said, puffing out her chest like an angry quail and letting out a loud belch.

'Take this woman back to the cells until she fully sobers up,' the magistrate said, and, turning to me, added portentously, 'You are dismissed from court.'

I was hauled over the coals for that one. I couldn't see the harm in it, talking to people while they were waiting to go into court – it wasn't as if they were murderers or child molesters – but no, it was them and us and never the twain shall meet and Leslie Pugh, the stipendiary magistrate, warned that I'd be out on my ear if it happened again.

'This is a court of law, O'Grady, not a Tupperware party,' I remember him saying, although the chances of finding Marlene at a Tupperware party are open to debate.

A professor from Liverpool University who drank in the Bear's Paw and with whom I'd become friendly compared Liverpool's 'vibrant underground gay scene' (as he called it) and the sub-culture that existed in the docks of the city to the Shanghai of the twenties. 'If Shanghai was the whore of the Orient,' he said, 'then Liverpool is the Very Naughty Aunty of the North West.' I was spending so much time in the Bear's Paw that Gordon, the manager, said I might as well come and work behind the bar.

I felt I'd hit the jackpot. I was able to go out clubbin' and get paid for it at the same time, with the added advantage of being able to chat up the customers across the bar that I'd previously been too shy to approach. One night I was asked if I'd like to go for a meal on a Chinese ship after work. I'd liked what little Chinese food I'd tasted in the past and so I went.

'Watch out they don't slip you a Mickey Finn and pack you off in a crate to South East Asia,' Brian the barman warned.

I had a great time. We gathered in the large galley and the crew crouched down along the walls to eat, shovelling noodles into their mouths at an alarming speed. The food was delicious; to this day I've never tasted Chinese food to equal that meal. I drank a gallon of Singha Beer and, untouched by human hand, Chinese or otherwise, went home in a taxi and not in a crate as predicted by Brian.

He had a lot to say the next night at work, shuffling around behind the bar in the manner of a cod geisha girl, fanning his face with a beer mat and singing 'The Ying Tong Song'.

'Have you met our new yum-yum girl?' he said to a customer. 'She Shanghai Lily, the Deadly White Flower of the Wirral.'

I'd vowed I'd never be called by a girl's name but the

nickname stuck, and much to my annoyance some of the customers started to call me Lil.

Tony thought it a fabulous name and gave me a copy of William Walton's popular song with the opening lines 'Lily O'Grady, silly and shady, wanted to be a lazy lady'. 'It was meant to be,' he said. 'It was written in the stars, you were destined to be a Lily.'

Since he thought it so bloody funny I rechristened him Ruby Arbuckle, a name he absolutely revelled in.

'The guy on the door said that someone called Shanghai Lil would look after me.' An extremely tall man in dark glasses and a white stetson was standing at the bar.

I wanted to crawl under it with shame. Who was this piss-taking cowboy? He stood out like a sore thumb among the regulars of the Bear's Paw. I dismissed him as a loon and carried on washing glasses.

'What can I get you, big feller?' Brian asked, looking at the stranger and grinning like the Joker, suddenly turning on the charm.

'These are on the house,' Gordon said, sidling up to the cowboy all smiles. 'Give LJB whatever he wants.'

Who was this guy that had the normally dour Brian running around after him and the notoriously parsimonious Gordon pressing him to have whatever he liked? Must be the Pope in disguise.

Suddenly the cowboy leaned over the bar towards me and stuck out his hand. 'Long John Baldry,' he said. 'Would you like to get your head out of that sink and join me for a drink?'

I looked over at Gordon, who gave me a nod of approval and opened the bar flap. 'You can come out from behind there, love, seeing as it's a quiet night and we're not very busy, and you can sit with Mr Baldry and have a drink with him.' He sounded like the proprietor of a hostess bar. I didn't know if I wanted to sit with Long John Baldry and have a drink. I wasn't very impressed. I'd seen him on the telly on *Top of the Pops* but his music didn't appeal to me. I liked T Rex, Motown, jazz and show music and I thought 'Let The Heartaches Begin', Baldry's 1967 hit, a bit naff and something strictly for the grannies and didn't appreciate at the time that I was having a drink with one of the great names of British blues.

Telling me that he was in Liverpool for a few nights playing a club date he seemed very laid back and affable as he chucked down the whiskies, but later on, back at his suite at the Atlantic Tower Hotel, his mood changed. He became morose and depressed, retreating into himself and his bottle of Scotch. I was a bit pissed and babbled on nervously, unsure how to deal with this strange man. We got on to the subject of music, his dark mood cleared momentarily and he spoke fondly of Elton John and Rod Stewart, laughing as he recalled the days when the Rolling Stones had been his support act. He quickly grew sad again at the mention of his recent album, *Everything Stops For Tea*, which he said had totally bombed in America. We lapsed back into silence.

I caught a glimpse of myself in the full-length mirror at the end of the room. A Stig of the Dump lookalike sat uncomfortably on the end of the bed with its chicken legs crossed, staring back at me. All I was wearing were my underpants, one of a pack of three from Owen Owen's, a Christmas present from Aunty Anne. Bri-nylon and bright red, they made my ghost-white skin seem even paler. I realized how stupid I looked and felt about as alluring as a bowl of cold Scotch broth. I made a move to get dressed.

'I don't know why we bothered getting stripped in the first place,' I muttered under my breath, angry with myself and annoyed with the situation. Nothing had happened. Long John, to put it delicately as I don't want to sound like a kiss-and-tell scrubber in the *News of the World*, had had one too many to drink, the whisky I assumed temporarily incapacitating him. It was either that or my red drawers that put the kibosh on the affair; in any case nothing had occurred.

'Where are you rushing off to in such a hurry?' he asked, looking up at me as I attempted to maintain my balance while trying to put my platform boot on and button my shirt at the same time. 'Don't go, stay and talk, drink a little whisky with me,' he said, waving the bottle and smiling for a change. 'What's your favourite song?'

I sat down again on the bed, avoiding the mirror, instead looking out of the window and over the dark waters towards the lights of Birkenhead and thinking of Aunty Chris. Her favourite song was 'Seven Golden Daffodils' as sung by Lonnie Donegan. It seemed a respectable enough choice, one that wouldn't make me sound like a complete pleb, and so I told him.

'Really?' he said, brightening up and looking at me in a new light. 'So you like skiffle and the blues, eh?' He stood up in the middle of the room wearing nothing but a pair of cowboy boots and started to sing it. His voice was rich and deep with a hint of gravel in it that filled the room and most of the hotel. Within minutes Reception was on the phone to say that a number of people had complained about the noise and did we know that it was 3 a.m.? Long John carried on regardless. I don't think he'd been aware that the phone had even rung, he was so lost in song – that and being ten parts pissed. Eventually a security guard came up and banged on the door. Long John opened it, warmly inviting the man in for a drink. The security guard politely declined the offer, and if he wondered why I had one leg in my jeans and why Long John was stark naked apart from his cowboy boots he was too much of a gentleman to mention it, accepting Long John's assurance that there would be no more singing that night as well as a fat tip before going on his way.

We lay on the bed waiting for dawn to break. He turned to

me and said out of the blue, 'I think I'm going mad.' I ignored him, putting it down to the ego of a troubled and frustrated star.

Later on he was institutionalized for mental health problems. I was shocked when I read it in the *NME*. Despite his mood swings I'd liked him and had spent quite a few evenings with him since that first encounter. I'd come to realize, as we chewed the cud over a bottle of whisky, that I was in the presence of someone who was truly out of the ordinary.

My mother answered the phone to him one night when he rang me at home.

'Sex, it, dabble tu.'

'Yeah . . . Hi . . . Is Paul in?'

'Yis, whoose spicking plis?'

'It's Long John Baldry.'

'Don't be so bloody 'ard-faced, I was only asking your name out of politeness, you cheeky sod. Paul! There's one of your fool mates on the blower who thinks he's a comedian.'

Shame she didn't believe it was him as she quite liked him.

When I told Tony what had happened to poor old Long John his reply was typical. 'You see, a couple of nights with you and you drive them insane.'

Coppers that I'd seen hanging around the courts would turn up at the Bear's Paw from time to time expecting free drinks. Much as he hated giving away free booze, Gordon would oblige, not wanting to upset them and risk a raid.

'Does your boss at the Magistrates Court know that you're working in a queer club?' one of them sneered as he collected yet another round of free drinks.

'And does your boss know that you're drinking on duty?' I snapped back, causing Gordon, who was hovering nearby, to hyperventilate.

'Mind your manners, you mouthy cow,' he said, flashing me

a look and steering the copper away from the bar. 'Take no notice of him, officer, he's a bit political.'

Because I was still going to the odd CHE gathering Gordon saw me as a political activist. He didn't like or trust 'those student types' as he called them, making trouble and giving out about gay rights. I wasn't in the least bit political. The only demonstration I'd ever been on was the Free Angela Davis protest march at the Pierhead the year before, and that wasn't due to any political motivation or because I felt impassioned about Ms Davis's incarceration. To tell the truth I didn't even know who she was. The only reason I was keen to join the protesting masses was because the television cameras were out in force and I fancied being on *Granada Reports*.

I did, however, object strongly to being expected to pander to the police to avoid harassment from them, and refused to be amenable to any who showed up at the bar.

Gordon was contemptuous of gay rights. He preferred the old days when customers knocked three times furtively on the door to get in and everything was kept under wraps.

I'd been to the first National CHE Conference at Morecambe, much to Gordon's annoyance ('You'll only get yourself arrested, daughter, and put me and your real mother in hospital'), and had taken Tony with me. He wasn't at all interested in what he called 'political bollocks', ending up instead doing his bit for the gay cause by going through Carlisle University's Gay Soc like a dose of salts. Over five hundred gay men and a smattering of women descended on the town that weekend, and it was a revelation being surrounded by so many gay people. Of course there was a bit of fuss from some of the locals. I suppose it was a shock for them to be confronted by a coachload of screaming homosexuals singing 'Walking Back To Happiness'. There was also the predictable abuse from yobs on street corners.

I wasn't as liberated as I made out. I still squirmed with

embarrassment at the sight of two grown men holding hands in public; in fact, any public displays of affection would have me cringing. I remember sitting in the afternoon sunshine on the steps of a disused cinema with a very intense young man, listening to him talk about a German doctor named Hirschfeld who he said was the father of the gay rights movement and who had remarked that 'the liberation of homosexuals can only be the work of homosexuals themselves'. We shared a packet of Beech Nut chewy and I'd have liked to share a lot more with him, but he was way too wrapped up in the theory to get down to the practical. I can picture that yellow and green Beech Nut wrapper on the step and taste the sharp mint of the gum as if it were this morning.

I thought a lot about what this Dr Hirschfeld had said on the minibus home and realized that the only way forward was to be honest. I could picture my parents' faces if I was to drop that little bombshell on them over corned beef, chips and peas.

'What would you say if I said I was gay?' I asked my mum a few days later. She was clearing out the cupboard under the stairs. Backing out, she turned to me holding a birdcage.

'Is there any point keeping this old thing?' she asked, completely ignoring what I'd said. 'Let's face it, I've no intention of getting another budgie. Dirty, messy things, scattering their seed all over the bloody house.'

Our budgie, Joey, had recently died. He was an ancient old bird, about to celebrate his twentieth birthday when he tipped forward on his perch and went to that great aviary in the sky.

'It's a blessing really,' my mother sighed as I lowered his little corpse, wrapped in a Kleenex, into a hole under the garden hedge. 'Make sure you've dug it deep enough, we don't want those bloody cats digging him up.'

Joey hadn't responded to a wolf whistle or a 'Who's a pretty boy then?' in years, neither had he chirped or peeped at his

317

reflection in his little mirror with the bell. He was silent and morose, recalling the glory days perhaps when he still had his full complement of feathers and could fly round the front room, landing on my dad's specs to take a bit of biscuit out of his mouth. He no longer took to the air – he couldn't any more – and so he sat hunched on the furthest corner of his perch, his head tucked under his scrawny wing or glaring at you through the bars of his cage with his one good eye.

My mother wasn't keen on having a caged bird in the house; she considered it unlucky. She wasn't keen on having any animal in the house really, yet over the years Holly Grove played host to a variety of creatures. My dad had brought a beautiful border collie back with him from Ireland, an ex-working sheepdog named Bran who went slightly mad for the want of something to do. His predecessor, a border collie puppy, a sickly little thing bought from Wirral Pets for my tenth birthday, had to be put down after a few weeks as he had distemper. He was impossible to housetrain. In the little deposits that he left around the house I'd find worms, which I'd lower down the plughole in the bathroom with my mother's tweezers before she saw them and threatened to throw the pup out. The shed in the back yard was full of guinea pigs, rats, mice, hamsters, gerbils, rabbits, catfish and tench and a ferret. My ma was wary of the ferret. It would stand up on its hind legs and wrinkle its nose up at her on the kitchen step as she was cooking the tea.

'Paul, gerrout here and see to this rat, it's threatening me again.'

'Did you hear me? I said what would you do if I said I was gay?' I asked again.

'Yes, I did hear you, thank you very much,' she snapped, 'and I'd be obliged if you didn't go talking like that in front of your father. You've already made him ill with your shenanigans.'

'Well, what would you do?' I'd gone this far so I might as well be hung for a sheep as a lamb.

'If what?'

'If I said I was, you know, gay.' My nerve was starting to go.

'I'd say that nothing would surprise me about you,' she said, chortling. She took the birdcage out to the bin in the back yard. 'Just don't let me catch you wearing my clothes. Gay? Gay me arse.'

The subject was never mentioned again.

I told Diane. She refused to believe me, insisting that my 'gayness' was just a stage that I was going through and, with the help of the right woman, it was something I would eventually grow out of. Maybe she didn't really want to acknowledge that I might actually be gay, our relationship had come too far for that. I felt she was becoming too possessive, making me feel uneasy in her company in case I said the wrong thing. I was constantly skating on thin ice in a situation that suddenly felt claustrophobic. We were really close friends who occasionally slept together – at least that was how I saw it – but for her it was a little more than that. I was too insensitive, or just didn't want to acknowledge what was happening, and buried my head in the sand and carried on, business as usual, treating her like one of the boys. She was also blinkered to the truth, kidding herself that I really was 100 per cent heterosexual and that I would eventually come round. Consequently our relationship deteriorated into a series of bitter recriminations and jealous accusations that eventually drove us apart. I was immature, irresponsible and needed to grow up, and not surprisingly my behaviour infuriated her. I didn't want to settle down with anyone, male or female, and tried to make that clear without hurting her feelings, but it fell on deaf ears. Sailors were a lot easier to deal with: women were far more complex creatures who required careful handling. A word to the wise: ladies, try not to fall in love with gay men. You're not only barking up the wrong tree, you're in the wrong bloody forest. Mark my words, as the old crone said, it will always end in tears.

Diane pestered me to take her to the gay bars. I didn't want her going to the Bear's Paw as the less she knew about my activities in there, the better. Instead I took her to the Lisbon and Sadie's Bar Royale, to give it its full title.

CHAPTER EIGHTEEN

'ARE YOU A MEMBER?' SADIE, THE FEARSOME CHATELAINE OF the Bar Royale, shouted down to us from a second-floor window. The name Bar Royale was a bit of a misnomer for the two rooms that awaited us upstairs, and nobody called it that anyway; it was known all over Liverpool simply as Sadie's. 'Who the fuck's she?' Sadie said, opening the door and glaring at Diane; Sadie was a total misogynist and panicked if he thought that there was a chance of the club's becoming 'over-run with women'. He'd rather have had a plague of rats.

'She's a friend of mine, Sadie,' I mumbled, handing over the forty-pence admission fee for both of us.

'Bloody fish,' Sadie hissed, letting us pass and following us up the long flight of stairs. 'I hope you know that this is a gay bar, so don't be causing any bloody trouble or you'll be out. Bloody straights. Don't be bringing any more in here or you'll be banned.' Sadie was a foul-tempered old queen with the profile of Mr Punch and, on a good day, the demeanour of an anaconda with toothache. He ran the club along the lines of a Singapore Borstal, terrorizing his patrons if they dared to put a foot wrong, yet despite the Draconian rules and the abuse, back we went for more.

Sadie's was very popular. It was nothing fancy, in fact it would be fair to say that it was commonly known as a bit of a low joint, a dump, attracting a 'rougher' clientele than the Bear's Paw did. However, it had a great atmosphere, and unlike the Bear's Paw it had the bonus of being open until 2 a.m. Diane had persecuted me, as I had Steve the Copper, to take her to a gay bar. Apart from tearing her hair out with curiosity she still refused to accept that I was in any way gay, and wanted to see how I reacted on my own territory, so to speak.

She was disappointed with Sadie's at first. She imagined all gay clubs would be sleazy Sodom and Gomorrahs, as I had done before actually setting foot in one. I sat her down at one of the tables and went to get the drinks. 'Don't be leaving me sitting on my own all night,' she said.

'Is that Nana Mouskouri over there?' Bunny the barman asked. 'If it is, I want her autograph for my ma.'

I glanced over to Diane, who was hunched with a martyred air on the end of her seat, staring morosely at the two elderly queens jiving energetically to 'Knock Three Times' on the tiny dance floor. With her re-entry-shield specs and streaked brown hair, parted in the middle and as straight as a yard of pump water, she just might have stood a chance of romping home with first prize at a Nana Mouskouri lookalike competition. I gave her a wave to show I hadn't forgotten her; she gave me a thin, watery smile in return. This was going to be a good night.

Sadie, standing at the end of the bar talking to his best friend Della, gave me a sour little nod. 'Thanks for letting my friend in,' I said, mainly for something to say. 'Would you like a drink?'

'No thanks, love,' Sadie said, slightly mollified, and bestowing upon me an expression that could easily be mistaken for the grimace of a gargoyle with crippling indigestion but was in fact a rare smile. 'Don't make a habit of it, that's all. They take over if you're not careful and before you know it the place is teeming with them, like a fuckin' aquarium.'

Della raised his eyes to heaven and drained his pint. He was the ugliest man in Liverpool, his battered face beneath the most unnatural-looking, shiny nylon wig in a shade of washed-out ginger a testimony to the many fights he'd had over the years. As Quentin Crisp once said, 'Some Roughs are really queer and some Queers are really rough.' Della would actually go out 'straight-bashing'. Any unfortunate who had been the victim of a gay-bashing could rely on Della to rally to the cause, root out the offenders and give them a taste of their own medicine. He was as hard as nails, a ferocious, whisky-drinking streetfighter who stood for no nonsense from the jeering homophobes he encountered, and consequently spent a lot of time shuttling in and out of prison for his trouble. He had a heart of gold and I liked him, as well as admiring his bravery.

When I got back from the bar with the drinks Diane was talking to Penny.

'Oh, hello, girl,' Penny drawled, raising his glass to me. 'Not on the ships tonight?'

Diane spluttered into her warm Bacardi and Coke. I knew it had been a mistake to bring her.

'I was asking Di here if she could guess who that picture was hanging on the wall,' Penny went on, pointing lovingly to an enlarged black and white photograph of a strange-looking woman with a Dusty Springfield hairdo framing a hard, ferret-like face. 'She had no idea that it was me, did ya, queen?' he squealed proudly, delighted with himself. 'That was taken when I won Miss Bar Royale, in the . . . er . . . late sixties. Everybody said I should've been a model.'

We made appreciative noises, and oohed and aahed in amazement that Sadie's very own Mona Lisa was actually our Penny.

'D'ya wanna gerrup for a dance?' Penny asked Diane. He lifted his empty glass from the table and turned to me. 'Get us a half of lager, will ya? I'm gagging for a bevvy here.'

'Yes, get Penny a drink,' Diane said smugly, heading for the dance floor, thrilled with her new best friend. 'And I'll have one as well.' I bought another round and went back to our table, where I lit a ciggy and sulkily drank my cider, watching them mooch around the dance floor. A clammy hand grabbed my arm.

'You couldn't give us the loan of your Hide and Heal, could ya? I wanna cover me love-bite up.'

Two Quid Trish, so christened because of his reputation for going in toilets with older men and attending to their physical needs for the princely sum of two pounds, was pointing to a purple welt on his neck.

Rimmel's Hide and Heal was supposedly wonderful at covering up spots, dark circles under the eyes and the odd love-bite. At least that was the theory – in practice it sort of worked, if you didn't mind going round with what looked like a dollop of magnolia emulsion daubed on your defects.

'I went back to the Holiday Inn with this feller last night,' Trish was saying, sitting down and helping himself to one of my cigs. 'He had the biggest dick I've ever seen, like a baby's arm holding an orange.' He swung his own arm back and forth by his side, clenching his fist to demonstrate the mammoth proportions of Mr Holiday Inn's genitalia. Diane, returning to the table, gave us both a frosty smile.

'Not disturbing anything, am I?' She simpered sarcastically. 'Who's your boyfriend?'

I hated these jealous swipes, and even though I wouldn't have touched Trish with a two-foot bargepole, the feeling no doubt being mutual, I was tempted to throw my arms round him and stick my tongue down his throat just to wind her up.

'Anyway, as I was saying,' Trish carried on, oblivious to Diane, 'I lay there and told him straight, I said, "If you think you're throwing that thing up me, mate, then you've got another bloody think coming." '

'So what did you do?' I asked distractedly, desperate for this torrid tale to end. Out of the corner of my eye I could see Diane enjoying herself watching me squirm.

'Well, he offered me a tenner,' Trish said with the resigned air of a queen who knew what hard times were. The wolf was no stranger to Trish's door; in fact it had moved in with him years ago. 'So what was a girl to do when she's offered that kind of fortune?'

Diane was fascinated. 'What did you do?'

'Opened my lallies, of course, and bit the pillow. Now for Christ's sake, have you got that Hide and Heal or what?'

We didn't stay very long. When Diane started asking Penny what happened on the ships I thought it was time to get our coats. I put Di in a taxi. She'd got on my nerves with her jealous accusations. For someone who, up to a few hours ago, had refused to accept that I was gay, she was now giving a very good imitation of being convinced that I'd slept with the entire gay scene and most of the navy. 'A slight exaggeration on your part,' I told her, 'it's only half the navy,' closing the cab door behind her and taking myself off to get the tunnel bus back to Birkenhead.

My dad was still up when I got in. The atmosphere between us was still tense. He disapproved of my 'nocturnal rambling' as he called it, objecting, quite rightly, to my using the house as a hotel. The previous week we'd had a particularly nasty row which had culminated with his throwing a chair at me and slamming out of the house. I can see him now, striding across the park in his shirtsleeves, with no idea where he was going as long as it was far away from me. He ended up getting blind drunk, which was almost unheard-of for him, and was barely able to stand when he returned home in the small hours of the morning. 'You've broke your poor dad's heart,' my mother said sadly when I came in the next day. 'And to think you were the apple of his eye when you were a little boy.'

The row had been over an all-nighter at the Wigan Casino. The soon-to-be-legendary club had only been open for a few weeks but its reputation was already spreading fast, and I wanted to go with a couple of my workmates from the courts. Previously an old theatre, it had been turned into a dance hall, the seating in the stalls ripped out to provide an extensive dance floor. The club opened at half past midnight and went through till eight in the morning. It was two quid to get in; there was no booze on sale and, in the early days, very few drugs. It really did have an amazing atmosphere. People came from all over the country to dance all night to the sounds of northern soul. Pete and Dave, my mates from work, told me to bring a change of clothes in a bag as dancing all night in the heat of the packed Casino made you very sweaty. I knew full well that I'd leave the dance floor the same way I left the football pitch at school – not a bead of perspiration on me – but I dutifully packed a few clothes in a bag to show willing and took myself off to Liverpool to meet them as arranged in Yates's Wine Lodge before hitting Wigan.

'How the hell are we going to stay awake all night?' I asked Dave. I liked my kip and was worried that I wouldn't last the course, and would shame us all by falling asleep on our bags and coats under the table.

'Aha, I've got these,' Dave said, taking a tube of pills out of his pocket. 'A couple each and we'll go all night.'

'Drugs?' I squeaked.

'Don't be daft,' Dave scoffed, popping a couple of pills in his mouth and washing them down with wine. 'You can buy these over the counter in the chemist. They're hardly tabs of acid. Here, take a couple,' he said, casually putting the tube in my shirt pocket.

I was rigid with fright. Dave was a drug addict. He unashamedly takes pills in front of everyone and has just dropped a tube of God knows what in my pocket, in full view of a packed pub. What if someone calls the police? What if Dave overdoses and dies? What am I going to do? I was so green I must have been breastfed chlorophyll.

'Hurry up,' Pete said, elbowing me in the side, 'I want a couple. I could do with a little lift.'

Oh my Lord, Pete was at it as well. I bent down, pretending to tie my shoelace, and slipped the tube out of my pocket so I could take a look.

'Oh, for pity's sake,' Pete said, exasperated. 'Just take them.'

I read the label. It said *ProPlus* and it promised to relieve tiredness and make you feel wide awake. I'd never heard of them, but as they didn't look as if they'd been bought in a Dock Road opium den I braced myself and took two, waiting apprehensively for them to kick in.

'D'ya think anyone can tell that I'm out of my mind?' I asked Dave after a couple of minutes, nervously licking my lips, my eyes darting manically round the room in the manner of one of the cast from the film *Reefer Madness*.

'Don't be such a twat and drink up. We've got to get to Wigan,' Dave said pityingly. 'Two ProPlus and he thinks he's Jimi Hendrix.'

We stood for hours in a queue that stretched literally the length of the road, waiting for the bouncers in their frilly shirts and bow ties to open the door. I have to admit that it was worth the wait. Once inside I could see why the change of clothes was necessary. Lads in trousers with waistbands that came up to their armpits and feather-cut hair chucked themselves energetically around the floor. It was quite unlike the dancing in the Bear's Paw: here they were doing the splits, back-flips, handstands – the whole three-ring circus. If you wanted to dance you didn't need a partner, you just took yourself off and did your own thing in among the mass of thrashing bodies. It was liberating to be lost in my own world, out of my drug-crazed mind on two ProPlus, dancing (or what passed for dancing in my case) to the likes of 'Cry No More' by Ben E. King and 'That's No Way To Treat A Girl' sung by Marie Knight.

Innocent as it all was, my dad didn't like me staying out all night 'roaming the streets'. He liked to think that the members of his tiny household were all indoors, tucked up safely in bed with the door locked, before he pulled out all the plugs and retired for the night. He had time on his hands since his retirement, and he'd taken up various hobbies to keep himself occupied: a rug-making kit that took two years to complete, the end result a hideous chocolate-brown shagpile monstrosity with navy blue and green chrysanthemums painstakingly handwoven into it that now sat proudly in front of the gas fire, clashing with the multicoloured front-room carpet. He redecorated the front room, encasing the chimney breast in pine tongue and groove, which we all thought was the height of style; painted the hall; built a cupboard for the bathroom that shook violently when you opened it and leaned dangerously towards the bath. He even took up making jewellery, intending to sell the fruits of his labour and make his fortune. That didn't last long. It was painstaking and fiddly work fitting tiny marcasites into the back of a brooch, so he used up every bead and stone he had in his 'Jewellery-Making Made Easy' kit ('Make and sell your own jewellery from home!'), dispensed the resulting brooches and bracelets among my mum and the aunties and called it a day, returning to visiting the sick and the elderly for the Knights of St Columbia and drinking in the Black Horse with his mates.

I hated coming home from a night out to find him still up, sitting quietly, wanting to know, not unreasonably, what I'd been up to and where I'd been till one in the morning, questions guaranteed to drive a resentful teenager into a paranoid sulk and wild accusations of 'persecution'. The night of my visit to Sadie's I just wanted to sit quietly for half an hour before turning in. After putting Diane into the cab I'd had to wait ages for the bus that ferried the night owls through the Mersey Tunnel and then tackle the long walk uphill in driving rain, wondering if it was all really worth the hassle for the pleasure of a night sitting in a shitty garret with a jealous girl-friend and a few ropy old queens. I was in a strange mood that night, feeling for some reason unsettled and tense. In the words of Mrs Garbo, I vanted to be alone. Fortunately my dad wasn't up for talking; he was on his way to bed. 'Dry your hair before you go up or you'll catch your death,' was all he said, adding, 'And don't be making a racket. Your mother hasn't been feel-ing too good. Try to think of others for once if you can.'

I sat on the sofa drinking a glass of milk and eating a bag of cheese puffs, listening to the floorboards above me creaking as my dad got into bed. He was right. I was out nearly every night, I spent my wages on clubbing and clothes and selfishly thought of little else. I was in a day job that was bearable and a part-time job of a night that I loved, I had lots of friends, an interesting and busy sex life and money in my pocket, and apart from strained relations with my parents life was good. So why wasn't I really, sincerely enjoying it? Two little words: Catholic guilt. It's inherent in me. When the going's good there's a niggling feeling in the back of my mind that at any moment it'll be payback time, that the clock will strike mid-night and Cinders will be back to rats and pumpkins again, quick as a flash; this little voice whispering in your ear that all good things inevitably must be paid for and that in all proba-bility an unforeseen and unexpected calamity is lurking round the corner just waiting to pounce. 'The winds of remorse whistling down the lobby, stirring up the leaves of emotion' was how Aunty Anne would describe the way I was feeling. Aunty Anne was a fan of Catherine Cookson and could be quite florid, if a little over-dramatic, herself when foretelling the approach of impending doom. The way to break the curse was to put something back, do something beneficial for others. Not just any old thing – you had to really put yourself out, show that you meant it. It was time to do something good, hopefully proving to my dad that I wasn't quite the lost cause he imagined at the same time.

I'd read an article in one of the thousands of *Reader's Digests* that occupied the house about the work of Sue Ryder and felt that I'd like to help out. I'd done some voluntary work in a Salvation Army hostel while I was at Steers House. I'd enjoyed the work and admired the practical yet caring approach of the Salvation Army so much that I briefly toyed with the idea of joining up. That's right, you heard me. You see, I fancied myself standing outside Robb's in Grange Road wearing a smart uniform, banging a drum and belting out a rousing chorus of 'Rejoice'. I still can, really.

I got the details of the Sue Ryder home in Suffolk from the reference library and wrote to them offering my services.

If they took me on then I planned to travel down on the odd weekend. Two days later I received a phone call: yes, they'd love to have me on board, they needed a strong pair of hands so why didn't I jump on a train and come down to see them. Blinded by their enthusiasm and confidence in me and also by the saintly glow of helping others I went one further, offering my services for a week. My mum and dad were off on a caravan holiday with my sister and her husband and kids at the end of the month and didn't like the idea, not surprisingly, of leaving me alone while they were gone.

'I'm over eighteen now, Mother. I'm an adult.'

'You're a gobshite, you mean, one who can't be trusted, and that's why you're going to stay at Annie and Chrissie's, my lad.'

I'd take a week's holiday from work and go off and do my

penance while my parents went on holiday, thus solving the problem. As usual my mother was deeply suspicious as to my motives, and even after ringing the home and getting to speak to the great lady herself couldn't quite believe that I was giving up a week's holiday to work with the survivors of the concentration camps. Aunty Chris was equally sceptical. 'The poor buggers,' she said. 'Haven't they suffered enough? A week with you and they'll be wishing they were back in Belsen.' My mother put Sue Ryder on the same level as Mother Teresa and Padre Pio. She couldn't believe that she'd spoken to her on the phone, a woman whom she considered a living saint, and went about for the rest of the day in a state of religious ecstasy. My dad was less impressed with Sue Ryder's husband, Leonard Cheshire, questioning his activities in the war, as he did Churchill's. Confused as they were by my overnight change from sinner to saint, they nevertheless gave me their blessing and I arranged to spend the week at the home.

Cavendish was, and probably still is, a beautiful Suffolk village, not that I saw much of it on that occasion. I didn't stop from the moment I got there until the time I eventually threw the towel in and left four days later. I only met Sue Ryder once. She was small and thin, a little bird in an Hermès headscarf, who never seemed to sleep. 'That's right, shoulder to the plough,' she shouted cheerfully to me one morning as I was taking bags of rubbish out to the bin. I didn't mind a bit of hard work, but I drew the line at slavery. It was chaos. There were not enough staff to go round and so from seven in the morning till ten at night I scrubbed and cleaned, changed beds, washed the faeces from the sheets in the sluice, sat with the residents, washed 'em and shaved 'em and fed those who were unable to do it themselves, lifted and carried, lugged and dragged, and all in all acted as general dogsbody and skivvy.

The residents of the home were mainly Polish. I could hear them crying out in the night as, too exhausted to sleep, I lay on the camp bed in my cupboard of a room. This place made the Wheatsheaf look like the Ritz. One man, who had survived Auschwitz but had watched his entire family go to the gas chambers, was obsessed by the idea that the Gestapo were out to get him. Small wonder when you consider what he'd been through. How could he possibly put his trust in anyone again, coming from wartime Warsaw, a dark place of mistrust and suspicion where even your closest friends turned informer or appeared one day dressed in the hated Nazi uniform?

The staff worked like Trojans. I don't know how they coped with it. Complaining to a nurse one night, as I washed a mountain of dishes in the kitchen, about how exhausted I felt, I was told to be careful what I said. The year before, a voluntary matron had persistently complained to Leonard Cheshire and Sue Ryder that the workload was impossible and that the standard of care and cleanliness was abysmal – and she'd been found dead by the lake in mysterious circumstances. The official verdict had been suicide but the staff gossiped that it might have been otherwise. 'You'll never get out of here now,' the nurse said darkly. 'They'll never let you go.'

That was enough for me. I reckoned that I'd earned my wings, having put in sixty hours' voluntary labour in four days, so I did a bunk, taking myself off to London for a few days before going home. I stayed with a couple I'd met through a friend in Liverpool, who lived in north London in a cramped little flat over a shop. They were the archetypical show tunes queens, the walls of the flat covered in posters of every musical ever made, every conceivable surface adorned with framed photographs of film stars, all female. *To Chris and Billy, Yours Sincerely, Mae West.*

I hardly knew them but they'd invited me to stay when I was in London so I took them up on their offer. Although their home was a shrine to the goddesses of the silver screen, they didn't take too kindly to less celestial females and distrusted them every bit as much as Sadie did, refusing to have a woman in the house. I didn't get this mindless misogyny and brought back a girl I'd met at the Galtymore, an Irish dance hall in Cricklewood. I didn't fancy her in the least, nor she me. We were a pair of oddballs who'd hit it off and she stayed the night rather than face the long trek home to Watford. That move didn't go down very well, particularly with Billy, a vicious little Scot with long fingernails and yellowing fangs who permanently reeked of French cigarettes. Discovering us curled up in a blanket on the living-room floor, he unceremoniously threw us out the next morning.

Back at home they'd returned from a lousy holiday. They all came back ill, and my mother, suffering from pains in her chest, took herself off to the doctor, but owing to the fact that she didn't have an appointment was told by the gorgon of a receptionist to come back in two days and not to worry as chest pains like hers invariably turned out to be nothing more serious than trapped wind. The next morning at work cleaning the Sandpiper club she had a massive heart attack and was rushed to St Cath's. My sister rang me at work and Joe Black, my long-suffering boss, allowed me to go home.

My dad was waiting in the corridor outside the intensive care unit by the time I got to the hospital. He was sitting with his head in his hands, barely holding back the tears, hardly able to say hello without his bottom lip wobbling like a child's.

A doctor came over to him. 'Mr O'Grady? Hello, yes, do you think I could have a word with you?' You could tell by the tone of his voice that the news wasn't good. 'It's touch and go at the moment, I'm afraid,' I heard him say. 'We're keeping a close eye on her but I have to be honest with you, things aren't looking good.' A stupid thing to say, I thought. What was wrong with being a little more optimistic? Hadn't I heard someone say that where there's life there's hope? I wanted to go over and shake him and point out that those three little words 'touch and go', so carelessly spoken to a desperate man, had in a single moment shattered my dad's world.

'Can I see her?' my father asked, ashen-faced. He was allowed by her bedside for a few brief minutes, returning with the tears streaming down his face.

'Take your father home,' the doctor said. 'There's no point in your hanging around here all night. We'll ring if there's any change.'

It was only a ten-minute walk back to our house from the hospital, but it felt like a day's journey. My father was beside himself. 'What'll I do without her?' he kept repeating through his tears as we walked up the road. 'What'll I do without my Molly?' It was hard to keep up with him, he was walking so fast, but when we got to the park he stopped and put his arms round me. Please don't, Dad, I screamed out inwardly, please don't do this in the street. We were not a touchy-feely family. 'What are we going to do if she dies?' he whispered, hugging me tightly. 'I can't live without her.'

Suddenly I was scared. Everything I loved was crumbling before me. I wanted to run away, to hide somewhere and pretend that none of this was happening. What if my mother died? What would we do? Life without her was unthinkable. Was this my punishment for not sticking it out for the full week at Sue Ryder's? If so, then God was one petty bitch.

My dad's sorrow turned to anger. He refused to come home with me, not until he'd paid a visit to the doctor's and let his hapless receptionist know exactly what he thought of her ill-judged prognosis. Aunty Chris, who had been waiting anxiously at the house with my sister Sheila for us to come back from the hospital, went after him. She said the entire surgery cheered as he wiped the floor with Dr Barlow's receptionist. She was a harridan, there's no other way to describe her. She saw the patients as a necessary evil, a bunch of malingering time-wasters who had no right to bother the doctor, and like revolutionaries storming the Bastille they roared their approval at hearing this uncaring bully get a long-overdue roasting from the local Robespierre, my normally placid father.

Later that night, after Aunty Chris and Sheila had gone home, I sat with my dad, both of us wrapped in a blanket of despair. I could feel the room closing in on me, the atmosphere unbearably claustrophobic. I wanted to scream out loud and thought I'd go mad if I didn't get out for a while.

'Don't go out tonight,' my dad pleaded, seeing me changing my shirt. 'Stay here with me.' I didn't know how to cope seeing him like this, desperate and defeated, his eyes raw from crying. He scared me and to my eternal shame and regret I refused to stay, leaving him alone while I went for a drink in the Bear's Paw. I didn't stay out very long. I regretted coming. It felt wrong being in a club full of people whose only concern was whether or not they'd cop off tonight. I left pretty well immediately and went back home, anxious for news.

As I sat on the train I thought about how many times I'd made this journey with my mother over the years, how many conversations she had enjoyed with complete strangers on the journey from James Street to Green Lane, expounding many a crying shame, airing her opinions on subjects as diverse as apartheid and varicose veins. She couldn't die. She was a powerhouse, permanently striving towards a new goal, whether it be the search for yet another 'little job' or a bus ride into unknown territory to explore a church she'd heard about. Inquisitive by nature, she still retained that thirst for knowledge she'd had as a little girl and would try to infuse me with it. Staring out of the window into the darkness of the tunnel, I could hear her voice.

'By 1903 this was the first electrified line of its type in the world, and it's still going today. I'm all for modern technology, me. Marvellous.' *Please don't die, Mum . . .*

There was no more news. All the hospital would say was that my mother was 'peaceful'. She'd never been peaceful in her life. I lay in bed, listening to my father worrying in the room next door, counting the minutes until morning, waiting in the dark for the phone to ring.

By 6 a.m. we were up and back at the hospital. There was still no change. My dad sat by the bed staring intently into the face of the woman he'd loved since he first clapped eyes on her at an Irish dance, gently stroking her hand and silently willing her to live. For the first time, I saw them not just as my parents but as a couple very much in love.

There was no point me hanging around, my dad said; I'd be better off at work. I disagreed but went, reluctantly, to keep the peace. Halfway through the afternoon session I was called out of the court and told once again by Joe Black to go home. This time it was my dad who'd had the heart attack.

Sheila was waiting for me at the hospital. He'd had two more coronary arrests and had been put on life support. 'He told Father Lennon that he was going on a journey,' she said through her tears. We thought it best to tell my mother, who had recovered slightly but was still very ill, that he'd caught a bad cold and was keeping away until it got better in case he passed it on to her. She'd have seen through this feeble lie in an instant if it hadn't been for the drugs fogging her mind.

My dad was dying. The Irish relatives gathered round his bed to say the rosary. He'd been taken off the life support machine now; there was no point. It wouldn't be long before he embarked on his 'journey'. The light over the bed cast shadows across his face, every vein visible through his waxen, transparent skin. I stood at the end of his bed, listening to his laboured breathing and the repetitive drone of the relatives as they chanted the rosary. He sat up for a brief moment and laughed. 'That bugger'll be all right,' he said quite clearly, pointing at me, before lapsing into sleep again.

It was time to tell my mother that her husband was dying. I hid behind a cupboard in the corridor as she was slowly wheeled into the intensive care unit, frail and vulnerable in her hand-knitted pink bedjacket, to say her last goodbyes.

'Where's Paddy?' she was saying in a small anxious voice. 'Where's my husband?' I was unable to face her, incapable of witnessing her grief, crouching on the floor in the dark at the side of the cupboard, eyes closed and hands over my ears, desperate to blot this heartbreaking image from my mind. She stayed with him until the doctor sent her back to the ward. On the way, she stopped the wheelchair to speak to me. 'This is you, this,' she said accusingly. 'You've put him in there with your shenanigans and your bloody carry-on.' Painful as it was, I was glad to see that there were still traces of the old Eve. Then she reached out and grabbed my hand, as if suddenly regretting her outburst. 'Have you had your tea?' she asked, wiping her eyes with a hanky that I noticed had the word Laxey printed on it, a souvenir of happier times and a holiday on the Isle of Man when she'd walked arm in arm with my dad along the prom for a drink in the Empress Hotel. 'I'll get me purse out of the locker and you can go down the Chinese and get yourself some of that muck you like. And then get to bed – you're the colour of boiled shite.'

My dad died in the early hours of the morning. He couldn't face a life without my mother, and, thinking that she was dying, slipped away himself. The doctor said that if he could put cause of death as 'Broken heart' on the death certificate he would have.

The normally inscrutable Aunty Chris, who loved my dad dearly, was chain-smoking furiously in the corridor, looking for a victim to vent her anguish on. I felt much the same. If she wanted a fight I was up for it, even though I knew she'd tear me to shreds within seconds. 'You're coming back to stay at ours,' she said, her voice cracking as she fought back her tears. 'And I don't want no bloody trouble either.'

I told her no, I was going home first, and ran off before she could get her claws out.

The house looked as it always did, only unnaturally quiet, my dad's pipe sitting on the mantelpiece, his football coupon, untouched, on the arm of his chair. In the kitchen a mug and bowl were stacked neatly on the draining board, evidence of his last meal. I sat in the dark on the stairs, numb with shock. My father was dead. Hard to take in at that age – at any age, really. I found the sudden sense of loss overwhelming. There were so many things I wanted to say to him, to thank him for, and now it was too late. Was it my fault he'd died? Had I brought on his heart attack? Years later, sitting in a cinema in London watching Maximilian Schell's documentary about Marlene Dietrich and hearing the lady herself recite Ferdinand Freiligrath's poignant 'Love as Long as You Can', I recalled that moment on the stairs again, and felt the same overwhelming regret as I did then.

Oh love as long as day may dawn,
The hour will come,
You'll stand beside a grave and mourn
Whoever gives his heart to you,
Oh, show him all the love you own,
And fill his waking hours with joy,
And never make him feel alone
And watch your tongue as best you can,
A wicked word is quickly spoken,
'Oh God, I didn't mean it so'
The other goes away heartbroken,

Then you kneel down beside the grave
Forgive me please for hurting you,
Oh God, I didn't mean it so,
But he can't see and can't hear you,
He can't be welcomed back, somehow.
The mouth that kissed you oft before,
Can't say that all's forgiven, now . . .
He did forgive you, long ago,
But many hot tears fell, my friend,
About you and your bitter word,
Oh, he's at rest, he's reached the end.

Enough to bring a bloody tear to a glass eye, as Aunty Chris probably would've said.

I was more than a little worried that the shock of my father's death might kill my mother, making me an orphan at eighteen. Lady Bracknell, or rather Tony's impression of her, sprang to mind: 'To lose one parent may be regarded as a misfortune; to lose both looks like carelessness.'

'Please God, let her get better and I'll never be bad again.' The old familiar petition that I'd employed since childhood was brought into use again. I had a mental image of St Peter in his long flowing beard and robes, standing in front of a pair of ornate gates on a fluffy lump of cloud, holding a phone out to the Almighty. 'It's Paul O'Grady, boss, he says he'll never be bad again?'

'Tell him I'm not in.'

The phone rang on the little hall table that my dad had built a lifetime ago, startling me out of my thoughts. I let it ring. It was probably Aunty Chris seeing 'what I was up to', so I ignored it and went to bed, getting into my parents' bed instead of my own. I could smell them on their pillows. On my mum's a faint whiff of Honeysuckle and setting lotion, on my dad's, cigarettes and sweat. I lay there in the dawn light, listening to a solitary foghorn from a ship on the Mersey. It was a surprisingly misty morning for September and it was chilly in the bedroom. The phone rang again. Reluctantly, I went to answer it.

'Paul?' It was Diane. 'How are you?'

'Well, me dad's dead and me mother's at death's door. Things couldn't get worse, really.'

I could hear her sobbing at the other end of the line.

'Oh, God, they could and they have,' she said, catching her breath.

'What do you mean?'

'I'm pregnant. You're going to be a father.'

INDEX

ABC cinema, 138–40
Abelard and Eloise, 266, 295
Aboud, Mr (dentist), 2–3
Alf (coalman), 11
Angela Chapman Employment Agency, 277
Ashe and Nephew, 272–3
Ashton, Susan, 195–6
ATS (Auxiliary Territorial Service), 102, 103
Audrey (barmaid), 233–5
Avengers, The, 148, 156, 169–70, 175, 193, 205

Babaloo club, 294
Baldry, Long John, 312–15
Ball, Lucille, 93
Bankhead, Tallulah, 167
Barlow, Dr, 334
Barney's the barber, 86–7
Batman, 171, 205
Bear's Paw club: ambition to visit, 282, 289; Diane wants to visit, 320; first visit, 289–91; mother's illness, 335; opening hours, 322; Persian sailors, 307; police at, 315–16; regulars, 294, 311
Begley, Betty, 226–8
Begley, Kim, 226, 227–8
Begley, Sally, 226, 227–9
Bernadette, St, 69, 71, 72, 144
Bidston Hill, 20–2
Bill, The, 305
Billy (in north London), 332–3
Birkenhead: 23 Holly Grove, 6–12, 19–27, 47, 61, 67–8, 89, 102, 103–4; Horden House, 232, 241; 29 Lowther Street, 83–5, 87–91, 95, 10–5; North End, 166–7, 205
Birkenhead General Hospital, 87, 188
Birkenhead News, 29, 34, 136, 208
Birkenhead Technical College, 215
Black, Joe, 333, 336
Black and Tans, 53–4
Blackler's Store, 218–19
Blackman, Honor, 226, 249
Blessed Edmund Campion School, 165–8, 171, 179

Boggins, Billy, 137
Boggins, Pat, 137
Bolger, Miss (teacher): discipline, 116, 135, 151; first teacher, 107–8, 110–16, 133; school dinners, 116–20; school reports, 108
Bowie, David, 303
Boys' Amateur Boxing Club, 192
Brailey, Thelma, 237–9, 241, 244, 251, 268, 275–6
Brian (barman), 311–12
Brindle, Miss (deputy matron), 5
Broad, Mr (teacher), 186
Butlins, 37

Cammell Laird's, 6, 47, 90, 209
Campaign for Homosexual Equality (CHE), 278, 279–81, 285, 316
Carlton Players, 224–9, 231
Carol (barmaid), 252–3, 256–7, 263
Carson's of Birkenhead, 301
Carter's Corner Place, 302
Casey, Bill, 94
Catcher in the Rye, The, 204
Chef and Brewer, 254–5
Chertsey Magistrates Court, 277
Cheshire, Leonard, 331, 332
Chris (trainee manager), 253–5, 257, 259–60, 264
Christian Brothers: discipline, 135, 150, 155, 163; St Anselm's, 141, 150, 163, 171, 207; television restrictions, 148
Christine (clerical assistant), 219
Co-op, 16, 86
Coleherne pub, 302
Coolidge, Calvin, 55
Corby, Marlene, 309–11
Corpus Christi High School, 15–16, 191
Cousin's café, 221
Covent Garden, 298
Creggs pub, 200–1
Crisp, Quentin, 323
Cubs, 181–2
Cunard Line, 85
Cunningham, Mrs (at the chip shop), 177–9

Daily Mail, 280
Daily Mirror, 96, 149, 214
Dave (clerical assistant), 219
Dave (friend from work), 326–7
Davies, Chamois, 113
Della (Sadie's friend), 322–3
Dennis (at Bear's Paw), 289–91
Department of Supplementary Benefits, 219–20
Diane (girlfriend), 293–4, 319–20, 321–5, 329, 340
Dietrich, Marlene, 61, 93, 295, 296–8, 338
Docherty, Mrs (Mrs Dock), 49
Dominion pub, 306–7
Dors, Diana, 261–3
Dot (prostitute), 308
Dougal (schoolboy), 16
Doughty, Dora, 15–16
Downey, Anne, 201
Doyle, Father, 145, 180, 183–5
Duane, Annie, 55

Eatock, Winnie, 48–9
Eddy (boxing trainer), 192–3
Edwards, Miss (teacher), 135–6, 151
Ennis, Brother, 147–8, 160, 161
Evelyn (schoolfriend), 279

Fawcett, Anne (Annie Savage, aunt): appearance, 80; author's career, 214; betting, 97–100, 199; birth, 67; bushbaby, 90–1; care of father, 76, 79–80, 105; cat, 89–90; childhood, 80–1; children, 105; Christmas at Holly Grove, 271–2, 273; education, 127; housekeeping, 83–4, 85–6, 97; husband's death, 237, 273; language, 128, 325–6; marriage, 63, 80; mother's death, 79; relationship with sister Chrissie, 97–100; singing, 83–4; sister Molly's garden thefts, 19; sister Molly's teeth, 3; work as cleaner, 282–3
Fawcett, Harold (Uncle Al): appearance, 80; bushbaby, 90–1; career, 85; death, 237, 273; drinking, 93–4; home, 85, 89; marriage, 63, 80; stories, 136
Fawcett, Ma, 63, 64
Fawcett, Maureen (cousin), 42, 85, 88
Fawcett, Michael (Mickey, cousin), 8, 85, 162
Fawcett, Old Ned, 63, 64–5
Fawcett, Tricia (cousin), 70, 85, 105, 199
Fawcett, William, 63
Finch, Paul: appearance, 252; dismissal of author, 268–9, 275; drinking, 260, 267; treatment of trainees, 258, 259, 262, 264; welcome to Wheatsheaf, 252–3; Wheatsheaf status, 252, 257
Flo (clerical assistant), 219–20
Frances (queen), 287–8, 306–7
Franconia, RMS, 54–5, 56
Frank (next-door neighbour), 12, 13

Gay News, 280, 304
Gayton, 294

George V, King, 67
Glinsk, 51–2, 53, 107
Glyndebourne, 298–9, 300–1
Grace (chambermaid), 41
Grady, *see also* O'Grady
Grady, Bridget (aunt), 57–9, 70, 123–4, 204
Grady, Bridget (Biddy Brittain, grandmother), 52–6
Grady, James (great-uncle), 53, 54, 60
Grady, James (uncle), 57, 112, 123–4
Grady, Mary (aunt), *see* Schillaci
Grady, Mickey (cousin), 174, 204
Grady, Patrick (father), *see* O'Grady
Grady, Patrick (grandfather), 51–2
Grady, Sarah-Ann (Sadie, aunt), 52, 54–6, 60, 63
Grafton club, 294
Grange Mount Hospital, 104
Great Barrier Reef, 129–32
Gypsy, 183, 302

Heath, Ted, 293
Hello Dolly!, 109
Henshaw, Eileen, 28, 29–34, 149–50, 182, 216–17, 285
Henshaw, George, 29, 30–2, 149
Henshaw's shop, 28, 29–34, 136, 149
Heswall, 206
Hiawatha, 157–61
Hirschfeld, Dr, 317
Holy Cross School, 191, 195

Isle of Man, 39–42, 189, 194, 337

J., Lady, 303–5
Jacko (dog), 4, 13
Jean (North End girl), 201–2
Jens (Streisand fan), 110–11
Jinksy (cat), 89
Joey (budgie), 317–18
John, Elton, 264
John (mate), 168–9, 221–4, 309
John Paul II, Pope, 72
Johnstone, Ma, 86
Johnstone's shop, 86

Kearney, Brother, 153–4, 155
Keeler, Christine, 149
Kemp, Lindsay, 303
Knights of St Columbia, 271, 328

Lake, Alan, 261–3
Lalley, Vera, 84, 104, 196
Langford, Bonnie, 302
Lansbury, Angela, 302
Laura (in Virginia Water), 265
Legion of Mary, 31
Lennon, Father, 39, 147, 201, 336
Lever's, 47, 80, 188
Lewis, Rosa, 123
Lifeline (employment agency), 237–9, 251
Lily Savage, 42, 46–7, 95, 160, 310

342

Lion in Winter, The, 226–7, 232, 295
Lisbon pub, 286–9, 320
Listen with Mother, 17
Littlewoods Pools, 104
Liverpool: CHE, 279–81, 285; gay scene, 289, 311; Steers House (Canning Place), 217–20, 232, 330
Liverpool Echo, 5, 29, 30, 32, 33, 74, 198, 209, 210, 214, 277, 278, 293
Liverpool Magistrates Court, 285, 309–11
Livingstone, Ken, 101
London, 242–9
Long, George, 27, 46, 47
Long, Jean, 134
Long, Michael, 45
Long, Rose: appearance, 43; caravan, 42, 153; relationship with Aunty Chris, 43–6, 49–50, 104–5; relationship with Molly, 20, 42, 43, 47, 48, 208; relationship with neighbours, 48–9; religion, 43, 144
Look and Learn, 147–8
Lourdes, 68, 69–71

McGee, Miss (Lulu), 150–1, 173
McGrath, Clare, 145
McGregor, Miss, 117, 119–20
Mack, Mrs (bar steward), 236, 260, 273–4
Macmillan, Lenny, 283–4
Madame Arthur's club, Copenhagen, 108
Man from UNCLE, The, 156
Mansfield twins, 195
Mardi Gras club, 294
Martha, Sister, 80
Mary, Queen, 67
Mary Cleophas, Mother, 132
Mary (next-door neighbour), 12–13, 134
Mary (shop assistant), 215–16
Masquerade Club, 289
Michell, Keith, 295
Millie (in Virginia Water), 265–6
Mooney, Celia, 110, 138
Mooney, Francis (Franny): altar boy, 179–80, 183; appearance, 110, 137, 179; ATC, 191; bullied, 137; burglary attempt, 206; family, 137–8; first communion, 145, 146; first day at school, 110–16, 133–4; friendship with author, 136–7; school dinners, 117, 119–20, 133–4; tonsils removed, 186–7
Mooney, Mr, 138
Mulligan family, 39–40
Murphy, Brendan, 129, 132
Murphy, Fat Pat, 103

New Southport Theatre, 296
New York, 55–6
Nora (cook), 40

O'Brien, William, 52
Official Secrets Act, 216, 217
O'Grady, *see also* Grady
O'Grady, Brendan (brother): childhood, 6, 58, 61, 127; education, 162; marriage, 194; relationship with brother Paul, 152, 193–4; work, 91
O'Grady, Keith (nephew), 194–5, 237
O'Grady, Mary (Molly Savage, mother): accent, 17, 21, 141, 172; appearance, 1, 18, 134; birth, 67; birth of son Paul, 5, 6; budgie, 317–18; cat poisoning, 25–7; childhood, 79, 80–1; at chip shop, 177–8; cinema going, 13–14; courtship, 63–4; crossing roads, 177; decoration of son Paul's bedroom, 174–5; dress, 18, 61; dressmaking, 158, 161; education, 127, 132; fan of Johnnie Ray, 295–6; father's death, 60; finances, 10, 30, 39, 60–1, 181; first meeting with Paddy, 51, 63; gardening, 19–27, 35; heart attack, 333–5, 340; holidays, 37, 40–3, 153, 330–1; home, 7–12, 67–8, 77–8; home perm, 134; home remedies, 19; Irish visits, 57–9; morning routine, 232–3; mother's death, 67, 79–80; Paddy's death, 336–7; relationship with Eileen Henshaw, 28, 29–30, 32–3, 216–17, 285; relationship with Rose Long, 20, 42, 43, 47, 48, 153, 208; religion, 68–72, 124, 147; robin, 23, 25, 27; scent, 16; sex education, 196–8; son Paul's appearance, 199–200; son Paul's appendicitis, 188–9; son Paul's career, 209–10, 216–17, 271–2, 282–3, 285; son Paul's career as altar boy, 181–3; son Paul's career in hotel, 240–2, 270–1; son Paul's criminal record, 207–8, 276–7; son Paul's eating difficulties, 124; son Paul's education, 134–5, 136, 141, 147, 152, 155–6, 161–3, 165, 172–3; son Paul's first communion, 145; son Paul's friendship with Tony, 294; son Paul's social life, 325–6; stories, 23; suspected of poisoning animals, 25–7, 34; swimming, 127–8; taking dope, 72–7, 81; taking to her bed, 38–9; teeth, 1–5; thyroid operation, 87, 91; view of homosexuality, 278–9, 317–19; view of Marlene Dietrich, 298; view of prostitutes, 166–7; wartime experiences, 6–7, 47–8; wedding, 64; work as auxiliary nurse, 5, 48, 260; work as cleaner, 48; work as domestic servant, 39–40, 132
O'Grady, Patrick (Paddy, Pakie, father): aftershave, 200; Anderson shelter, 47; appearance, 51, 61; arrival in Birkenhead, 51, 61–3; birth, 52, 56–7; character, 33; childhood, 53–4, 57, 59–60; cinema going, 14; coal, 24; courtship, 63–4; death, 5, 336–8; dress, 61; drinking, 199, 201, 325; education, 107; family background, 52–3; father's death, 51–2; fear of water, 128; finances, 60–1, 136; first meeting with Molly, 51, 63; hobbies, 328; holidays, 41, 330–1; home, 7, 11–12; Irish visits, 57–8, 173–5; Knights of St Columbia, 271, 328; Molly's heart attack, 333–6; naming of son, 6; relationship with son Paul, 107, 148, 193, 201, 206–7, 209, 212, 293, 318, 325–6, 328–9, 335;

O'Grady, Patrick (*cont.*)
  religion, 147, 184; sister–in–law Chris's
    baby, 103, 105; son Paul's career, 209–10,
    221; son Paul's career in hotel, 240–2,
    275–6; son Paul's criminal record, 206–8,
    277; son Paul's education, 136, 141, 147,
    162, 165, 173, 187; son Paul's first com-
    munion, 146; son Paul's paper round, 32–3;
    view of homosexuality, 278; visits to den-
    tist, 2; war service, 50, 128–9; wedding, 64;
    work, 91, 152–3, 209
O'Grady, Paul: family background, 51–7,
    59–64, 67, 79–81, 85; birth, 5, 6; name, 6;
    early memories, 14, 16–18, 21–2, 29–30;
    holidays, 37, 40–3; first day at school, 109–16,
    133–4; St Joseph's, 107–8; St Anselm's, 141–2,
    150–6; Blessed Edmund Campion, 165–9,
    171–3, 185–6; appendicitis, 186–9; burglary,
    205–8; leaving school, 209, 213; first job as
    civil servant, 214–15, 216–20, 232, 236–7;
    journey to London, 242–4; arrival in London,
    244–9; at Wheatsheaf Hotel, 251–7; arrest,
    267–8; dismissal from Wheatsheaf, 268–9;
    return to Birkenhead, 269–70; Chertsey
    Magistrates Court sentence, 277; CHE,
    279–81; trainee clerk of the court, 285, 309–11;
    at Glyndebourne, 299–301; at Sue Ryder
    home, 330–2; mother's illness, 333–6;
    father's death, 336–7
  APPEARANCE: accent, 151–2, 173; dress,
    145, 199–200, 296, 299–301; hair, 88,
    174, 199–200, 300
  EDUCATION: Blessed Edmund Campion,
    165–6, 167–9, 171–3, 185–6, 209,
    212–13; exams, 141–3, 161–3, 209,
    212–13; learning to read, 107; St
    Anselm's, 141–2, 150–6; St Joseph's,
    109–10, 132–3, 135–6, 142–3; sex, 196–8
  EMPLOYMENT: bar work, 233–6, 260–1,
    273–4, 282–4; career plans, 209–14;
    237–8; DHSS, 216–20, 232, 236–7, 241;
    office work, 277, 280; paper round, 5, 26,
    30–4, 205; rent boy, 205; shop assistant,
    215–16; Sue Ryder home, 330–2; trainee
    clerk of the court, 285, 309–11;
    Wheatsheaf Hotel, 239–40, 251–7, 268–9
  HOME: 23 Holly Lodge, 6–11, 14, 89;
    staying at 29 Lowther Street, 87–91
  INTERESTS: acting, 142–3, 157–61, 228;
    altar boy, 178, 179–85; amateur dramatic
    society, 224–9; attitude to death, 122;
    attitude to food, 121, 123–5; *Avengers*,
    148, 156, 169–70, 175, 193, 205; Barbra
    Streisand, 110–11, 189; Batman, 171, 205;
    boxing, 192–3; burglary, 205–8; cinema,
    14, 139–41; Cubs, 181–2; drinking, 70,
    200–1, 205; marine cadets, 178, 191–2,
    193, 205; Popeye, 124–5, 309; radio, 17;
    reading, 148, 204; snorkelling, 129–32; tel-
    evision, 133, 148, 183; theatre, 295, 302
  RELIGION: altar boy, 178, 179–85;
    church-going, 147, 205, 273; education,

142–4; first confession and communion,
    143–6; prayers, 273, 339
  SEXUALITY: CHE, 279–81; childhood, 46;
    Diane, 293–4, 319–20, 340; early sexual
    experiences, 5–6, 168–9; friendship with
    Tony, 294–5, 298–302; gay scene in
    Liverpool, 281–2, 286–91, 294, 321–5;
    girls, 191, 196, 201–3, 205, 266–7, 279,
    284–5, 293–4; John, 168–9, 221–4; men,
    193, 245; Persian sailors, 306–8; Steve the
    Copper, 281–3, 284, 285–91
O'Grady, Sheila (sister): birthmark, 47;
    childhood, 6, 61, 127; children, 205, 330;
    dress, 199; holidays, 330; miscarriage, 237;
    mother's illness, 333, 334, 335; relationship
    with brother Paul, 125–6, 129, 146, 271;
    wedding, 162; work at St Cath's, 5, 91
Orange Lodge, 43, 144

Paul (Persian sailor), 307–8
Penny (friend in bar), 288–9, 306–7, 308, 323
Pete (friend from work), 326–7
Piccadilly, 246–8
Piggott, Lester, 97
Plug (at St Joseph's School), 117–20
Poll, Aunty (great-aunt), 76, 77, 81, 132
Popeye, 124–5, 309
Portmeirion, 305
Prescott's (newsagents), 5, 198, 215–16
Pritchard, John (JP), 298–306
Profitt, Mrs, 28–9
Proust, Marcel, 15, 16
Pugh, Leslie, 310–11

Ray, Johnnie, 295–6
Rigg, Diana, 266, 295
Robin (of CHE), 279–80, 285
Roscoe, Fanny, 283
Rowson, Harold, 224, 227
Rowson, Norma, 224–5, 227
Royal Airforce Association (RAFA) club,
    233, 238, 254, 273–5, 282
Ryder, Sue, 330–2, 334

Sabina, Aunt, 125
Sadie (of Sadie's Bar), 321–2, 333
Sadie's Bar Royale, 282, 290, 320, 321–2,
    329
St Anselm's College, Redcourt: discipline,
    135, 150, 153, 155–6; eleven-plus results,
    161–3, 172; elocution lessons, 151–2, 167,
    173; entrance exam, 136, 141–2;
    Hiawatha, 157–61; pupils, 152–3; staff,
    150–1; studies, 153–5; uniform, 142
St Catherine's Hospital: author's birth, 5, 208,
    271; Evelyn's training, 279; father's death,
    5; Franny's tonsillectomy, 187; mother's
    illness, 333; mother's work, 5, 48; patients,
    215; present-day, 6; sister's work, 5
St Helens Star, 210
St Hugh's School, 161, 165, 167
St Joseph's Church, 145, 147, 179–85

INDEX

St Joseph's School, 109, 132–6, 142–3, 151, 179
St Laurence's Church, 64, 80
St Margaret's Convent, 76–7
St Werburgh's Church, 147, 167, 199, 201–2
Salvation Army, 330
Sandpiper nightclub, 283–4, 333
Savage, Anne (grandmother), 67, 78–9
Savage, Christine (Chris, Chrissie, aunt): appearance, 92–3, 95–101, 234, 243; author's career, 214; author's first communion, 146; birth, 67; brother-in-law's death, 337–8; bushbaby, 90–1; childhood, 80–1; Christmas at Holly Grove, 271–2, 273; in convent orphanage, 76–7, 81; dress, 61; education, 127; feud with Rose Long, 43–6, 49–50, 104–5; friendships, 84; hairdressing, 49; language, 181; model for Lily Savage, 46–7, 95; Ned Fawcett's suicide, 64; pregnancy, 102–4; relationship with Keith, 194; relationship with sister Anne, 83–4, 97–8; relationship with sister Molly, 3, 104, 105; sayings, 32, 87, 92, 94, 137, 144, 157, 209, 242, 267, 277, 331; sex education, 196–8; sister Molly's illness, 334–5; smoking, 49, 85, 99–100, 198; son, 45, 104–5; as teenager, 94; teeth, 3; view of drinking, 93–4, 272; view of ghosts, 88–9; war service, 102; work as clippie, 92–3, 101, 272; work at off-licence, 272–3
Savage, John (cousin), 45, 85, 104–5, 162
Savage, Lily, 42, 46–7, 95, 160, 310
Savage, Michael (Mick, grandfather), 63–4, 67, 76–7, 79–80, 105
Savage, Miss (school secretary), 187
Schillaci, Joe, 56
Schillaci, Mary (Grady, aunt), 52, 54–6, 57, 60
Seaview (boarding house in Isle of Man), 40–1
Selfridges, 248–9
She Club, 294
Shearer, Gordon, 289–90, 312, 315–16
Shell Oil, 91, 211
Shelley, Jim, 220
Simon, Carly, 279
Smith, Mr (teacher), 150
Snowdon, Lord, 302
Song of Bernadette, 69
Stefan (houseboy), 304–5

Steve (gay policeman), 281–2, 284, 285–91
Streisand, Barbra, 108–9, 189
Stubb's confectioners and bakers, 17–18
Summerfield, Monica, 195
Susan (girlfriend), 284, 285
Sutherland, Joan, 302
Szwelski, Hannah, 157
Szwelski (at St Anselm's), 156–7

Talacre, North Wales, 42
Thorpe, Jeremy, 293
Thorson, Linda, 170–1
Times, The, 305
Tina (neighbour), 33–4
Todd, Sweeney, 88–9
Tony (friend): appearance and character, 294, 339; dress, 296; friendship with author, 294–5; friendship with JP, 298–9, 303–5; social life, 295, 299–302, 306–8, 316; work, 294, 306
Tranmere Methodist Church, 116–20
Triplett, Reg, 226, 228
Trish, Two Quid, 324–5
Tufty Club, 134

Ugly's club, 294
Union of Catholic Mothers, 68–9, 74, 196
United Irish League, 51, 52
Upstairs, Downstairs, 245

Victoria Coach Station, 243–5
Virginia Water, 238–9, 244, 251, 256, 264
Visit of the Old Lady, The, 301

Walsh, Deirdre, 135
Watch with Mother, 133
West, Mae, 295, 332
Wheatsheaf Hotel, Virginia Water: accommodation, 253–4; arrival, 251–2; bars, 260, 264–5; clientele, 261–3; dismissal, 267–9, 275; food, 258–9; recruitment, 239–40; staff, 252–3, 255–6, 257–8; uniform, 254–5, 261; work, 256–7, 259
Wigan Casino, 326, 327–8
William III, King, 46
Williams Ellis, Clough, 305

Yentl, 108